Theory and Tradition

in

Eighteenth-Century Studies

Edited by
Richard B. Schwartz

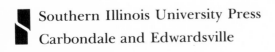
Southern Illinois University Press
Carbondale and Edwardsville

Edited and designed by Donna E. Butler
Production supervised by Natalia Nadraga

Library of Congress Cataloging-in-Publication Data

Theory and tradition in eighteenth-century studies / edited by Richard
    B. Schwartz.
        p.   cm.
    Papers presented to a NEH-sponsored conference held at Georgetown
University on April 1–3, 1987.
    Includes bibliographies and index.
    1. English literature—18th century—History and criticism—
Theory, etc.—Congresses. 2. Literature and history—Great
Britain—History—18th century—Congresses. I. Schwartz, Richard
B. II. National Endowment for the Humanities.
PR442.T44 1990
820′.9′005—dc19   88-36814
ISBN 0-8093-1561-0   CIP

for JIM CLIFFORD

Contents

Part 3
Challenges and Accomplishments

Preface

THE PAPERS in this volume originated as plenary session addresses at a conference held at Georgetown University on 1–3 April 1987. Fifteen years had elapsed since the last serious look at the state of eighteenth-century literary studies conducted by the English Institute, and I thought it useful to assemble a group of senior scholars in the field to examine issues that we face daily as students of the period. The most important of those questions is the position (or relative nonposition) of contemporary literary theory in contemporary eighteenth-century studies. While open to the insights of theorists and prepared to apply those insights whenever they are helpful, most eighteenth-centuryists have been resistant to the tendency to elevate theory to a position of prominence. Moreover, having seen what followers can do to the original thought of important thinkers (e.g., Newton), they have been far more respectful of the progenitors of theoretical movements than of their popularizers.

Thus, I asked the speakers to consider a number of issues as they prepared their papers. No one was asked to focus on a specific topic, but I felt that our present situation raised several key questions. Why have our colleagues often resisted the blandishments of theory? How have they used theory in their own work? What traditions of scholarship have informed their work? What key tasks remain to be performed by students of the period?

These questions are interrelated. Some have argued, for example, that literary studies have changed in response to the fact that more traditional approaches have been exhausted. The principal questions, in short, have been answered, and our flogging of dead horses is of small interest to our students and, indeed, to our colleagues. That the task of the literary historian has been completed is absurd; on the other hand, many continue to focus on the same subjects in largely the same ways with, essentially, the same results. Do we need new methods or do we need abler users of traditional methods?

The speakers who were chosen represent a good cross section of the traditions of eighteenth-century scholarship as they were developed under specific individuals at specific institutions (e.g., Crane/Chicago, Clifford/Columbia, Mack/Yale, and Bronson/Berkeley).

Given our current interest in the state of our profession, seen from the vantage point of its history, it is important to consider how our field has been conceived and shaped and how individuals have been shaped within institutions. Thus, I invited the speakers to offer personal reflections on their own experiences as students and scholars as well as on the manner in which the structure and history of their institutions have determined their research agendas.

The three divisions of this book approximate the categories I suggested. The first section deals directly with the position of theory within eighteenth-century studies. The second views studies of fiction and drama with an eye on the ways in which theory can aid literary scholars by challenging their presuppositions and sharpening the focus of their work. The thrust remains historical (as Maximillian Novak so ably demonstrates) but a historicism informed by multiple points of view. These papers are closer in spirit to the first four than they might at first appear, for one underlying theme in the discussions during the conference was that while historicism remains dominant in eighteenth-century studies, no one is prepared to defend the naive historicism that, in many cases, brought on the alternative approaches now commanding attention.

Many argued, for example, that the eighteenth-centuryists— schooled in the Enlightenment critique of the falsifications of history— have been especially active as revisionists and have advanced arguments that, in their time, were met with opposition and even outrage. Eighteenth-centuryists share the impatience of both the New Critics and the newest critics with simple-minded literary history, as Donald Greene shows.

At the same time, they challenge attacks on historicism per se and bristle at the ahistorical or antihistorical conclusions of some theorists. In other cases they are in agreement with much that the theorists say, but as John Middendorf argues, they feel there is little in what is said that is essentially new. Many of the voices inspiring contemporary writers of theory are nineteenth-century voices, and many of the positions taken by contemporary theorists appear very familiar once they are clarified and defined.

The final set of papers examines conditions within the field, addressing the issues of what has been done and what remains to be done, issues anticipated in earlier papers by, for example, Howard Weinbrot and Paul Hunter. Increasingly, as a profession, we have begun to focus upon the temporal and economic conditions affecting our work, matters that both John Middendorf and Shirley Kenny examine in the context of textual scholarship. While demonstrating the accomplishments of modern eighteenth-century scholarship, Gwin

Kolb (like Morris Brownell) also offers a personal account of the specific conditions that have affected his own work.

That literary studies are now in flux is more than a truism. The situation has led to a communications problem comparable to that in many fields of science where knowledge grows so rapidly that the purpose of formal publication is purely archival, since word of mouth and the circulation of prepublication manuscripts is the actual medium of communication. This is not to suggest that our knowledge is growing at breakneck speed but that events are occurring constantly with which we all must conjure.

Since the conference in April 1987, for example, revelations concerning Paul de Man's collaborationist activities with the Nazis have been announced, attacked, excused, and interpreted. For some he has functioned as an exemplum of the tendencies of (conveniently) ahistoric poststructuralism. Much has also been made of Heidegger's naziesque sympathies and of the importance of his thought for many contemporary writers such as Derrida. The contrast between the world of the withdrawn theorist and the real world of human struggle and suffering has recently been drawn in strong and moving terms by David Hirsch ("Paul de Man and the Politics of Deconstruction," *Sewanee Review* 96 [Spring 1988]: 330–38).

The new historicism continues to press its claims though its novelty is more a matter of emphasis and orientation than an instance of real methodological innovation. The "battle of the books," exemplified by Stanford's tinkering with its curriculum but waged intently across the entire landscape by feminists and third worlders, continues apace with charges and countercharges flying. The *New York Times Magazine* has even run a feature article on the phenomenon (5 June 1988) with particular attention devoted to the doings at Duke. Quite apart from this *People* magazine approach to literary study (anticipated to some extent by Imre Salusinszky's interview book *Criticism in Society*), one is struck with a sense of embarrassed déjà vu. For example, Jane Tompkins talks about the study of American popular literature in tones and terms suggesting radical breakthroughs, while in fact Leslie Fiedler (now past his seventieth birthday) has been doing that sort of thing for decades. Throughout the conference, participants pointed out that many activities were enriching thought and scholarship but that claims of novelty had been inflated and the underlying bedrock of historical methodology was far more secure than the debate suggested. In the year since the conference these impressions have been reinforced, particularly as the Marxists and feminists continue to dissociate themselves from poststructural theorists and focus our attention on life and on society.

The root issue here is the relationship between art and thought on the one hand and the academy on the other. A system of institution-alized criticism that broadens the gulf between writing and society has been fostered, while a system of patronage and instruction that has all but destroyed poetry has evolved. Two studies that have appeared since the conference should be mentioned in this regard: Gerald Graff's *Professing Literature* and Russell Jacoby's *Last Intellectuals: American Culture in the Age of Academe*. If we are to bridge the gulf between the academy and the lives of the members of our society (something presumably favored by a significant portion of the members of our profession), few models to which we might turn offer more compelling examples than the experience of the eighteenth century.

This collection is dedicated to the memory of a man who remains a model for many of us who write and talk about eighteenth-century literature, a man who both enjoyed and chronicled controversies but always did so in the larger context of an ongoing conversation among friends and colleagues participating in a common enterprise in a spirit of generous cooperation.

The conference upon which this collection is based was made possible by a grant from the National Endowment for the Humanities and a grant from Dean Royden B. Davis of the College of Arts and Sciences at Georgetown. The advice and encouragement offered by both Dr. Crale Hopkins of NEH and Fr. Davis of the college were the sort that could bring Jim Clifford to mind. We are all in their debt.

Contributors

DONALD GREENE is Bing Professor Emeritus at the University of Southern California.

MORRIS R. BROWNELL is professor of English at the University of Nevada, Reno.

RICHARD B. SCHWARTZ is professor of English and dean of the Graduate School at Georgetown University.

HOWARD D. WEINBROT is Vilas and Quintana Professor of English at the University of Wisconsin, Madison.

MAXIMILLIAN NOVAK is professor of English at the University of California, Los Angeles.

J. PAUL HUNTER is professor of English at the University of Chicago.

JOHN H. MIDDENDORF is professor of English at Columbia University.

SHIRLEY STRUM KENNY is professor of English and president of Queens College of the City University of New York.

GWIN J. KOLB is Tripp Professor in the Humanities at the University of Chicago.

Part 1

Theory and the Eighteenth Century

1

Literature or Metaliterature?: Thoughts on Traditional Literary Study

DONALD GREENE

A PSYCHIATRIST acquaintance of mine once coined an apho-
rism that has long stuck in my mind: "People who like pigeonholes
don't like pigeons." At times I have been tempted to apply it to the
occupation that has engaged me for the greatest part of my life, the
study of literature, and over the years I have sometimes wondered
how many of my teachers and colleagues have really liked literature
at all.[1] But I suppose that such a doubt cannot be confined to one
academic specialty. I have certainly known musicologists who, I suspected, did not really care much for music, art historians who seemed
more interested in the peripheral aspects of their subject than in art
itself, and indeed theologians who did not much seem to like God.

I suppose this is understandable. Pigeons are flighty, unpredictable creatures; they come in a bewildering variety of colors and sizes;
their behavior, as Gertrude Stein poetically observed, is sometimes
embarrassing to those who consort with them. Rather than try to deal
with them directly and individually, it is easier and less damaging to
one's amour propre to spend one's time at the drawing board design-
ing ingenious blueprints of neat compartments into which they might
be fitted, even though, when approached, large numbers of them may
stubbornly refuse to enter their designated apertures. To drop the
metaphor, direct response to literature and the products of the other
arts—or to genuine religious impulse—is not easy for many people.
Lionel Trilling said of the modern novel (and the same might be said
of much other literature, certainly including that of the eighteenth
century): "Its greatness and practical usefulness [lie] in its unremitting
work of involving the reader himself in the moral life, inviting him to
put his own motives under examination, suggesting that reality is not

3

as his conventional education has led him to see it."[2] To be called on to do so is disturbing for many and, paradoxical as it might seem, so disturbing for some who earn their living by professing to teach literature that they are basically hostile to the texts on the pages they are forced to present to their students. Thus, they do their best to neutralize them by subordinating them to various a priori systems and theories, for which the function of the literary text is to serve as raw material.

Only very rarely do they recognize or admit their hostility. One exception was the head of the English department when, long ago, I had a precarious year-to-year teaching position in a North American university. When my copy of *PMLA* arrived and I picked it up in the departmental mail, I was always careful to hide it behind my back as I made my way back from the mailroom past his office for fear that he might see it and add it to the already large number of discredits against me. Early in my career there I had foolishly attempted to organize an English literary club among the students and younger instructors. When I asked our head if he would be kind enough to say a few words of blessing at the initial meeting, the response was an outburst of rage. He had, it seemed, suffered through several years of postgraduate work in order to obtain the Ph.D. degree needed to qualify him for his position and thought it all a lot of vicious nonsense. He was widely acclaimed as the most popular teacher on the campus. He conducted courses in recent Canadian and American literature, found a great deal in it that could be made fun of—as, of course, there was—and had the students rolling in the aisles with laughter.[3] When, many years later, the then dean of the college asked me whom, as a student, I had found the best teacher of English, he was astonished when I did not name this gentleman, but rather my teacher of Old English, a former pupil of Kittredge at Harvard, who suffered a slight speech defect and was denied promotion for many years. He was intensely devoted to his subject and believed that *Beowulf* is a great poem, as it is. But few have been as candid about their detestation of literature as Professor X, our head.

As is already evident, a good deal of this paper is going to be autobiographical, but I am not too apologetic. Much literary criticism—perhaps in the end all of it, however much those who profess to be objective about it may demure—is essentially autobiographical. I think of Samuel Johnson on *Julius Caesar*, "I have never been strongly agitated by it, and think it somewhat cold and unaffecting," and on *King Lear*, "I was many years ago so shocked by Cordelia's death that I know not whether I ever endured to read again the last scenes of the play till I undertook to revise them as an editor."[4] T. S. Eliot's preference of Dryden to Milton surely has something to do with his High Churchmanship, and Leavis' enthusiasm for D. H. Lawrence with his own social background and experience. Are not these, and many other examples that could be cited, instances of what has been proclaimed a great novelty, reader-response criticism?[5] The complaint that Pope's versification was "too uniformly musical" Johnson dismissed as "the cant of those who judge by principle rather than perception"—principles of pigeonhole construction rather than perception of actual pigeons. Would such critics, he asks, really take more pleasure in Pope's poetry "if he had tried to relieve attention by studied discords?"[6]

Of several texts I might address myself to here, I have chosen a challenge issued by Joel Weinsheimer, founding editor of the journal *The Eighteenth Century: Theory and Interpretation*. He wanted to know "the reason why scholars in our field have been relatively unresponsive to new critical systems and literary theories—semiotics, phenomenology, reader-response criticism, structuralism, deconstruction, hermeneutics—and continue, by and large, to consider the literature of the eighteenth century in the more traditional ways—textually, biographically, bibliographically, historically."[7] A pragmatic, if perhaps cynical, answer might be that wise scholars are hesitant about climbing aboard a bandwagon at a time when others are beginning to drop off it. A more thoughtful reply might be that such critics as Aristotle, Dante, Dryden, Johnson, Lessing, Coleridge, Arnold, Sainte-Beuve, Eliot, Leavis, and Edmund Wilson seemed to be able, using traditional methods and without recourse to newly discovered -isms and -icses, to furnish the world with what is still regarded as valuable literary criticism and that there seem to be no signs of any potential Johnsons, Eliots, or Wilsons emerging from the ranks of the practitioners of deconstructionism and the rest.[8]

My first purpose here is to argue that Weinsheimer's account of the traditional ways of studying eighteenth-century literature is a gravely defective one, and I want to illustrate my contention by a brief account of my own experiences with the study of literature during— *horresco referens*—the past sixty-five years. Like many children from reasonably literate families, I was reading things like nursery rhymes, *Peter Rabbit, Little Black Sambo,* and *The Three Billy Goats Gruff,* when I was five or six years old. Thank heaven television had not yet been invented, though perhaps I am being too self-congratulatory in surmising that a few exposures to Captain Kangaroo would have quickly sent me back to Beatrix Potter. I later made my way under my own steam—thank goodness no adults ever tried to direct my spare-time reading—through the Oz books, the Alger books, the Henty books, eventually developing, by massive exposure to progressively more rewarding levels of junk—a kind of process of natural selection, or survival of the fittest—a taste for adult literature.

At school we encountered readers, one per grade, increasing in textual difficulty. We did not have those colossal bores Dick, Jane, Spot, and Puff. Johnson was right when he said, "Babies do not want to hear about babies; they like to be told of giants and castles and of somewhat which can stretch and stimulate their little minds." When Mrs. Thrale objected that edifying children's books like *Tommy Prudent* and *Goody Two Shoes* had large sales, he retorted, "Remember that parents *buy* the books, and that children never read them"[9]—except, of course, when the schools force them to involve themselves in the drab middle-class suburban lives of Dick and Jane. We had Aesop's fables, fairy tales from Grimm and Andersen, Greek and Roman myths, stories of Robin Hood and his merry men, and simple verse like "The Wreck of the Hesperus" and "Oh, young Lochinvar has come out of the West!" By the fifth and sixth grades we got our teeth into the Cratchits' Christmas dinner, Ruskin's *King of the Golden River*, David Copperfield's encounter with the greedy waiter, and "the story of the caskets" from the Lambs' *Tales from Shakespeare*.

The eighth reader in the series I am describing[10]—the content of the various readers put out by different publishers was much the same—is impressive in its scope and variety and in the power of comprehension expected of students. There is no simplification: the original text is given. There are the opening scene of *Hamlet* and Caesar's funeral in *Julius Caesar;* Gray's *Elegy;* Macaulay's "Horatius"; Byron's "Prisoner of Chillon"; the opening stanzas of *The Faerie Queene* (in the original spelling, though with a glossary); the Nausicaa episode in the *Odyssey* in the Butcher and Lang translation; the death of Socrates in Jowett's translation of the *Phaedo;* Tennyson's *Ulysses;* and Arnold's "Forsaken Merman" (this seems to be a strange choice for thirteen- and fourteen-year-olds but perhaps not). The most shrewd device of the compilers of such volumes was to include long excerpts from classic works in the expectation—certainly fulfilled in my case— that they would arouse our curiosity sufficiently to make us go on and read the rest of the work: Don Quixote and the windmills; the tournament and the siege of Torquilstone in *Ivanhoe;* the discovery of the map of Treasure Island; the opening chapter of *Vanity Fair,* with Becky Sharp hurling Johnson's *Dictionary* back at her schoolmistress; Maggie Tulliver's attempt to run away and join the gypsies. The last two were particularly attractive to youngsters, who at times would have liked to do similar things. What, I asked, was going to happen to these young rebels? There was only one answer—read the book.

Some selections, such as moral bits of Carlyle and Ruskin, were boring, but most were enjoyable. We got the impression that there was a world out there with wider horizons than our narrow, isolated little farming community, a world that afforded richer opportunities for emotional and intellectual involvement. Johnson's maxim that poetry—literature—instructs by pleasing had not yet been forgotten, and by "instructs" he meant much more than inculcating moral precepts.[11] And it was made clear that there was an almost unlimited supply from many centuries and many parts of the world.

One of the most depressing phenomena during my years in academia has been the gradual reduction of the familiarity with literature generally expected of students in English. In my days as a graduate student we were expected to have not only a fairly detailed knowledge of the literature of one or more centuries but at least a nodding acquaintance with considerably more. At Columbia in the 1950s we had to demonstrate some reading knowledge of at least three foreign languages to qualify for admission to the Ph.D. program. (Curiously, some of my late colleagues who urged the reduction or abolition of foreign language requirements also volubly advocated an internationalist rather than an isolationist stance in American politics.)

My surmise that hostility to literature in general, a suspicion and fear of it, exists among the teaching establishment seems supported by the way in which the requirement of a broad acquaintance with the literature of many centuries was readily abandoned in favor of a minute scrutiny of a few texts, often contemporary American works whose chance of more than an ephemeral life seems dubious. Edmund Wilson, who took all literature for his province and began the study of Russian and Hebrew late in life in order to come to grips firsthand with the literatures of those languages, remarked concerning the popularity of T. S. Eliot in courses in English literature: "The point is that Eliot's work is fatally suited to the needs of American teachers of courses in English. In the first place, there is very little of it. . . . These English professors are lazy. They rarely know anything but English Lit., and they rarely read anything in English that they do not have to read for their degrees and their courses or to get themselves a little credit by writing in some critical organ about one of their accepted subjects."[12] Of course, Eliot's work does deserve careful study; but one hesitates to say the same about this or that recently discovered novelist or poet who is much touted today but who will probably be forgotten the year after next. And of course we can advance beyond minimalist reading of selected texts and study merely literary theory in vacuo, where the choice of works, if any, to be read is as irrelevant as the choice of a particular frog for the student of biology to dissect in order to learn batrachian anatomy and the technique of dissection.

To return to the autobiographical mode—during these early school years, we did not get much theory, but we had plenty of interpretation. The hermeneutics were simple. Each day we were assigned a sizable chunk from the reader to prepare. We were instructed to look up the unfamiliar words in our dictionaries and, if necessary, to analyze grammatically (we had been taught to do that) the often involved sentences of Scott and Washington Irving. The next day, in a session of perhaps forty-five minutes, we were quizzed in turn on our comprehension of what we had read, sometimes reading the piece aloud, paragraph by paragraph. Poetry was always read aloud, and sometimes recited from memory, while attention was called to the elements of prosody. In dramatic works, parts were assigned to different pupils and sometimes acted out at the front of the classroom. (*Macbeth* in particular was great fun, with paper crowns and wooden swords.)

Exposition of necessary background was given either by useful annotation in the textbook or by the teacher. History, as Weinsheimer points out, was an important part of that tradition. For a minimal understanding of "The Charge of the Light Brigade" or "Horatius," we had to know something about the Crimean War and the early history of Rome. Geography too sometimes came into it. A simple sketch map of the Mississippi valley added greatly to our comprehension of *Huckleberry Finn* (why was the fog at Cairo so crucial to the story?), and a map of Scotland to our comprehension of *Kidnapped*. There was some biography too. Dickens' boyhood helped us to empathize with the protagonist of *David Copperfield*. There was bibliography, in the sense that our attention was called to other plays by Shakespeare and other novels by Dickens and Scott that we might want to look into someday, with brief, appetite-whetting accounts of what happened in them.

All this was done in a low-key, undogmatic manner. Such bits of outside information were presented as ancillary to our response to the text. The text was not regarded merely as a quarry from which evidence could be extracted for construction of literary history or speculative psychobiography, such as Edward Dowden's famous "De Profundis" and "Out of the Depths" (third period) and "On the Heights" (fourth period)—"Whatever [Shakespeare's] trials and errors may have been, he had come forth from them wise, large-hearted, calm-souled."[13] During our high school years we read six of Shakespeare's plays, using the old Oxford and Cambridge editions, probably the most heavily annotated school editions ever published. There were three sets of notes, in ascending order of scholarly subtlety, in the margin, at the foot of the page, and at the end of the volume, some of the latter calling attention to the textual variants available in the early editions. But memorization of the whole lot was not required; as Johnson did, we were allowed to regard them as necessary evils and to pick and choose among them, although the glossarial ones were rightly regarded as the most important. To be sure, such a passage as "Pistol's cock is up" (*Henry V*, 2.2.55) had to wait for Eric Partridge's *Shakespeare's Bawdy* for full annotation, without even such a commentary as that of Dowden in Joyce's *Ulysses*, "Life ran very high in those days," though I am sure most of my fellow adolescents had no trouble in appreciating its polysemy.

General interpretations of the plays were suggested, but not insisted on, manifesting themselves in such examination questions as "Was Hamlet mad?," "Write a character sketch of Falstaff," and "What can be said in defence of Macbeth?" I am grateful to my twelfth-grade teacher who—when I argued, contrary to his and the then majority view, that Hamlet seemed very sane indeed and that the little failings of the tragic hero Macbeth were not all to be blamed on the dire influence of his villainous wife—gave both my papers an *A*. I was pleased when I learned much later that Tom Stoppard, in *Rosencrantz and Guildenstern Are Dead*, and Mary McCarthy, in her fine essay "General Macbeth," agreed with me.[14]

In short, the study of literature considered textually (that is, with regard to the authenticity of the text being read), historically, biographically, and bibliographically—the approach Weinsheimer seems to deplore—was certainly part of the tradition that I grew up with. But the overriding element in that tradition was what the French call, or used to call, explication de texte (there does not seem to be an English equivalent), and the other activities were of value in literary study only so far as they furthered it. Moreover, I believe that the most distinguished literary scholars who have worked in these disciplines have been well aware of the priorities: for instance, Phillip Harth, whose studies of the intellectual history of the seventeenth century have contributed much to our fuller understanding of the writings of Dryden and Swift; the late Irvin Ehrenpreis, whose monumental biography of Swift enables us to read his writings with greater appreciation of their subtleties; and Fredson Bowers, editor of *Studies in Bibliography*, who memorably defends textual scholarship: "As a principle, if we respect our authors, we should have a passionate concern to see that their words are recovered and currently transmitted in as close a form to their intentions as we can contrive."[15]

Such activities are not to be sneered at as old hat and fuddy-duddy; they are absolutely essential to serious literary study and always will be. This is not to say that we were allowed to be unaware that differing explications of the same text were possible and that there was no heaven-sent formula for deciding which of them was the "correct" one. There are always various degrees of probability, and only the reader can decide what the criteria of probability are. Perhaps, as one recent critic has maintained, the word "Still," in the climactic line of Johnson's *Vanity of Human Wishes,* "Still raise for good the supplicating voice," is to be read in the twentieth-century sense of "however," "nevertheless," "even if it may do no good," a word that is "powerfully, if sadly, concessive here in its acknowledgment that we cannot expect to see results," rather than in its usual seventeenth- and eighteenth-century sense of "always," "continually," "without ceasing," so that the message Johnson is giving his readers in the poem is a profoundly pessimistic rather than a hopeful one.[16]

There is no way of deciding such a question. A majority vote of the experts will not do it: such a vote, if one had been taken in the year 1200, would have shown conclusively that the sun revolves around the earth. Nor, as W. K. Wimsatt pointed out, does the author's intention decide the meaning of a text. When Robert Browning, misreading a seventeenth-century text, referred in *Pippa Passes* to a nun's "twat," he thought the word meant, and no doubt intended his readers to take it to mean, an article of her vesture, and no doubt a large number of the innocent Victorian maidens who worshipped Browning so took it to mean.[17] Does the fact that a large number of their more worldly brothers knew another meaning for it help us to decide which explication is the correct one? Not in the least; there is really no answer to such a question. Perhaps that is all Jacques Derrida's long-drawn-out lucubrations about decidability amount to (more on that below). But we knew something about all this in our high school years.

But in the later years of high school I also began to encounter metaliterature—getting above or away from literature, pigeonholing. Here we were informed of the existence of something called "the Romantic revival"[18] (or "revolution"), which apparently occurred in or about 1798. Perhaps the thinking was that since there was a political revolution in France at that time, there must have been a corresponding revolution in human sensibility and literary practice, although other political revolutions—those of Britain in 1688, America in 1776, and Russia in 1917—seem not to have required such a postulate. This revolution, we were told, displaced what Edmund Gosse casually dismissed as "the decay of taste" of the eighteenth century (like the ancien régime in France).[19]

It became clear that the works we were being told to read were chosen not for their possible appeal to our emotions and intellects but as evidence to bolster this thesis and to convince us that post-1798 rural (or nature) poetry, having mercifully superseded the pre-1798 prosaic "verse" of "city poets" such as Pope, was the right stuff. (It was not simply that it was more recent; when T. S. Eliot came along in the 1920s with *The Waste Land,* very much a city poem, it was denounced by Arthur Waugh, a figure of some consequence in critical circles, as the mad raving of a drunken Greek helot.) Those of us who lived with the rural delights of shoveling snow and manure, of trudging to school in forty-below-zero weather, and of coping with dust storms and plagues of grasshoppers during the drought of the 1930s were less appreciative of the glamor of nature than the more sheltered Wordsworth and Shelley. Nevertheless, the edict had gone forth, and I remember the evening before the eleventh-grade final examination memorizing "Oh, cuckoo, shall I call thee bird / Or but a wand'ring voice?" and "Hail to thee, blithe Spirit! / Bird thou never wert," for possible use next day (I was indeed able to make use of them) and wondering what cuckoos and skylarks were like. We did not have them on the western prairies, or fields of daffodils either.

Robert Burns, in particular, as the John the Baptist of the "movement," became a drag. Much later I was able to appreciate Burns' minor talent as a verse satirist. But it was not his satirical verse we were exposed to; that would have put him back in the heartless, unimaginative, tasteless eighteenth century (in which he actually lived). Instead, we had "To a Mountain Daisy" and "Wee, sleekit, cow'rin', tim'rous beastie." Carlyle's "Essay on Burns" was on the list of books we were supposed to have read for the twelfth-grade examination— the subject of a fine piece of American folk poetry and folk literary criticism:

> As I was laying on the green,
> A little English book I seen.
> Carlyle's Essay on Burns was the edition;
> So I left it laying in the same position.

I noticed that in every previous examination there had been an optional essay topic dealing with the work, differently worded from year to year but all to the effect: "What a great guy Burns was!" (Of course, neither Carlyle nor our teachers mentioned his prowess as a fornicator; he might have interested us more if they had.) So, with a sixteen-year-old's shrewdness, the week before the exam I composed and memorized an all-purpose essay to this effect and reproduced it on the examination paper. I forget what the stated subject was, but it did not matter—I got high marks.

When I made it to the university, Burns was nearly my nemesis. I enrolled in a compulsory course in "romantic" literature (I recall no course in eighteenth-century literature ever being offered while I was there). The first assignment was to go to the library and find as many definitions of romanticism as we could. I got as far as fourteen before my time and patience ran out (many of them mutually contradictory and all of them refuted in a fine article by Irving Massey some years ago).[20] Our second assignment was an essay explaining why Burns embodied the essence of romanticism, and I got into serious trouble for not burbling loudly enough about him. Honest response to a piece of writing was not wanted; what was required was adherence to externally imposed dogma. Literature had been displaced by metaliterature.

Such was my introduction to a different tradition of literary study from the one I had encountered in my early school days. In a paper I gave some years ago at the English Institute, I attempted to trace its origins.[21] It seems to have begun in the midnineteenth century, when the formal study of English literature was first introduced into academia, as the poor stepsister of the old and haughty disciplines of classics and mathematics. Its teachers seemed not quite to know what to do with it. Indeed, when much later someone proposed its introduction into the last holdouts Oxford and Cambridge churlish dons asked, "How can English literature be taught, anyway?" The assumption was that anyone who came to college with the kind of preparation in school that I have described was perfectly capable of reading and comprehending anything written in his or her native tongue for general consumption. There was also, perhaps, a feeling of inferiority to the older disciplines, which appeared to require the construction of a pseudoscientific systematization that students could be forced to memorize and regurgitate in examinations. Otherwise, how could one examine students on the subject? Merely to ask questions like "What do you think of Lemuel Gulliver?" or "Did you like *Rasselas?* If so, why? If not, why not?" would not do; it would be difficult to give the answers a pass or a fail.

In illustration I quoted Esther J. Trimble, Professor of Literature in the State Normal School, West Chester, Pennsylvania, who wrote a *Handbook of English and American Literature for the Use of Schools and Academies* (1883). "One of the most important lessons that . . . the genuine student learns," she affirms, "is that of sifting"—that is, of getting rid of part of the material being dealt with, in this case literature. She continues, "It is of the utmost importance to learn to generalize, to take in as nearly as possible the general and prominent features of a subject. . . . The work is divided into seventeen chapters, each chapter representing an era. . . . The prominent features of each era could be given in one lesson, enabling the pupil to get through the outline of the subject [presumably the whole of English and American literature] in a few lessons."[22] For each of her seventeen eras, Trimble provides a neat list of "points" to be memorized in the course of "getting through the outline" and no doubt to be reproduced in the pupil's examination paper. One era whose contents get thoroughly sifted out is the Restoration, the outstanding point of which is that "the prevailing taste in literature was low."

Thus arose the proliferation of -isms. Successive sections in Legouis and Cazamian, the standard history of English literature when I was a student (first published in the 1920s and much reprinted in the 1930s and 1940s), bear the titles "The Preparation for the Renascence," "The Flowering of the Renascence," "The End of the Renascence"—an era must necessarily have a rise, then a flowering, and then a decline and fall—"Classicism," "The Survival of Classicism," "The Pre-Romantic Period," and "The Romantic Period." Individual works had to be fitted into these pigeonholes. When I resurrected my old copy, I was surprised to discover even Quiller Couch, not the most exigent of critics (except when dealing with T. S. Eliot), demurring a little in his preface: "I feel that here and there in the second part . . . M. Cazamian has been forced back upon his Gallic instinct for logical neatness to overstrain it somewhat: that he is driven to classify our authors by 'movement' and 'tendencies' rather than by individual merit."[23]

But the urge to pigeonhole persists. Northrop Frye and others have created an Age of Sensibility in the later eighteenth century. In almost every number of the *Times Literary Supplement* one finds a reference to a mysterious entity called "Augustanism," which has nothing to do with Augustus Caesar and whose chronological bounds are hazy, to say the least.[24] Not long ago W. J. Bate published a book in which he reclassified the older "eras" as The First Temple, The Second Temple, and The Third Temple.[25] The search for the "essence" of such eras continues, though what good it does one if and when it is discovered is hard to say. It seems to be a kind of hedge anthropology or social history, unsupported by the kind of statistical evidence that might make its conclusions credible (just how many people abandoned a neoclassical for a romantic mode of thinking and feeling in 1798 or were afflicted by a dissociation of sensibility in 1660?). If this is what Weinsheimer means by traditional concern with history, I heartily agree with his suggestion that students ought to be occupied more profitably—though of course it is not really history, only literary history.

The search for essences extends not only to periods but to individual authors. When I recently published an anthology of Johnson's writings containing much that was unfamiliar to most readers, W. W. Robson, the Masson Professor of English in the University of Edinburgh, reviewing it in the *TLS*, asked, "Does it give the essence of Johnson?" so as to be of greater use to students writing examinations set by him. He recommended that the more unfamiliar parts of its contents be scrapped and replaced by reports of Johnson's conversation, taken presumably from Boswell—even though serious doubts have arisen about the authenticity of many of those reports—since Johnson "is best known as a conversationalist."[26] That, it has been authoritatively decided, is his essence. Such a procedure, of course, saves us the labor of reading much of Johnson's writing, fine as it is. The spirit of Trimble is still with us: Johnson has been well and truly sifted.

I also agree with Weinsheimer's suspicion of much so-called literary biography, in which biographers attempt to "get into" their subject's psyche—which usually means assimilating it to their own—with very little attention to how that psyche manifested itself in their subject's writings. An old Oxford don, resisting the movement to introduce an English honors program into the university, predicted that its content would consist of "chatter about Harriet." Chatter about the personalities and psychological quirks of Jonathan Swift, Samuel Johnson, Jane Austen, Evelyn Waugh, to mention a few, whose chatterers display minimal acquaintance with their writing and minimal interest in them, still flourishes. A few remarks by Germaine Greer will suffice.

> If Shakespeare had had a biographer he would not now be great. . . . It will be argued that biographers excite and maintain interest in their subjects, who would not remain in the public eye without them. This is demonstrably false, the case of Shakespeare being sufficient to prove the point. Contrariwise, there is the case of Byron, who has had more biographers than the sun breeds maggots in a dead dog. All of them sell well, to people who have never read a line Byron wrote. . . . Transmitted through Boswell, Johnson became less. *The Vanity of Human Wishes* and *London* are worth all of Boswell's scribbling together. But they remain unread. Boswell is easier to take.[27]

This is not to say that serious, down-to-earth biographies, such as Ellmann's Joyce, Edel's Henry James, and Clifford's two volumes on the earlier Johnson do not make it easier to understand their subjects' writing by showing us the circumstances in which that writing originated. Such biographers recognize that it is only their subjects' achievement as writers that makes them worth writing biographies about at all. The other kind is merely another of the many ingenious methods of rejecting literature.

Pigeonholing was what I was chiefly exposed to during my first two years of college. When I returned after four and a half years of military service during World War II, although Legouis and Cazamian were still the bible, there were hints that another tradition was beginning to make its way into the upper reaches of academia—a tradition represented by T. S. Eliot's analyses of Donne and Dryden (though his early, mysterious "dissociation of sensibility" was a little too much like Trimble for me to be entirely comfortable with it) and by I. A. Richards' *Practical Criticism,* followed by a number of other collections, which audaciously omitted names of authors and dates of poems, so that one could not tell what period they belonged to or rehearse the conventional wisdom about the author (from some potted biography), but asked one simply to read the texts and see what could be made of them. Cleanth Brooks and Robert Penn Warren's *Understanding Poetry* shuffled the pigeons about so that it was difficult to fit them into preassigned holes, and one was forced to contemplate the pigeons themselves. This new tradition was also represented by Richards' *Principles of Literary Criticism* and his and C. K. Ogden's *Meaning of Meaning;* William Empson's *Seven Types of Ambiguity* and *Some Versions of Pastoral,* which demonstrated that Gay's *Beggar's Opera* was more than a quaint little period piece; Brooks' *Well Wrought Urn,* which showed *The Rape of the Lock* to be something more than a piece of dainty filigree and pointed out that its subtext, to use current jargon, really has to do with rape; and Maynard Mack's "Muse of Satire," which indicated that it is somewhat naive to take the "I" of Pope's satires as always being literally Alexander Pope, 1688–1744.

Naturally this approach was bitterly opposed by the "periodizers." When F. R. Leavis saw an affinity between Marvell's "Tortur'd, besides each other part, / In a vain head and double heart," and Pope's "Bounded by Nature, narrowed still by Art, / A trifling head, and a contracted heart," F. W. Bateson would have none of it. Knowing the essential difference between the seventeenth and eighteenth centuries, he was able to affirm that in the Marvell passage "head" and "heart" are concrete images, "picture language," and that "the sense-impression predominated," whereas in the Pope passage, since Pope was an "Augustan," "the words are primarily conceptual," merely "grey abstractions."[28] Before 1700 people visualized, after 1700 they conceptualized, and there's an end on't. Such are the uses of a priori theory when applied to the reading of a text.

This group was nicknamed the New Critics, and their method of close examination of a text, without much concern for what period it belonged to, the New Criticism. As far as I was concerned, there was nothing new about it. It was a return to the tradition of my early exposures to literature in elementary and secondary schools—explication de texte; it was a return to Johnson's way of close reading and pondering the possible meanings and effect of individual words. Why not drop the pointless "new" and call it "explicatory criticism," or the like? This was the tradition that appealed to me. When I returned to college after the war, I had thought of majoring in mathematics or chemistry, at which I had done reasonably well, rather than surrendering again to the -isms and pseudohistory of Legouis and Cazamian. Now it seemed there might be some future in academia for the serious study of literature itself instead of ersatz theories about it. For me, this *was* the tradition, and for a time, in the 1940s and 1950s, it was the predominant one. It is astonishing that Weinsheimer overlooks it completely in his list of the traditional occupations of students of eighteenth-century literature. Those I have mentioned did not engage in textual, biographical, bibliographical, and historical study merely as ends in themselves but as means to an end, the fuller comprehension of literary texts. I see no reason why it cannot go on being the tradition in eighteenth-century literary scholarship, in the service of helping intelligent and sensitive readers become more sharply attuned to the fine and subtle literature of that century. There is still plenty to do. As the motto of what might almost be called the house organ of that tradition, quoting Dryden, puts it, "The last verse . . . is not yet sufficiently explicated."[29]

Naturam expelles furca, tamen usque recurret. Plus ça change, plus c'est la même chose. Weinsheimer, like Trimble, is in favor of abandoning the study of literature for that of metaliterature—not, as with Trimble and her successors, factitious eras and their essences, but another set of metaliterary disciplines. Certainly there is no harm in a professor of literature, if he or she is interested in them, deciding to learn something about semiotics, the study of signs, or about structuralism, an approach to anthropology or linguistics that teaches that structure rather than function is important, or about phenomenology—one assumes that Weinsheimer refers not to Hegel's (1806) but to Edmund Husserl's. But I do not understand why he calls them new systems. Husserl was born in 1859, did important work in the nineteenth century, and published his *Phänomenologie* before the First World War. The eleventh edition of the *Encyclopaedia Britannica* (1910) has a substantial article on "Significs," which seems to be synonymous with semiotics, drawing on such nineteenth-century work as that of C. S. Peirce and Bréal's *Sémantique.* Saussure, so often mentioned in work on semiotics, lived from 1857 to 1913. Perhaps Weinsheimer means only that they are new to him. More probably, though, it is simply their newness, their current fashionableness in academic literary circles, that is intended to recommend them; he does not even attempt to show what value they might have for literary study. This seems a rather cynical approach to scholarship, as if to say, "Waistlines are lower and hemlines higher in Paris this year, so discard or alter your old wardrobe." It might be wiser to put it in mothballs, since who knows whether in a few years it may not become the vogue again?[30]

There are perhaps three elements involved. First is a continued manifestation of the inferiority complex of Trimble and her contemporaries who felt that something more imposing was needed to justify their salaries than merely trying to read and explicate and getting students to read and explicate literary texts. They therefore contrived the elaborate structure of neoclassicism, preromanticism, romanticism, modernism (postromanticism?), postmodernism, and post-postmodernism ("What, will the line stretch out till end of doom?"). Second is academic empire-building. Some of those empires have become well entrenched, in particular romanticism. However great one's skepticism that the word has any real meaning, it is not likely in the foreseeable future that courses, journals, and scholar-specialists who carry that banner will be displaced. It is the prospect of hitting a similar jackpot with some new -ism that makes the ambitious young scholar's eyes light up. And third, there is the excuse to avoid the time-consuming and toilsome occupation of reading and explicating a great many difficult texts by such authors as Chaucer, Shakespeare, Milton, Dryden, Pope, Joyce, Eliot, and Pound—that is, the same old dislike of literature exhibited by my first department head.

Still, such terms as those flourished by Weinsheimer can be impressive, and if a candidate for appointment or promotion can tell a dean that he or she is a specialist in hermeneutics—something literary and biblical scholars have been practicing for over two millennia, from Aristarchus of Alexandria, through Augustine, Origen, and Aquinas, down to the latest proposer of a better explication of "The onlie begetter of these insuing sonnets, Mr. W. H."—the dean, perhaps a hard-headed organic chemist or zoologist who has never heard the term before, may be impressed. Of course, the danger of investing heavily in a current fashion is that the bottom may suddenly fall out of the market and let one down. Twenty or thirty years ago Weinsheimer would have felt compelled to include existentialism in his list of desiderata. Where are the existentialist literary critics now?

So at last we come to deconstruction. I can not resist referring to a hilarious account in the *Los Angeles Times* of the reception at the University of California at Irvine of the news that J. Hillis Miller was moving there from Yale University. It was headed "UCI Will Try Deconstructing with Yale Critic," and it reported that in Irvine "profes-

sors were dancing in the streets." Some of the rapture may have
been dampened by the reporter's quotation from an anonymous Yale
academic: "When we're done with [a movement] here, it is exported
to the provinces." Miller was reported as having described his introduction to deconstruction by Jacques Derrida (who later joined the hegira
from Yale to Irvine) in a seminar at Johns Hopkins University: "I
thought it was terrific. He was reading texts by Rousseau, Plato, and
Mallarmé and seeing things nobody ever saw. . . . For example, he
noticed that Plato repeatedly used a Greek word *pharmakon,* which
means both remedy and poison. Derrida's conclusion was that the
meaning of Plato's work was 'undecidable.'"[31]

Well! "Seeing things nobody ever saw"! The small Liddell and
Scott Greek-English dictionary that I used as an undergraduate tells
me at once that *pharmakon* can mean either "remedy" or "poison" (and
several other things as well).[32] Anyone who has ever walked into a
pharmacy knows that the pharmaceuticals on its shelves can be either
remedial or poisonous, and it will always be undecidable whether a
particular user will take a couple of Valium tablets to relieve nervous
tension or gulp down a handful in order to commit suicide. If this is
all that is needed to convert us to a belief in deconstructionism, there
would appear to be no reason for us all not to be converted at once.
The truth, of course, is not only students of literature but also ordinary
intelligent readers have known for ages that words have multiple
meanings and that, if and when their meanings seem decidable (and
often they are not), it can only be through a study of the context in
which people have used them. Every student can think of many places
in the texts of Shakespeare where ambiguities exist that critics have
argued over and will probably never be decided. Indeed, William
Empson, long ago in *Seven Types of Ambiguity,* welcomed the undecidability of language as contributing to the emotional complexity and
evocativeness of poetry. When Lady Macbeth, learning of Duncan's
proposed visit to Glamis Castle, tells her husband, "He that's coming
must be provided for," is she speaking as a conscientious housewife,
concerned that proper accommodation be arranged for the royal
guest, or as a potential assassin? Both, no doubt, and she is probably
enjoying the black humor of the remark. My attention was called to
this undecidable double meaning in the eleventh grade.

I have not been able to see what deconstruction has added to what
traditional readers already knew about the nature of the language
they encountered in the texts they read. "If anything is destroyed in
a deconstructive reading," one translator and editor of Derrida writes,
in as clear a statement of what he is getting at as I have encountered,
"it is not meaning but the claim to unequivocal domination of one

mode of signifying over another." But who in the world had made such a claim? "This," she continues, "of course implies that a text signifies in more than one way, and to varying degrees of explicitness." Among the ways "the discrepancy is produced," she lists "a double-edged word" (like, one supposes, Lady Macbeth's "provided"); "when the figurative level of a statement is at odds with the literal level" (is this much more than our old friend the mixed metaphor, like Hamlet's "take arms against a sea of troubles"?); and "when the so-called starting point of an argument is based on suppositions that render its conclusion problematic or circular."[33]

Those of us who have made our way through a fair amount of writing about literary theory have had ample opportunity to recognize circular argument. There is certainly no unequivocal way of determining the claim of one signification of Lady Macbeth's "provided" or Browning's "twat" over another, and it is hard to think of any serious critic who has ever advanced such a claim. With the first, we are quite content to let the two significations exist simultaneously. With the second, that Browning intended his noun to mean something no other speaker or writer of English ever took it to mean (except, perhaps, naive readers of Browning who never encountered the word elsewhere) does not give that meaning a claim to dominate the other signification or vice versa. Few students are going to lose much sleep over these pseudoproblems, any more than Johnson did about taking arms against the sea: "I know not why there should be so much solicitude about this metaphor. Shakespeare breaks his metaphors often, and in this desultory speech there was less need of preserving them."[34]

"Surely a man of no very comprehensive search may venture to say that he has heard all this before, but it was never till now recommended by such a blaze of embellishment" (Johnson again, this time on the *Essay on Man*).[35] We long ago learned to live with undecidability in language, even, as with Empson and Brooks, to welcome it.[36] This however is not to say that a fair amount of agreement about the signification of particular words and passages in particular contexts will not continue, even if there is no way to guarantee its hundred-percent certainty. Hume demonstrated that no matter how many millions or billions of times the sun has risen in the past, there is no logical or rational way of predicting that it will do so tomorrow; yet we are so constituted that we go on acting as if it will. Most people who hear a husband described as "a good provider" will not think that "a good assassin" is meant, although conceivably someone with a Shakespearean capacity for irony might. Perhaps some scholar will uncover proof that Browning had access to some obscure text in which "twat" signified "wimple," or improbably, some religious order will one day decree that that designation be given to some part of its members' attire. But until that happens, the rank and file of vulgar speakers, on hearing the word, will go on taking it to signify what the *Oxford English Dictionary* calls, in the decent obscurity of a learned language, the *pudendum muliebre*.

Without some measure of agreement, however tentative or temporary, on the ordinary signification of a large part of the language in use, it is hard to see how much useful communication can take place, not merely between the writer of a book and its readers but among human beings in general. The vast majority of readers, when the text tells them that King Duncan was murdered or that Huck and Jim traveled down the Mississippi on a raft or that the Ancient Mariner shot an albatross with his crossbow, will accept the primary significance of those statements without demur; a world in which they did not would be a very strange one, as would a literature in which their primary meaning could not be trusted. True, all these examples may also have symbolic significance—the mariner's albatross quickly became a widely used metaphor for a burden of guilt, and the Mississippi may be "a strong brown god"—but a reading of the text in which they were not, in the first place, a bird and a river would be, to say the least, difficult. Yet there is no law to prevent readers from so reading it if they choose, any more than there is a way to prevent people from ordering their affairs as if the sun were not going to rise tomorrow; who is to decide? As Hume pointed out, it may not.

That language, an activity of fallible, unpredictable human beings, is never ultimately decidable has always seemed to bother Continental, especially French, scholars more than it has those brought up to communicate as best they can in the vast, sprawling, imprecise, mutable vernacular called English.[37] The original purpose of the great *Dictionnaire* (1st ed., 1694) of the Académie Française was to establish norms of usage and meaning to which speakers and writers of French were supposed to conform. Samuel Johnson, on the contrary, in the midst of a century when Great Britain and its English-speaking colonies were beginning to expand into a worldwide Anglophone community, poohpoohed any such attempt at "fixing" a language and invoked "the spirit of English liberty" against French academicism and authoritarianism.

Mathematics, too, is a humanly contrived language. A recent study of deconstructionism relates it to the controversy that arose in the early twentieth century when the German mathematician David Hilbert proposed his *Entscheidungsproblem*—the problem of decidability: whether mathematical theorems can be shown to be either provable or unprovable within the framework of the mathematical system in which they were created.[38] The Czech logician Kurt Gödel showed that they cannot. Gödel's challenge to Hilbert was made in 1928. If it has taken the deconstructionists so long to catch up with it, it seems to me that as with Weinsheimer's other desiderata, there is something rather old hat about it. "Ah, what a dusty answer gets the soul / When hot for certainties"—or decidability—"in this our life!" But Meredith said this a century before Derrida.

In short, from the rise of general literacy to the present, the efforts of a large number of those who have professed to be mediating literature to readers have been motivated by a distrust of it and have been intent, whether consciously or not, on subverting it (a nice Derridean situation, incidentally). In the mideighteenth century, John Newbery initiated the still-flourishing trade of publishing do-gooding children's books that parents would buy and children not read. In the twentieth, the advent of progressive education, or something of the kind, replaced fairy tales, myths, and fables in the school readers with the Dick-and-Jane vignettes of how a white middle-class suburban family conducted, or ought to conduct, their conformist lives. When English literature made its way into the upper levels of education, the first concern of most of its teachers was to protect those exposed to it from its immoral effects. "The gems with which it is so copiously adorned," pronounced the first professor of English literature at the University of London—perhaps the first professor of English literature anywhere—"sometimes require to be abstracted and exhibited with a careful hand, lest they convey pollution with the foul mass of daring profaneness or disgusting wantonness in which they are too often encrusted. Never," he continued, "will I suffer the eye of inexperienced youth to be dazzled by the brilliancy of genius, when its broad lustre obscures the deformity of vice."[39]

But perhaps even this moralizing attitude, which at least took literature seriously, if only as serious menace, was preferable to that of those who, to convince themselves that they were rivaling their colleagues in the sciences, took a rigorously objective, taxonomic approach to it, sorting it out into periods, movements, and -isms like a microbiologist at the microscope classifying a collection of bacteria. A reviewer of the latest published volume in the *Oxford History of English Literature,* on the mideighteenth century—a work much delayed in publication and evidently owing much to the late author's training in the Oxford school of English in the 1920s—commented that its account of the habits and adventures of the "greater ode" and the "lesser ode" sounded like a chapter from *The Birds of Rutlandshire.*[40] It was during the same 1920s at Oxford that Robert Graves was warned, "I understand, Mr. Graves, that the essays which you write for your

English tutor are, shall I say, a little temperamental. It appears, indeed, that you prefer some authors to others."[41] Graves' tutor would surely feel at home in a deconstructionist setting where value judgments and expressions of personal preference are taboo. One text is as good as another to practice deconstruction on; to become emotionally involved with them is beneath the dignity of one engaged in so academically elite an occupation as the pursuit of theory.

"Grau ist alle Theorie, und grün des Lebens goldner Baum," wrote Goethe—gray is all theory, and green life's golden tree. Still, I am not wholly against theorizing about literature, if the theory has some credible basis, such as that language and literature, both literary composition and the response to it, are manifestations of human behavior. Since Weinsheimer and others imply that not to concern oneself with literary theory is to be beyond the pale, I shall provide an easy one. It is stated very simply by the editors of a "new critical" anthology of poetry: "The poet is conscious of an experience; to him, from the point at which he starts to write, the poem is not the original experience but the experience which *these words* 'mean' to him. The reader must use these words, in reverse order so to speak, to create in himself an experience." [42] If something more impressive is wanted, I can put it in the form of a diagram:

$$S \longleftrightarrow R = s \longleftrightarrow r$$

S is the external stimulus or stimuli that impels a writer to put pen to paper. The first arrow represents the writer's nervous system, conditioned by years of experience, through which these stimuli pass and are enhanced and modified so as to produce the response R, the literary artifact. (The reverse arrow represents the feedback from drafts of the work, which causes them to act as stimuli to impel the writer to revise until he or she is reasonably satisfied with the effect.) The final product R, the poem, story, or whatever, then becomes s, the stimulus for the reader. It in turn acts on the reader's nervous system, conditioned by his or her own experience, so as to produce r, the reader's emotional and intellectual response to the work. (The $s \longrightarrow r$ process may be repeated in subsequent readings, in each of which the reader's nervous system has been further conditioned by the earlier readings—perhaps this is what reader-response criticism is dealing with.)[43]

There is nothing novel or alarming about this account of how literature works. It can be found in Leonard Bloomfield's masterly *Language* (1932), a work that in my opinion has not been superseded, Chomsky or Derrida to the contrary notwithstanding, and is implicit in such works as Ogden and Richards' *Meaning of Meaning* (1923),

Richards' *Principles of Literary Criticism* (1925), and Thomas Clark Pollock's unfortunately neglected *Nature of Literature* (1942). There is little in literary criticism that is not taken care of by this model. Derrida's (and others') polysemism, for instance, is the natural product of the immense amount of variation between one conditioned nervous system and another or between different stages of conditioning in the same nervous system. Conditioning is the result of the changing patterns of electrochemical connections (synapses) between nerves; neurobiologists estimate that the average number of synapses in the human brain is approximately 10^{15}, or ten quadrillion. No computer with ten quadrillion transistors or microchips has yet even been imagined.

The overt effects of stimulus-response in literature are well known. Sir Walter Scott used to say that he could never read the closing lines of *The Vanity of Human Wishes* without tears. When the film *The Exorcist* was shown, scenes caused members of the audience to vomit. Male readers may recall that, in their younger days at least, the reading of such erotic literature as *Fanny Hill* or Shakespeare's *Venus and Adonis* could produce interesting changes in the male anatomy. I have no doubt that Pavlov's dog could have been conditioned to salivate at a recitation of "She was a phantom of delight." If this seems farfetched, a story is told of the horse ridden by Laurence Olivier in the film *Henry V*, which had been trained to gallop at appropriate places in the script. It was given to Olivier as a memento, and he took it to his country place, where he once put it in a trap and drove it to the station to meet Noël Coward, who was coming to visit him. The horse ambled along at a leisurely pace, and Coward, growing impatient, asked whether its speed could not be increased. "Oh, certainly," said Olivier, and he began to recite "Once more into the breach, dear friends, once more." The horse immediately broke into a gallop. (I suppose a deconstructionist horse would have turned its head, looked knowingly at the two passengers, and pointed out that, even though they might not be conscious of it, "breach" has a significant homonym. But there have been earlier experts in occult signification, going back at least as far as Swift's Hack in *A Tale of a Tub*.)

Some may be alarmed at the thought of the so-called lower animals being susceptible to aesthetic stimuli along with us superior human beings, and no doubt far more subtle transactions take place in the far more highly developed human nervous system. I am not arguing that greater knowledge of the latest advances in neuroscience will be of great value to the student or teacher of literature, only that if one is looking for a theoretical basis for solving the problem of how literature works, such a neurobiological model offers a more credible and promising one than the alternatives suggested by Weinsheimer. "The denial of the importance of psychology," T. C. Pollock writes—or its hand-maid neurobiology—"in literary studies . . . implies that literature has no important relation with what we call the minds of men,"[44] a denial that Northrop Frye, as much as anyone on this side of the Atlantic, was responsible for promulgating. What are the roots of this desire to divorce literature from human experience? Is it that life, with which literature tries to cope, is too frighteningly various and complex? Does the pain of living curl up the small soul in the window seat behind *The Anatomy of Criticism?*

Perhaps the best my neurobiological theory can do at present is to call attention to the importance of the second arrow in the diagram above. Neuroscientists argue that some electrochemical synaptic trans-ferences may be excitatory and some inhibitory. Richards' *Practical Criticism* demonstrates how inhibitory conditioning can keep one from responding fully to literature's potential for stimulation—how a reader who has never seen a grand piano but only upright ones is put off by D. H. Lawrence's poem in which a little boy sits under a piano; how response to literature can be stifled by conditioning in stock responses. It is presumably our job as students and teachers of literature to try to remedy such inhibition, to enable readers of a novel, as Trilling wrote, to involve themselves in the moral life, to put their own motives under examination, more deeply to respond, aesthetically, emotion-ally, intellectually, to the world outside their present limited experi-ence of it. Or, to quote Johnson, "The only end of writing is to enable the readers better to enjoy life, or better to endure it,"[45] and I am not sure whether the study of semiotics, phenomenology, structuralism, and deconstructionism (all escapes from direct contact with literature) can contribute much to that end. Trilling and Johnson of course assume that literature is related to human experience, and Johnson, at least, assumes, that language is a form of human behavior. If those assumptions are not granted, the advocates of metaliterary disciplines recommended by Weinsheimer will presumably conclude this discus-sion with the ultimatum issued by the truculent businessman in a recent *New Yorker* cartoon, talking on the telephone to a recalcitrant colleague: "This conversation's going nowhere if you keep injecting the human factor."[46]

Notes

1. I am not the first to make this observation; cf. Edmund Wilson, reviewing Joseph Wood Krutch's *Samuel Johnson* (1944): "There is a tendency in scholarly writing done by professors and composers of theses that sometimes becomes rather exasperating to the reader outside the college world. This tendency may be briefly described as an impulse on the part of the professors to undermine their subjects or explain them away. . . . The professor would be made most uncomfortable if he had to meet Whitman or Byron; he would not like him—he does not, in fact, like him. But he has gone in for studying literature and he must try to do something to advance himself in that field" ("Re-Examining Dr. Johnson," in *Samuel Johnson: A Collection of Critical Essays,* ed. Donald Greene [Englewood Cliffs, N.J.: Prentice-Hall, 1965], 13).

2. "Manners, Morals, and the Novel," in *The Liberal Imagination* (Garden City, N.Y.: Doubleday, 1957), 215.

3. Every beginning instructor in English should be required to read Virginia Woolf's devastating essay on a similar popular spellbinder, Sir Walter Raleigh, first professor of English literature at Oxford: "He joked, he told stories. He made the undergraduates rock with laughter. He drew them in crowds to his lecture room. And they went away loving something or other. Perhaps it was Keats. Perhaps it was the British Empire. Certainly it was Walter Raleigh. But we should be much surprised if anybody went away loving poetry, loving the art of letters" (*The Captain's Death Bed* [London: Hogarth Press, 1950], 86). A colleague of mine once observed that the talents most likely to lead to "best teacher" awards in universities are those of the stand-up comic. In the two volumes of Raleigh's letters Virginia Woolf is reviewing, she comments, "It would be difficult to find a single remark of any interest whatever about English literature," and she quotes Raleigh, "[I] can't read Shakespeare any more. . . . Not that I think him a bad author, particularly, but I can't bear literature." Raleigh later found his true métier as a historian of the Royal Air Force, and my department head as chairman for many years of the local socialist party.

4. The Shakespearean comments are from the concluding notes on *Julius Caesar* and *King Lear* in Johnson's edition of Shakespeare.

5. I once heard Stanley Fish, just beginning his career as the pundit of reader-response criticism, deliver a splendid talk on *The Pilgrim's Progress* to a group of faculty and graduate students at the University of Southern California. It consisted largely of a description of his response to the work the first time he read it and his heightened response the second time round. This is excellent; there should be much more of this kind of thing. But is it not what good teachers of literature have always done?

6. *The Lives of the English Poets* [Pope], ed. G. B. Hill (Oxford: Clarendon Press, 1905), 3:248.

7. *Johnsonian News Letter* 44 (March–December 1984):31. Lawrence Lipking (*Eighteenth-Century Studies* 21 [Fall 1987]:109) is similarly puzzled: "Why do people write books about Samuel Johnson? The answer does not seem to be that many of them have something new to say. The effort of revaluation that spurs literary studies of most great authors, testing them by the critical methods or ideologies of the present day, has passed by Johnson with hardly a murmur, as if he occupied a sanctuary where structuralism and post-structuralism, feminism, the new historicism, or assaults on the canon must repectfully lower their voices." I suppose people go on writing books about Johnson for the same reason they go on writing books about Shakespeare. The implied injunction to "revaluate" literary texts using the "critical methods or ideologies of the present day" is ominously reminiscent of the Hack's program of critical modernism in *A Tale of a Tub*. Such strident PR on behalf of poststructuralism, deconstructionism, and the rest may indicate a certain sense of insecurity on the parts of their advocates. "Indeed," Lipking continues, "many books on Johnson seem to take pride in leaving him undisturbed. At its best, this urge to protect the work from intruders can result in better editions and more accurate historical research." In the remark about the urge to protect Johnson from intruders, is there just a suggestion of the existence of a conspiracy?

8. The one book so far published that seems to have tried to heed Weinsheimer's and Lipking's exhortations to "make it new" (*The New Eighteenth Century,* ed. Felicity Nussbaum and Laura Brown [New York: Methuen, 1987]) has not proved a conspicuous success. See a long review of it by Howard Weinbrot, forthcoming in volume 3 of *The Age of Johnson* (1989). The impression one gets from the book is that the new eighteenth century is just the same old immoral, insensitive, hypocritical, class-ridden eighteenth century so fervently denounced by the Victorians, with a privileged elite grinding the faces of the downtrodden poor. Its writers deplore its "maldistribution of wealth, bourgeois, capitalist virtues" the "prevailing social and economic disparities," and its oppression and exploitation of women. It is still the eighteenth century of Dickens' *A Tale of Two Cities* and *Barnaby Rudge*. One writer even laments the rise of illegitimacy in the century: one would like to see some statistics about the comparative incidence of illegitimacy in England from the time of the bastard William the Conqueror down to the liberated 1980s. One of the editors has published a monograph demonstrating that Pope was a hireling lackey, a running dog of capitalist imperialism, toadying to his aristocratic masters—such as, no doubt, King George II and Queen Caroline, Sir Robert Walpole, and Lord Hervey. It is introduced by Terry Eagleton, a much-acclaimed critical innovator, who writes of the century's "squalor and exploitation, the material destitution and imperialist violence." "[After Laura Brown's study] it should be less easy to mistake the patrician values of Alexander Pope ... for the unchanging truths of the human heart." A similar combination of demonology and smug self-righteousness is found in "We instinctively feel the great, the immeasurable distance that severs this age, so proud of its truth, its earnestness, its energy, its high and noble aims, from

the heartlessness, the indifference, the frivolity, in one word, the utter worldliness of the eighteenth century." The Victorians' favorite historian John Richard Green wrote this in 1859 (Brown, *Alexander Pope* [Oxford and New York: Basil Blackwell, 1985], vi–vii; Green, *Studies in Oxford History, Chiefly in the Eighteenth Century* [Oxford: Clarendon Press, 1901], 28).

9. Hester Lynch Piozzi, *Anecdotes of the Late Samuel Johnson, LL.D.*, ed. Arthur Sherbo (London: Oxford University Press, 1974), 65. The psychiatrist Bruno Bettelheim enters a powerful defense of fairy tales in *The Uses of Enchantment: The Meaning and Importance of Fairy Tales* (New York: Knopf, 1976). In *The Second American Revolution and Other Essays* (New York: Random House, 1982), Gore Vidal has an excellent essay on the virtues of the Oz stories. No doubt the influence of Dick and Jane had something to do with the response of the little girl reported by David Riesman (*The Lonely Crowd* [New Haven: Yale University Press, 1950], 83), who when asked whether she would like to be able to fly, replied, "I would like to be able to fly if everybody else did, but otherwise it would be kind of conspicuous."

10. *Everyday Classics: Eighth Reader*, ed. Franklin T. Baker and Ashley Thorndike (New York: Macmillan, 1920).

11. The maxim is found in the preface to Shakespeare (*Yale Works of Samuel Johnson* [New Haven: Yale University Press, 1968], 7:67. I once ventured to paraphrase this as "Literature, by involving the reader emotionally, effects desirable changes in the patterns of his nervous system"—another way of putting Lionel Trilling's comment on the function of the modern novel, indeed Aristotle's *katharsis*.

12. *The Bit Between My Teeth* (New York: Farrar, Straus, and Giroux, 1965), 381.

13. Edward Dowden, *Shakspere* (New York: D. Appleton, 1878), 60.

14. In *The Writing on the Wall and Other Essays* (Harmondsworth: Penguin, 1973), 9–19.

15. *Textual and Literary Criticism* (Cambridge: Cambridge University Press, 1959), 8. Bowers tells (29–30) the story of F. O. Matthiesen's delight over the "soiled fish of the sea" in Herman Melville's *White-Jacket*—the "shudder" that resulted from this "frightening vagueness," the *discordia concors* (a sound deconstructionist stance)—and how "soiled" turned out to be a misprint for "coiled." Nevertheless some critics praised the misprinted expression as an improvement over the original, thus making an incompetent typesetter a greater artist than Melville.

16. Murray Krieger, *The Classic Vision* (Baltimore: Johns Hopkins University Press, 1971), 14.

17. The *Oxford English Dictionary*'s entry for the word gives a good account of Browning's involvement with it.

18. "Revival" stems from the curious notion held for a time in the nineteenth century that the first "romantic" period occurred in the reign of Elizabeth I. When Edmund Gosse first delivered his ill-fated lecture series in America in 1884, he gave it the title "From Shakespear to Pope; A History of the Decline of Romantic Poetry." When, the following year, he gave it as the Clark lectures at Cambridge University and printed it, he retitled it *From*

Shakespear to Pope: An Enquiry into the Causes and Phenomena of the Rise of Classical Poetry in England—which did not prevent it from being torn to shreds by Churton Collins.

19. In the article "Song" in the *Encyclopaedia Britannica*, 11th ed., 1910. In an article "The Rise of Modern Science and the Genesis of Romanticism" (*PMLA* 97 [January 1982]), Hans Eichner referred to "the decline of poetry in the eighteenth century." The article was awarded the Modern Language Association's William Riley Parker Prize for the best article of the year in *PMLA*.

20. "The Romantic Movement: Phrase or Fact?," *Dalhousie Review* 44 (1965): 396–411. Ian Jack (*English Literature, 1815–1832* [Oxford: Clarendon Press, 1963; vol. 10 of the Oxford History of English Literature]) also rejected the use of the term.

21. "The Study of Eighteenth-Century English Literature: Past, Present, and Future," in *New Approaches to Eighteenth-Century Literature*, ed. Phillip Harth (New York: Columbia University Press, 1976), 1–32.

22. (Philadelphia: Eldridge and Brother), iii–iv. I have been accused of sexism for picking on poor Esther Trimble. In fact, I am paying her a compliment by quoting her rather than some of her far sillier male colleagues. For instance, William Francis Collier, LL.D., of Trinity College, Dublin, in his *History of English Literature* (London: T. Nelson & Sons, 1873), divides it into nine eras and fulminates against the fifth (1674–1709).

> Men and women were alike immoral—nay depraved. . . . All the comedies and much of the poetry written from the Restoration to the close of the century, and later too, are disgustingly vicious. It took many a long year to root out the poisonous weeds that, sown in this age, spread their tangling fibres through the best soils of English poetry. Even yet the English stage has hardly been cleansed from the pollutions heaped upon it by the playwrights, who manfactured highly flavoured vice for the delectation of the wicked men and women that hung by the skirts of the worst of our Stuart kings. The satires, songs, and novels also bear the brand and scars of vice, and flaunt them openly in the eyes of all (219–22).

Trimble's restrained "the prevailing taste in literature was low" seems liberal and enlightened by comparison. But rooting out literature and cleansing it (Lipking would say "revising the canon" and "revaluating" it) and "testing" it by "the ideologies of the present day" was clearly regarded as the most important function of academic teachers. In the 1880s, the ruling ideology was the maintenance of sexual morality; this has been replaced in the 1980s by various other selected ideologies. (But why "of the present day"? Where, except in academic literary study, is Marxism still taken seriously? Not even, it seems, in Russia and China. Or simon-pure Freudianism, except among a small minority of practicing psychiatrists?)

23. Emile Legouis and Louis Cazamian, *A History of English Literature*, English tr. London: J. M. Dent, 1933 (first published 1926), vii.

24. Howard D. Weinbrot (*Augustus Caesar in "Augustan" England* [Princeton: Princeton University Press, 1978]) demonstrates the silliness of the epithet.

25. *The Burden of the Past and the English Poet* (Cambridge, Mass.: Belknap Press, 1970).

26. *Times Literary Supplement*, 26 Oct. 1984, 1221.

27. London *Times*, 1 Feb. 1986, 8.

28. *A Selection from Scrutiny*, ed. F. R. Leavis (Cambridge: Cambridge University Press, 1968), 2:280–308.

29. It is a mistake to say, as is often said, that the New Critics neglected history. They neglected and despised the pseudohistory of Trimble and of Legouis and Cazamian. But a glance at the actual criticism of Brooks, Empson, Richards, and the others shows that they welcomed whatever the real historical background of a work could contribute to our understanding of it. Brooks' fine edition of Percy's correspondence, displaying a meticulous regard for history and biography, should not be forgotten. The Dryden quotation is used as the motto of each number of *The Explicator*.

30. The stress on being "up to date," on using "critical methods or ideologies of the present day" is perhaps another effort to raise the lowly status of professors of literature and the arts to that of their colleagues in the physical sciences. It is of course necessary for physicists or molecular biologists to keep up with developments in their fields: new theories, based on new experimentation, invalidate and supersede older ones (though even here, Thomas S. Kuhn suggests, there may be an element of chance and faddishness). But it has never been supposed that the arts and criticism of the arts are "progressive" in the same way that John Cage and Andy Warhol and Allen Ginsberg supersede Mozart and Michelangelo and Shakespeare, that Derrida and de Man supersede Aristotle and Johnson, and that those who continue to perform Mozart or study Aristotle are obliged to give the "reason" for their bizarre behavior in clinging to these fuddy-duddy occupations. Of course other fields of endeavor have long been aware of the potency of the *argumentum ad novitatem:* "Use the new, improved Eezywash, and you'll never again be satisfied with the old-fashioned brands."

31. *Los Angeles Times*, 6 Mar. 1986, sec. 6, pp. 1, 12, 14. Miller's hysterical outburts in defense of deconstruction (*TLS*, 17–23 June 1988), after it was disclosed that his former Yale colleague Paul de Man had published anti-Semitic articles in a journal in Nazi-occupied Belgium, astonished many:

The real aim [of de Man's critics] is to discredit that form of interpretation called "deconstruction," to obliterate it, as far as possible, from the curriculum, to dissuade students of literature, philosophy, and culture from reading de Man's work or that of his associates, to put a stop to the "influence" of "deconstruction". . . . The target is literary theory or critical theory generally, for example the so-called "new historicists," or feminine theorists, or students of popular culture, or practitioners of so-called "cultural criticism." The rapid widening of the targets of hostility has been a conspicuous fact. . . . All deconstruction must be of a piece. De

Man was a Fascist. Now we know what was suspected all along. Deconstruction is Fascist. Therefore get rid of it.

Hell hath no fury like a leader of an avant-garde movement when it ceases to be avant and to attract new recruits. I suppose the charge of a conspiracy was inevitable. I assure Miller that my objection to deconstruction is not that it is Fascist, but that it is trivial, trite, and pretentious. Nevertheless it is disturbing, as Stanley Corngold points out (*TLS*, 26 Aug.–1 Sept. 1988), himself applying deconstructionist technique to the language, that words such as "deconstruct," "disassemble," "dismember," and "disarticulate" are "double-edged," and when read in a less figurative way than most of their present users, I am sure, are conscious of, they bear a gruesome resemblance to what de Man's Nazi associates were in fact practicing in Auschwitz and Belsen.

32. The unabridged Liddell and Scott gives even more. Miller would have found a far more wide-ranging and searching account than Derrida's of the history and multiple uses of *pharmaka* in the article "Pharmacy" in the *Encyclopaedia Britannica,* 11th ed. (1910), by a learned pharmacologist.

33. Jacques Derrida, *Dissemination,* trans. Barbara Johnson (Chicago: University of Chicago Press, 1981), xiv–xv.

34. *Yale Works*, 8:981. "Desultory," in Johnson's *Dictionary,* is "roving from thing to thing; unsettled; immethodical; inconsistent."

35. *Lives of the Poets,* 3:244.

36. A great deal of undecidability is built into all the Indo-European languages. For instance, in "John drove James to his house," there is no way of deciding whether the house is that of John or of James. French "sa maison" is no better. In Cree, spoken widely in northern Canada, one of the great Algonquian family of languages, the house, if John's, is "wikihk" (said to be in the proximate case and the pronominal suffix to be in the third person); if James', it is "wikiyihk" (obviative case or fourth person). If someone says to a friend, "We had a fine party last night," there is no way of deciding whether "we" means "I and you" or "I and some other persons." In Cree there are two first person plural pronouns, "keyanow" (first plus second person) and "neyunan" (first plus third person). Much current controversy about the use in English of the "sexist" pronouns "he" and "she" would be avoided by the sensible Cree solution of having two genders—animate and inanimate (neuter), instead of three; the pronoun "weya" means both "he" and "she." Over the centuries, huge tomes of philosophy and theology have originated from the use, in the Indo-European languages, of "to be" as both a substantive verb and a copulative verb. What is meant when we say, "There is a soul" or "What is its essence?" Such questions could not be asked in languages such as Chinese, where no such verb is found but which seem to get on quite well without it. Berkeley proposed a neat solution—get rid of the substantive verb in the Indo-European languages: *esse est percipi.* But this did not appeal to his fellow epistemologists, who would have been robbed of much employment.

37. Ironically, in his quest for something absolutely certain, Descartes left a splendid example of undecidability. In that quest, he says he spent a day alone in a "poêle" and came up with "I think, therefore I am" (whatever "am"

means). French-English dictionaries make "poêle" a frying pan or a pall (a canopy at a funeral) or a stove. The last seems most likely, but it presents difficulties. One standard translation of the *Discours de la Méthode* renders it as "a stove-heated room"; Bertrand Russell thought it one of the huge German porcelain-ornamented stoves seen in museums; the latest version I have seen makes it "a wall-oven." I suppose the only way to make this decidable would be if someone had been there with a video camera, and even then someone afflicted with "Cartesian doubt"—which does not seem to have been all that powerful—might argue that video and other tapes can be forged.

38. Floyd Merrell, *Deconstruction Reframed* (West Lafayette, Ind.: Purdue University Press, 1983). A more detailed account of the problem is given in Andrew Hodges, *Alan Turing* (New York: Simon & Schuster, 1983), especially pages 82–86, 92–94, 133–45. In 1952 I published an article, " 'Logical Structure' in Eighteenth-Century Poetry" (*Philological Quarterly* 21:315–36), which began with the statement that a firm basis for logic was impossible, since if one sought for it, one ran into "an infinite hierarchy of metalanguages." This view, now accepted by all mathematical logicians, derives from Gödel.

39. D. J. Palmer, *The Rise of English Studies* (London: Oxford University Press, 1965), 20.

40. P. N. Furbank, review of *The Mid-Eighteenth Century,* by John Butt with Geoffrey Carnall, *The Listener* (12 July 1979).

41. *Good-Bye to All That* (Garden City, N.Y.: Doubleday, 1957), 294.

42. *Reading Poems: An Introduction to Critical Study,* ed. Wright Thomas and Stuart Gerry Brown (New York: Oxford University Press, 1941), 743.

43. An excellent guide for the layman to recent research in neuroscience is a supplement, *The Brain,* to *Scientific American,* 1984, with essays by David H. Hugel (professor of neurobiology, Harvard University) and Bernard Crick (Nobel Prize winner and codiscoverer of the structure of the DNA molecule). During the past few years, *The New York Review of Books* has published informative articles and correspondence on current neurobiological research.

44. *The Nature of Literature: Its Relation to Science, Language, and Human Experience* (Princeton: Princeton University Press, 1942), 53.

45. *Samuel Johnson,* ed. Donald Greene (Oxford: Oxford University Press, 1984; The Oxford Authors), 536 (review of Soame Jenyns, *A Free Inquiry into the Nature and Origin of Evil*).

46. Cf. Tzvetan Todorov (*TLS,* 4 Oct. 1985): "If we wish to call a spade a spade, we must conclude that the dominant tendency of American criticism is anti-humanism," and Stanley Corngold on Paul de Man.

2

Doing without Theory: A Defense of Cultural History

MORRIS R. BROWNELL

THE TRADITIONAL literary historian today finds himself or herself in the position of John Partridge in Swift's Bickerstaff papers: he futilely protests he is still alive while all the world insists he is dead. Every day we read another obituary for cultural history. We are told that literary history is moribund and that the cultural historian has expired. The new literary theorists tell us that our texts have no determinate meaning, that our history is a fiction, and that our objectivity is a sham while they happily denounce us as hypocrites and imposters. Without a murmur of protest, theorists suppose, we have kissed their rod, hung our heads in shame, and retired to the archives to pursue our pointless research in lonely isolation.[1] I wish to offer a Bickerstaffian protest to these charges express and implied. I shall argue that literary history in eighteenth-century studies is alive and well, that its untheoretical premises are more sound than the literary theory now in vogue, and that much of the new theory is the work of the Spider in Swift's *Battle of the Books,* while modern cultural historians are doing the work of his Bee.

I believe that eighteenth-century cultural historians must resist the fatal Cleopatra of theory because its irrational premises make their work impossible and subvert their proven and tested methods of skeptical empiricism. I will call as my first witness for the prosecution Meyer Abrams, who explains how he does without theory in a discussion of his prize-winning book *Natural Supernaturalism.* I will then illustrate how the best recent eighteenth-century cultural historians dispense with theory and how little use I have found for theory in my own work on Pope and Johnson. Finally, I will conclude with a short jeremiad predicting that the fashionable linguistic philosopher of modern theory Humpty Dumpty is destined to fall of his own weight.

One could not ask for a more illuminating case study of the conflict between traditional scholarly method and new theoretical approaches to literature than the critical reception of Meyer Abrams' *Natural Supernaturalism* (1971). The debate originated in a Modern Language Association seminar on Philosophical Approaches to Literature in which Abrams and Wayne Booth participated, and it addressed issues raised in a review of the book by J. Hillis Miller in *Diacritics*.[2] *Critical Inquiry* published amplified versions of these papers and other contributions to the discussion by Miller, Morse Peckham, and James Kinkaid in a series of articles on "The Limits of Pluralism."[3] Although *Natural Supernaturalism* deals with the romantic period rather than the eighteenth century, the issue of the debate is the validity of Abrams' methodology as a cultural historian. I doubt whether a traditional work of cultural history has ever been exposed to a more searching test of its assumptions.

Reviewers universally praised Abrams' book as a masterful synthesis, a brilliantly organized and scrupulously documented demonstration of an original thesis about the romantic period.[4] Wayne Booth, acting in the dual role of apologist and devil's advocate questions Abrams' assertion that Wordsworth and his contemporaries in England and Germany wrought a romantic revolution of thought and feeling in their works by secularizing "inherited theological ideas and ways of thinking" (*NS*, 12). Abrams attempts to show "that the secular design of human history . . . is connected to the earlier religious design . . . by the relationship of continuity-in-change" ("Reply," 454). Booth Socratically pretends to have been seduced by Abrams' arguments without being able to explain why or how they should command our rational assent. "In short," Booth writes after summarizing Abrams' claims, "the scandal is perpetrated: by telling a persuasive story . . . Abrams overwhelms my possible objections and leaves me convinced about at least ten kinds of ambitious propositions, many of them evaluative" ("Historian," 434).

What, questions Booth, is the controversy about Abrams' arguments in *Natural Supernaturalism*? First, Abrams makes claims about causation—connections, parallels, analogies, and echoes "between Wordsworth's poems and what came before and after" —many of them "highly conjectural," "elusive," "ambiguous," and "troublesome" ("Historian," 416–17). These Booth mischievously classifies as "short stories," and he refers to Abrams' "large-scale causal theses" about the development of English and German romanticism as "novellas" ("Historian," 416). Second, Abrams maintains that Wordsworth is the exemplary romantic poet, speaking for the spirit of his age, thus invoking the Zeitgeist, a concept that "many philosophers and some historians say is illegitimate" ("Historian," 418). Third, Booth points out the arbitrariness of Abrams' epideictic ideas about the greatness and prophetic importance of Wordsworth and the romantic period. Abrams' "simple dialectic of sameness and difference could even be used to do a *negative* epideictic history—'proving' that Wordsworth and his time were not great" ("Historian," 438). Fourth, Booth questions Abrams' assertions about the relevance and value of romantic writers, their "positive, affirmative, 'redemptive stance'" ("Historian," 419) as opposed to the contemporary nihilistic vision of the modern adversary culture; "most modern theorists would simply dismiss [the romantics' metaphysical values] . . . as entirely out of the range of cognitive inquiry" ("Historian," 420). Finally, Booth notes with something approaching disbelief that Abrams seems actually to believe that he has told a true story about the past in *Natural Supernaturalism: "all of this happened*—this *story* is *true*" ("Historian," 421). But how can this be, Booth wonders, when Abrams concedes in his preface in the spirit of a critical pluralist that a history of romanticism with Byron as hero would tell a different story?

Booth then asks how Abrams validates these questionable claims in order to seduce his reader. The answer, Booth implies, is Abrams' style and rhetoric. Abrams' rigorous clarity and resistance to flourish "makes everything as clear and as interesting as the subject matter allows," producing "an air both of mastery and self-effacement" and an "*im*personal force" calculated to make the reader "trust the author's generalizations" ("Historian," 422–23). Moreover, Booth continues, the masterful structure and organization of Abrams' book, a series of circuitous journeys of interpretation out and back from Wordsworth's prospectus for *The Recluse,* illustrate the fallacy of imitative form and offer further evidence of Abrams' suspect "style-as-proof," his false appearance of objectivity, and his specious authority. Booth's Socratic apology praises Abrams' book more than it blames, but he asks throughout his discussion the disarming question whether *Natural Supernaturalism* does not more properly belong in his own *Rhetoric of Fiction* (1961).

Even more radical is the challenge offered by J. Hillis Miller in his *Diacritics* review of Abrams' book and in his contribution to the debate in *Critical Inquiry* that introduces us to the deconstructionist view of traditional literary history. Miller attacks Abrams' mimetic theory of language and his blind faith in the copiously cited texts supporting his thesis. He says that Abrams "takes his writers a little too much at face value, summarizes them a little too flatly, fails to search them for ambiguities or contradictions in their thought, does not 'explicate' in the sense of unfold, unravel, or unweave" ("Tradition," 11). Abrams is not interpreting, according to Miller, but imposing his univocal meaning on texts that are intrinsically ambiguous. As Booth summarizes Miller's indictment: "Abrams is not by any means a pluralist in his interpretive theory; he is a dogmatist of the most blatant kind . . . unaware of the radical ambiguity of all texts. . . . Each text is steadily, ploddingly assumed to mean exactly what Abrams says it means. . . . Abrams works throughout with a monolithic theory of interpretation which, by silently imposing the doctrine of 'the single interpretation,' is finally stultifying to the life of letters" ("Historian," 440).

Abrams' response to Miller's attack, a brilliant essay entitled "The Deconstructive Angel," contains the most lucid statement of deconstructionist critical theory that I have encountered—its origins in Nietzsche, its exposition in Derrida, and its practice by Miller. As Abrams explains, deconstructionist theory challenges the basic linguistic assumptions of the traditional cultural historian, namely, that the historian can rely upon written texts that, however ambiguous, have a core of determinate meanings competent readers can recognize and discuss. The deconstructionist critic, following Nietzsche's nihilist assumptions, denies the possibility of correct interpretation; since texts have no meaning in themselves, interpretation is merely an expression of the reader's will to power. What Abrams aptly calls Derrida's "graphocentric model" ("Angel," 429) of the text divorces writing from speech and from its contexts in cultural norms and conventions that limit, direct, and control meaning. The deconstructionist reader, according to Abrams, is therefore shut into a "sealed echo-chamber" of texts "in which meanings are reduced to a ceaseless echolalia, a vertical and lateral reverberation from sign to sign of ghostly non-presences emanating from no voice, intended by no one, referring to nothing, bombinating in a void" ("Angel," 431).

Miller's practice of deconstructionist criticism maximizes the free play of significance on the premise that all reading is misreading. He infallibly discovers in any text "a ceaseless play of anomalous meanings . . . 'indeterminable,' 'undecipherable,' 'unreadable,' 'undecidable'" ("Angel," 433), but it is clear that the deconstructionist theory is much more dogmatic than the logocentric model of the cultural historian it attacks. Seek and ye shall find, and the deconstructionist critic does infallibly find the aporia, the impasse, the uncanny moment when the text deconstructs itself. It is tempting to dismiss such an absurd theory out of hand, but Abrams reminds us unequivocally of what is at stake, nothing less than "the validity of the premises and procedures of the entire body of traditional inquiries in the human sciences" ("Angel," 426). Miller's charge, Abrams remarks, "is not simply that I am sometimes, or always, wrong in my interpretation, but instead that I—like other traditional historians—can never be right" ("Angel," 427). He concludes, "If one takes seriously Miller's deconstructionist principles of interpretation, any history relying on written texts becomes an impossibility" ("Reply," 458).

Thus we can deduce that cultural historians have no choice in the matter; if they wish to write their history at all, they must dispense with deconstructionist theory. Indeed Abrams admits that both of his superb historical studies, *The Mirror and the Lamp* (1953) and *Natural Supernaturalism* (1971), were composed "by taste, tact, and intuition." "These books were not written with any method in mind. Instead they were conceived, researched, worked out, put together, pulled apart, and put back together, not according to a theory of valid procedures in such undertakings, but by intuition" ("Reply," 447). Like William James, whom he quotes on the writing of his *Principles of Psychology,* Abrams asserts that he had "'to forge every sentence in the teeth of irreducible and stubborn facts'" ("Reply," 455). I will go further: even if the deconstructionist's graphocentric model of language were correct, we would have to invent a logocentric model in order to write our books. Cultural history and the community of rational discourse depend upon faith in the logocentric system, and I am prepared to say with Sir Thomas Browne that it is certain because it is impossible ("Certum est quia impossibile est").[5]

I wish now to review briefly the work of three students of eighteenth-century literary history who seem to do very well without theory. The first is Maynard Mack. Despite Mack's disclaimers in the preface, *The Garden and the City* combines history and biography with criticism; that is, it bridges what Jerome McGann has called the "almost unbridgeable" gap between scholarship and criticism.[6] Mack's book argues that "Pope's 'creation' of Twickenham constituted an act of the mythopoeic imagination. . . a 'composition of place' without which he could not have written his mature poems as we have them" (9). He supports this thesis with formidable literary and pictorial documentation of Pope's house, garden, and grotto at Twickenham, which prepares a highly speculative argument about the satire of innuendo directed at Robert Walpole's ministry in the *Imitations of Horace.* Like Abrams, Mack builds imaginatively, creatively, and speculatively on a scrupulously exact, well-documented factual record of evidence. As Mack remarks in his preface:

"This is a frankly speculative work. . . . I have not hesitated to ask questions of the evidence, and to leap from fact to inference, sometimes, I suspect, extracting more inference than the facts will strictly bear" (viii).

At least one reviewer was dismayed by Mack's seductive rhetorical skill, as Booth is by Abrams', in teasing out innuendoes of Pope's attack on Walpole that seem as suspect as Abrams' analogies.[7] But I believe that imaginative speculation grounded in the factual record—educated guesses and inference—are precisely the qualities that distinguish the creative from the compilatory in cultural history. Mack admirably expresses the intuition that controls a great literary historian's speculations: "These shapes are our own subjective creations, yet we sense at the same time that they answer to something in the person, constitute at least a plausible image of his mystery, even if they can never pluck out its heart" (viii). A plausible image of a mystery—it would be hard to think of a better definition of the biographer's or the literary historian's art.

My second example of an exemplary eighteenth-century scholar who dispensed with theory is the late James L. Clifford, friend, colleague, and hero of many members of this symposium. In *From Puzzles to Portraits* Clifford classifies his biography of Mrs. Thrale as a "'scholarly-historical'" biography unencumbered by theory: "There is always some selection of evidence, but no unacknowledged guesswork, no fictional devices, and no attempts to interpret the subject's personality and actions psychologically."[8] No one who ever attended one of Jim's lectures on Johnson's obscure middle years can forget his enthusiasm for fact, his love of the chase, and his evangelical zeal for his subject. Jim is one of Richard Altick's prime examples of the scholar adventurer.[9]

Yet Jim's biographies have no theory that I can discern save an insatiable appetite for fact, a shrewd skepticism of evidence, an ability to subordinate facts to an idea of character, and a talent for writing an economical and absorbing narrative. Witness the first sentence of *Young Sam Johnson*, classified in *Puzzles* as an "'artistic-scholarly'" biography (85): "Everyone thinks of Dr. Johnson as an old man. At the first mention of his name the vision rises of the familiar massive, wrinkled face, the bushy bob wig, and the dull-brown coat with metal buttons. It is as the Great Cham of literature, lumbering on an uncertain course down Fleet Street, or talking to his friends at the Mitre, that he lives. He has become almost a symbol of the wise old moralist, and many readers have the impression that he sprang to life full-grown. So fixed is the image that it requires a violent wrench of the imagination to think of him as young."[10] Every detail of this description is based upon fact, yet the result is an imaginative selection and recreation that belongs to the literature of fact.

Selection, synthesis, skeptical weighing of evidence, a willingness to make inferences while carefully distinguishing fact from inference, plus creative imagination—these are Clifford's qualities, and they are a far cry from the theorists' caricature of the literary historian as a dogmatic, univocal reader of texts. But we never hear any cant from Clifford about the biographer as artist.[11] (Compare the embarrassing appeals from theorists to consider their unreadable jargon as a new genre of literature.)[12] Yet it is true that great biographers, like Clifford, must be artists in order to account adequately for their facts. This is all the theory that I can find in Clifford's biographies.

Finally, with no pretense of impartiality, I want to pay tribute to my late teacher Bertrand Bronson and to ask what his *Ballads,* his *Ritson,* his *Johnson Agonistes,* his "printing," his *Chaucer,* and his selection of Johnson's notes on Shakespeare published last year have to do with theory. Bronson's biography *Joseph Ritson: Scholar at Arms*—his Yale dissertation under Chauncey Tinker, two definitive volumes on the waspish literary antiquary—is a book theorists will condescend to. Stylishly written, exhaustively documented, and handsomely illustrated, with a bibliography of Ritson's works, it is representative of the best of its kind in an era when publication of a definitive work was a requirement for the Ph.D. degree. The biography of Ritson anticipated Bronson's entire career of literary research. It led him to Johnson and to his collaboration with Arthur Sherbo on the Shakespeare volumes in the Yale Johnson; it led him to write his classic essays on Johnson and Boswell in *Johnson Agonistes;* it led him to investigate the nonliterary arts, particularly music, in the eighteenth century, exemplified by his essays on John Gay's *Beggar's Opera* and *Acis and Galatea;* and it led to his lifework and magnum opus, the four volumes of the variant tunes of the Child Ballads, an achievement of interdisciplinary scholarship unrivaled in our century.[13]

Modern dogma insists that we ask what Bronson's theory was. As far as I can tell, Bronson had no theory but a love of books from Chaucer to Johnson and a curiosity to learn all he could about the cultures that produced these books. He conveyed what he had learned about these subjects to his students in lectures and writings of unique gravity, allusiveness, and wit. (We called his course the Age of Bronson.) One sentence from a postscript to *Rasselas* in his anthology of Johnson illustrates the quality of his writing: "One by one, in their appointed sequence as the work moves deliberately forward, the rushlights of hypothetical earthly happiness gleam ahead of us but, when we come close to them, gutter out and leave us in the uncertain, but not unpeopled, dark."[14] Doubtless this sentence could easily be deconstructed by theorists, but in it we hear, as in every measured, lucid, and witty sentence he ever wrote, the consummate scholar and the great critic speaking in one voice.

Now, to compare lesser things to greater, I wish to explain how I have managed to do without theory in my own research. I never studied the art of literary research in Richard Altick's sense.[15] Whatever theory I learned resulted from Bertrand Bronson's teaching by example, particularly one standard assignment in his seminar that presented to us a facsimile of an autograph eighteenth-century letter without identifying sender, recipient, or date. Editing and annotating that letter was an experience that converted me to eighteenth-century literary research. Nor did I learn any theory in Maynard Mack's seminar on Pope at Berkeley, which he offered when he was delivering the Beckman lectures on *King Lear* in 1964–65.[16] In the class we were asked to present weekly oral and written reports, for example, an analysis of Pope's revisions from the facsimile of the manuscript of the *Epistle to Arbuthnot*. Textual editing, annotation, bibliography, and biographical research—this was all the theory we knew, and all we thought we needed to know. It should be obvious that I am describing an apprentice system, an oral tradition of literary research passed down from Chauncey Tinker to Bronson and Mack and subsequently to innocent graduate students including John Trimble and Morris Brownell who began their careers during the free speech movement at Berkeley, a period that coincides exactly with the dawning of the absurdist movement in literary theory.[17]

Born in Boston, educated in the Special Program in the Humanities at Princeton and in graduate school at Berkeley, I was destined to be a reactionary, and my research on Pope originated in a penciled note from Professor Bronson written on the back of a typescript page of his essay on Gay's *Acis and Galatea*. The note, which arrived in my teaching assistant's mailbox after I had floundered for a semester to find a subject for my dissertation, read: "Pope as a Critic of the Arts, precept, example, influence?" That untheoretical question determined the course of my research for the next ten years, and my subsequent work has been devoted to the study of the nonliterary arts in the careers of eighteenth-century English writers: after Pope, Johnson, and, soon to be started, Horace Walpole.[18]

In writing my dissertation entitled *Alexander Pope, Virtuoso,*[19] I decided to start with a chapter on Pope and sculpture because I thought if I could find something to say on such an unlikely subject, it would be downhill from there. As recently as the early sixties we took seriously the admonition of graduate committees to find a subject no one else had written on and to find out everything about the subject, and we lived in terror that we would discover that someone else might be working on our subject. Chapters on painting and architecture followed, but it soon became obvious that the history of landscape gardening was to be the heart of the project. How was I to study the history of an artifact that had disappeared from the face of the earth or had been altered beyond recognition? Here is a literal example of the deconstructionist's paradigm of literary history—tracing the untraceable. For the next ten years I looked for the answers in the Osborn collection at Yale where I read the proofs of Joseph Spence's *Anecdotes,* in English libraries and art galleries from the Bodleian to the Ashmolean, and in English estate archives from Chatsworth to Stourhead.

But what on earth did landscape gardening have to do with literature?, I wondered in response to the disbelief of friends and family. "Don't you have something new to say about *The Rape of the Lock* or the *Dunciad?*" "What's the point of poking around in garden history?" My rejoinders, had I been able to formulate them at the time, would have been that I found the subject interesting and that I was falling in love with cultural history. But the example of my teachers' work saved me from being satisfied with mere compilation, *wissenschafteslehre* to give it an honorific title. I was convinced that a compilation of facts about Pope's Twickenham and his gardening lords was not sufficient and that I had to find a thesis to unify my story and to help me sort the note cards that were beginning to fill up Bass boot boxes.

That unifying idea, after many anxious attempts to define and redefine a portmanteau word, turned into a thesis about Pope's sensibility to the picturesque—a concept that determined the structure, organization, and illustration of the book. The discovery of this thesis, after testing and abandoning many hypotheses, may be the closest I have come to being blessed by theory. I am happy to say that many of my reviewers appear to have accepted my thesis, although one found it endearingly "exaggerated," and another, John Dixon Hunt, has attacked it in a campaign, I am flattered to say, that continues to this day.[20] My only pretense to theory as a cultural historian, therefore, is that the moral of the tale one tells must be derived from stubborn and irreducible facts, documented scrupulously so that readers can decide for themselves whether those facts tell a different story.

After compiling an art catalog, *Alexander Pope's Villa,*[21] to keep my sanity while chairing my department, I looked for another eighteenth-century figure interested in the arts and lighted upon David Garrick, a writer I had written a seminar paper on for Bronson at Berkeley. I studied his enormous iconography, read the recent biography by Stone and Kahrl,[22] and looked into his letters, plays, and poetry, but I soon realized that I was not interested in Garrick's aesthetic sensibility. This led me to a sabbatical project on the arts in Johnson's circle but after delivering a lecture on "Johnson's Iconoclasm" at the Huntington Library, I realized that Johnson's prejudice against the arts was my subject.

The book I have just completed entitled *Samuel Johnson's Attitude to the Arts* challenges the traditional and persistent view that he knew little and cared less about the arts, explodes anecdotes about Johnson the philistine, and presents evidence that he was thoroughly familiar with the nonliterary arts of his time, contributing to their patronage as something of a Handelian, a patron of painters and architects, and a student of landscape more discerning than William Gilpin. Theorists will tell me that there is a theory lurking somewhere in this book, but I am conscious of no more theory here than in my earlier one. I want only to find the facts (if possible all the facts or at least as many new facts as possible) and to tell a true and interesting story about them.

For example, the subject of chapter 5—Johnson's patronage of the poverty-stricken painter Mauritius Lowe (1746–93); his assistance in getting Lowe's lost picture exhibited at the Royal Academy over the objections of the Academy's council; his indifference to fashionable contempt for a poor, half-blind artist; and his treatment of this rebellious reprobate as a son—struck me as a fascinating and moving story of a human relationship that had been ignored by biographers and art historians. My theory was to find every scrap of evidence about this strange artist.

Fortunately modern scholars had done some of the work without telling the story. Frederick Hilles had discovered the record of litigation in which Lowe was involved, when Lowe sued a client who had not paid for a design for an engraving and the judge ruled against him although the evidence was in Lowe's favor. Fritz Liebert had published the record of Lowe's testimony at Joseph Baretti's trial for murder. And Boswell's recently published journals contained Lowe's conversation with Boswell and Mrs. Desmoulins about Johnson's sexuality suppressed in the *Life*.[23] After applying to these facts tests of skepticism and relevance, I decided they belonged to the documentation of my story about Johnson's patronage of an unfashionable painter.

I applied the same theory—finding facts to tell a true story—to Johnson's pamphlet war with the young Scottish architect Robert Mylne (1733–1811) about the building of Blackfriars Bridge. In 1759 Johnson wrote three anonymous letters to the editor of the *Daily Gazetteer* supporting, in the competition for the commission, bridge designs of circular arches, chiefly those of his friend John Gwynn, and opposing the elliptical designs of Robert Mylne who eventually won the commission.[24] What was at stake in this chapter was John Hawkins' charge that Johnson was ignorant of architecture. I was able to show that Johnson prepared his brief carefully, consulted experts about the theory of arches, and read pamphlets involved in the Westminster Bridge controversy.

In the end it appeared that Johnson's anonymous letters had opened the public debate about one of the most important public buildings erected in London in his time. Out of the dusty reports of the *Journals of the House of Commons,* decaying articles in the *London Chronicle,* and anonymous pamphlets emerged a dramatic story of David and Goliath. The brash, cocky, twenty-six-year-old Scots architect wrote home to his mother for clean shirts, flattered fat City aldermen, and ran a brilliant public relations campaign that helped him to triumph over the leading architects and engineers of the time, including William Chambers, Robert Smeaton, William Dance, and John Gwynn. Gwynn was being supported by the greatest writer of the age whose three letters of special pleading in the *Daily Gazetteer* have been evaluated by a modern historian of bridge architecture as more sound on the theory of arch design than Mylne himself.[25]

To tell such a story hidden in facts ignored or overlooked is for me nothing less than exhilarating. This is the untheoretical demon that drives me to search the records, to go to the sources—*ad fontes*— in the spirit of Altick's scholar adventurers. And some interesting dividends occasionally reward the search, for example, discovery in a satirical engraving of the first piece of external evidence supporting attribution to Mylne of *Observations on Bridge Building,* the anonymous pamphlet in which Mylne sums up his case against Johnson's attack on his elliptical arches. The obscure engraving dated 31 October 1766 is entitled *Just Arriv'd From Italy / The Puffing Phaenomenon with his Fiery Tail Turn'd Bridge Building, Shewing the Artful Section of his Stones.*[26] Another example is the discovery of several additional paragraphs that I believe can be attributed to Johnson in the *London Chronicle* reprint of one of his letters on Blackfriars Bridge.[27] These are small potatoes compared to the discovery of the Boswell papers in this century, but it gratifies a fledgling Johnsonian to consider the possibility that he may have disinterred a few unknown sentences from Johnson's pen.

Allowing for a hidden theoretical agenda in my research that I am unaware of—a mystical sexist, political, linguistic, racist, bourgeois ideology—I try on principle to do without theory because a priori method is incompatible with the unceasing search for facts and irrelevant to the attempt to tell an interesting story about the facts discovered. As the facts change, so does the story—that is the be-all and the end-all of my theory. Theorists may well call it naive, antiquarian, and dull, but I prefer to think of it as pragmatic, empirical, and exciting.

It is hardly surprising that many of the secondary sources I rely on in telling my stories are compendiums of facts. Although I am aware this may seem to be simpleminded, I would like to ask what use theory might serve in reference works like dictionaries, catalogs, and calendars that are the sine qua non of my literary and art-historical research? Let us imagine for a moment Howard Colvin's *Dictionary of British Architects,* Dorothy George's *Catalogue of Personal and Political Satires in the British Museum,* and *The London Stage* devised according to deconstructionist principles.[28] Instead of finding an accurate reference to George Dance's design for Blackfriars Bridge in the Corporation of London Record Office—an evil-smelling dusty document measuring seven feet nine inches by 3 feet four inches, signed and dated by the architect—the deconstructionist dictionary would expunge the document from the records of our civilization, recording in its place a trace of a difference between signifier and signified that we could meditate about with *plaisir* if not *jouissance.*

But quite frankly, if this is not a damaging Freudian admission, I prefer to look at the documents. I obtain far more *plaisir* and *jouissance* looking at John Smeaton's design for Blackfriars Bridge at the Royal Society or at Raphael's drawing in the Royal Library at Windsor of the figure of Poetry decorating the ceiling of the Stanza della Segnatura in Rome—a drawing John Piper has suggested that Reynolds may be quoting in his earliest portrait of Johnson (1756).[29] Moreover, I am exceedingly grateful to Kai Kin Yung of the National Portrait Gallery for correcting the factual record of Reynolds' portraits of Johnson in a recent catalog: rejecting the portrait of Johnson in old age from Reynolds' work, redating two others, and reversing the order of the Streatham portrait (ca. 1772) and Blinking Sam (ca. 1775), which can now be plausibly identified as the "busy" portrait.[30]

Sometimes when catalogs do not serve, one has the still greater pleasure of discovering through friendship a picture not in the British Museum Catalogue. John Riely led me to *Scotch Worship of an English Idol,* a print in the Pierpont Morgan Library satirizing Boswell's *Tour.* John also told me about the complete drawings by Samuel Collings in the Princeton University Library for Rowlandson's *Picturesque Beauties of Boswell* (1786). Catherine Jestin of the Lewis Walpole Library helped me to *Signor Piozzi Ravishing Mrs. Thrale,* the print in the New York Public Library from Horace Walpole's collection with Walpole's annotation identifying Johnson. Bob Wark's student Pat Crown informed me that three drawings of the Royal Academy exhibition in 1784 (the last year of Johnson's life), formerly attributed to Johann Ramberg, were the work of Charles Burney's nephew Edward Francis Burney (1760–1848). They include figures Pat takes to be portraits of the artist and his sisters Fanny and Susan. Richard Altick's recent study *Paintings from Books*[31] added six more paintings to my list of Victorian subject pictures of Johnson that I am claiming influenced the double tradition of his reputation, for example, Henry Wallis' *Johnson at Cave's* (1854) and Eyre Crowe's *Penance at Uttoxeter* (1869). The earliest (ca. 1786) and most elusive of these subject paintings, appropriately entitled *Dr. Johnson's Ghost,* I located by accident in the National Portrait Gallery archives. The accession number for a different picture turned up a photograph of the original painting that Richard Owen Cambridge had commissioned from "an artist about the house" to execute his idea for a satire of Boswell's *Tour* derived from lines in Congreve's *Way of the World.*[32]

The London Stage, surely one of the monuments of eighteenth-century scholarship of this century, enabled me to establish the likely date, provenance, and occasion of Johnson's attendance at a performance of the *Messiah* with Mrs. Thrale. This fact, combined with his remarks on Handel in a review of Joseph Warton's *Essay on Pope* and his subscription to the first printed score of the *Messiah* in 1767, supports the claim I make in the book that Johnson was not as ignorant of music as he pretended.[33] (It occurs to me to wonder how deconstructionist theory might work on a musical score. Are there no wrong notes?) Another reference work, perhaps not as well known to students of eighteenth-century literature, is the *New Grove Dictionary of Music and Musicians.* It is filled with well-documented articles on the century's composers, and even on eighteenth-century concert halls, that helped me to explicate the rare mezzotint by John Raphael Smith entitled *The Promenade at Carlisle House* (dated 1781), depicting a concert hall in Soho run by the notorious Mrs. Theresa Cornelys from 1760 to 1772.[34] Chaloner Smith in his catalog of mezzotint portraits claims that the print contains the figure of Johnson talking to a lady in the hallway beyond a door in the right background.[35] The figure bears no resemblance to Johnson, but Smith's wishful thinking prompted me to make this picture the frontispiece of my book—emblem of an argument that attempts to exorcize the ghost of the philistine Johnson and replace it with a better-drawn figure who could have been seen in concert halls as well as theatres, who knew something about architecture, and who even appreciated landscape.

Christopher Thacker's recent book on garden history *The Wildness Pleases* provided me with another straw man, something few scholars with a thesis can resist.[36] Thacker reads Johnson's description and comparison in his *Diary* of his Welsh tour of two landscape gardens as a sober appreciation of the picturesque and sublime in landscape.[37] I read the same passages as Johnson's burlesque of John Brown's "Letter on the Lakes" (1767) in which Brown compares Dovedale and the Vale of Keswick to the advantage of the latter.[38] If my interpretation of this description is right, Johnson's irony supports the thesis that his distaste is not for landscape, as the anecdotal tradition has it, but for false, fashionable modes of description epitomized by John Brown and William Gilpin who belie landscape with false compare. Another recent scholarly study of landscape, Barbara Stafford's *Voyage into Substance,* helped me to account for Johnson's theory of natural description, which reflects the substitution of scientific for picturesque sensibility in European illustrated travel literature of Johnson's time.[39]

How then can I sum up my case for doing without theory as a cultural historian? I must admit that it would not have occurred to me to make a case had it not been for this conference and Dick Schwartz' invitation to expound my views. The approach of the deconstructionists, as it reached me through rumor, hearsay, and the occasional book I reviewed, seemed to me patently absurd, so that I dismissed it out of hand and tried to put it out of mind. But I now realize that a plea of nolo contendere is not enough and that the modern mania for theory threatens to discredit our enterprise unless we make ourselves heard.

Why then do cultural historians reject theory and resist appeals for more theory from the left and the right, from Jonathan Culler and from Jerome McGann?[40] How can we account for "the theoretical torpor of the best representatives of modern academic historiography," to quote Hayden White's fine study *Metahistory?*[41] First, cultural historians are compelled to reject the absurdist premises of the cognitive atheists (I borrow my terms from White and E. D. Hirsch, Jr.).[42] They refuse to abandon the empirical method,[43] to assassinate the author, and to transform the text into blips on a deconstructionist's theoretical screen. Second, cultural historians reject theory because theorists have abandoned the dialectic of critical discourse and truth-seeking conversation of scholars modeled on Abrams' paradigm. [Question:] "This is so, isn't it?" [Answer:] "Yes, but . . . " (Booth, "Historian," 415). Third, cultural historians reject theory because of its partisan, totalitarian, and nihilist ideology. Fourth, cultural historians are suspicious of theory because it is fashionable and because they find inflation of the critic at the expense of the author ludicrous. Fifth, cultural historians find much of the theory pouring from the presses today unreadable, and they remark of the modern Dunciad of deconstruction that "the Poem was not made for these authors, but these authors for the Poem."[44]

Finally, those of us working in the related fields of literary and art history find the theorists' brave new world of interdisciplinary studies a promiscuous witches' brew. The eighteenth-century art historian and connoisseur Robert Wark has recently reminded us that "the most helpful interdisciplinarians are those who keep their feet firmly planted on their own side of the fence while surveying their neighbor's yard."[45] And Lawrence Lipking warns, "At a time when interdisciplinary studies have become fashionable, the traditional kinship among the arts seems to offer a model for scholarship—always with the proviso, of course, that two half-understood 'disciplines' will never combine in a whole one."[46]

To conclude with a "jeremiadical" paragraph, let us remember the humanist tradition exemplified by Abrams, Mack, Clifford, and Bronson and ignore modern critic-artists congratulating themselves on their uncreating word of theory. Let us repudiate the "trahison" of the French clerks who devised their theory to spite an authoritarian university system completely foreign to the democratic tradition we cherish in our institutions of higher learning. The most eloquent and moving illustration of this tradition that I know is the anecdote Erwin Panofsky tells in the introduction to his book *Meaning in the Visual Arts*. He describes the visit of a physician to Emmanuel Kant in his last illness, who, half-blind and sick, rises from his chair and stands until his visitor has been seated, explaining in words that reduce them both to tears that his illness has not robbed him of his humanity: "Das Gefühl für Humanität hat mich noch nicht verlassen." Panofsky moralizes the tale to illustrate the ambivalence of the traditional meanings of humanism and the humanities—studies that inspire human beings to reach higher than they can and simultaneously teach them their limitations. "It is not so much a movement as an attitude which can be defined as the conviction of the dignity of man, based on both the insistence on human values (rationality and freedom) and the acceptance of human limitations (fallibility and frailty); from this two postulates result—responsibility and tolerance."[47] It is in this spirit that the greatest works of eighteenth-century cultural history have been written in our century. Let us not sell our birthright for a mess of pottage.

Notes

1. For a representative example of these attitudes, see Geoffrey H. Hartman, *Criticism in the Wilderness: The Study of Literature Today* (New Haven: Yale University Press, 1980), 227, 291.

2. See J. Hillis Miller, "Tradition and Difference," review of *Natural Supernaturalism: Tradition and Revolution in Romantic Literature,* by Meyer H. Abrams, hereafter cited *NS* in the text, *Diacritics* 2 (Winter 1972): 6–13, hereafter cited "Tradition" in the text.

3. For the debate about *Natural Supernaturalism,* see *Critical Inquiry* 2 (Spring 1976), 3 (Spring–Summer 1977), and, in particular, the following articles cited "Historian," "Reply," and "Angel" in the text: Wayne C. Booth, "M. H. Abrams: Historian as Critic, Critic as Pluralist," *Critical Inquiry* 2 (Spring 1976): 411–45; M. H. Abrams, "Rationality and Imagination in Cultural History: A Reply to Wayne Booth," *Critical Inquiry* 2 (Spring 1976): 447–64; M. H. Abrams, "The Limits of Pluralism—II: The Deconstructive Angel," *Critical Inquiry* 3 (Spring 1977), 425–38. For another trenchant analysis of poststructuralist critics, see M. H. Abrams, "How to Do Things with Texts," *Partisan Review* 46 (1979): 566–88.

4. See, for example, Thomas McFarland's review in the *Yale Review* 61 (Winter 1972): 279–88; E. D. Hirsch, Jr., *The Wordsworth Circle* 3 (Winter 1972): 17–20.

5. *Religio Laici, Works,* ed. Geoffrey Keynes, 4 vols. (1928; reprint, London: Faber, 1964), 1:18.

6. See Maynard Mack, *The Garden and the City: Retirement and Politics in the Later Poetry of Pope 1731–1743* (Toronto: University of Toronto Press, 1969), hereafter cited in text by page number; Jerome J. McGann, *The Beauty of Inflections: Literary Investigations in Historical Method and Theory* (Oxford: Clarendon Press, 1985), 91.

7. Pat Brückmann, "Edges of Analogy," *University of Toronto Quarterly* 42 (Fall 1972): 84–92.

8. See James L. Clifford, *Hester Lynch Piozzi (Mrs. Thrale),* 2d ed. (Oxford: Clarendon Press, 1968); *From Puzzles to Portraits: Problems of a Literary Biographer* (Chapel Hill: University of North Carolina Press, 1970), 85, hereafter cited as *Puzzles.*

9. See Richard D. Altick, *The Scholar Adventurers* (1950; reprint, New York: Free Press, 1966), 90–91, 118–21.

10. James L. Clifford, *Young Sam Johnson* (1955; reprint, New York: Oxford-Hesperides, 1961), vii.

11. Clifford writes of "'artistic-scholarly'" biography in *Puzzles:* "It in-

47

volves the same exhaustive research [as the "'scholarly-historical'" biography], but once the evidence has been assembled, the biographer considers his role that of an imaginative creative artist, presenting the details in the liveliest and most interesting manner possible" (85).

12. On the deliberately opaque and obfuscatory style of modern theorists, see John Sturrock, ed., *Structuralism and Since: From Lévi Strauss to Derrida* (Oxford: Oxford University Press, 1979), 15–17. On the critic as romantic hero personified by Harold Bloom, see Geoffrey Hartman, "Literary Commentary as Literature," *Criticism in the Wilderness*, chap. 8.

13. See Bertrand Harris Bronson, *Joseph Ritson: Scholar at Arms*, 2 vols. (Berkeley: University of California Press, 1938); "The Beggar's Opera," *Studies in the Comic*, University of California Publications in English, vol. 8 (1941), reprinted in *Facets of the Enlightenment: Studies in English Literature and its Contexts* (Berkeley: University of California Press, 1968), 60–90; "The True Proportions of Gay's *Acis and Galatea*," *PMLA* 80 (September 1965): 325–31; "The Double Tradition of Dr. Johnson," *ELH* 18 (1951): 90–106; *Johnson Agonistes and Other Essays* (Berkeley: University of California Press, 1965); "Printing as an Index of Taste in Eighteenth-Century England," *Bulletin of the New York Public Library* 62 (August–September 1958): 373–87, 443–62; *The Traditional Tunes of the Child Ballads*, 4 vols. (Princeton: Princeton University Press, 1959); *In Search of Chaucer*, The Alexander Lectures 1958–59 (Toronto: University of Toronto Press, 1960); *Johnson on Shakespeare*, ed. Arthur Sherbo, "Introduction" by Bertrand H. Bronson, *The Yale Edition of the Works of Samuel Johnson*, vols. 7–8 (New Haven: Yale University Press, 1968), 7: xiii–xxxviii; Bertrand H. Bronson, ed., with Jean M. O'Meara, *Selections from Johnson on Shakespeare* (New Haven: Yale University Press, 1986).

14. Bertrand H. Bronson, ed., *Samuel Johnson: Rasselas, Poems, and Selected Prose*, 3d ed. enl. with *The Life of Savage* (reprint, San Francisco: Rinehart Press, 1971), xx.

15. *The Art of Literary Research*, 3d ed. (reprint, New York: Norton, 1981).

16. *King Lear in Our Time* (Berkeley: University of California Press, 1965).

17. I borrow the term from Hayden White's excellent typology of modern criticism "The Absurdist Moment in Contemporary Literary Theory," *Tropics of Discourse: Essays in Cultural Criticism* (Baltimore: Johns Hopkins University Press, 1978), 261–82.

18. See Morris R. Brownell, *Alexander Pope & the Arts of Georgian England* (Oxford: Clarendon Press, 1978); *Samuel Johnson's Attitude to the Arts* (Oxford: Clarendon Press, 1989).

19. Diss., University of California, Berkeley, *DA* 27 (1966): 3421–22.

20. See Ronald Paulson, review of *Alexander Pope & The Arts of Georgian England*, *JEGP* 78 (July 1979): 431–36; John Dixon Hunt, "*Ut Pictura Poesis, Ut Pictura Hortus*, and the Picturesque," *Word & Image* 1 (1985): 87–107.

21. (London: Greater London Council, 1980).

22. George Winchester Stone, Jr., and George M. Kahrl, *David Garrick: A Critical Biography* (Carbondale: Southern Illinois University Press, 1979); Martin Anglesea, "David Garrick and the Visual Arts," M. Lit. diss., University of Edinburgh, 1971.

23. See Frederick W. Hilles and Philip B. Daghlian, eds., *Anecdotes of Painting in England . . . Collected by Horace Walpole* (New Haven: Yale University Press, 1937), 5:102; H. W. L. [Herman Wardwell Liebert], *A Constellation of Genius: Being a Full Account of the Trial of Joseph Baretti for the Murder of Evan Morgan Held at Justice-Hall in the Old-Bailey, On 20 October 1769 . . . Reprinted . . . with an Introduction and Notes* [Grolier Club Lecture, 20 September 1958] (New Haven: Yale University Press, 1958); James Boswell, *Boswell: The Applause of the Jury, 1782–1785*, ed. Irma S. Lustig and Frederick A. Pottle, *The Yale Edition of the Private Papers of James Boswell* (New York: McGraw-Hill, 1981), 11:109–10.

24. See "Considerations on the Plans Offered for the Construction of Black-Friars Bridge in Three Letters to the Printer of the Gazetteer," *The Letters of Samuel Johnson*, ed. R. W. Chapman, 3 vols. (Oxford: Clarendon Press, 1952), 1:446–52.

25. See Ted Ruddock, *Arch Bridges and Their Builders, 1735–1835* (Cambridge: Cambridge University Press, 1979), 67. For full documentation of Johnson's pamphlet war with Robert Mylne, see my *Samuel Johnson's Attitude to the Arts*, chap. 9.

26. See the unique copy at the United States Military Academy Library of the pamphlet by "Publicus" entitled *Observations on Bridge Building, And the Several Plans Offered for a New Bridge. In a Letter Addressed to the Gentlemen of the Committee, Appointed by the Common-Council of the City of London, for Putting in Execution, A Scheme of Building a New Bridge Across the Thames, at or near Black Friars* (London: J. Townsend, 1760). See also the etching in Frederick George Stephens, ed., *Catalogue of Political and Personal Satires Preserved in the Department of Prints and Drawings in the British Museum*, vol. 3 (1877; reprint, Ilkley, Yorkshire: Scolar Press, 1978), No. 3733.

27. [Samuel Johnson?], "Reasons Against Elliptical Arches and Iron Rails," *London Chronicle* 6 (1–4 Dec. 1759), 534–35.

28. See Howard Colvin, *A Biographical Dictionary of British Architects, 1600–1840*, 2d ed. (London: John Murray, 1978); Mary Dorothy George, ed., *Catalogue of Political and Personal Satires Preserved in the Department of Prints and Drawings in the British Museum*, vols. 5–7 (1771–1800) (1935–42; reprint, Ilkley, Yorkshire: Scolar Press, 1978); William Van Lennep, et al., eds., *The London Stage, 1660–1800*, 11 vols. (Carbondale: Southern Illinois University Press, 1960–68.

29. "The Development of the British Literary Portrait up to Samuel Johnson," *Proceedings of the British Academy* 54 (10 January 1968), 71.

30. Kai Kin Yung, *Samuel Johnson, 1709–84* [Exhibition Catalogue] (London: Herbert Press for the Arts Council of Great Britain, 1984), No. 78, pp. 110–12; No. 83, pp. 117–18; No. 103, pp. 135–36.

31. *Paintings from Books: Art and Literature in Britain, 1760–1900* (Columbus: Ohio State University Press, 1985), 157–58.

32. See my article "'Dr. Johnson's Ghost': Genesis of a Satirical Engraving," *Huntington Library Quarterly* 50 (Autumn 1987): 339–57. For subject pictures of Johnson, see *Samuel Johnson's Attitude to the Arts*, app., pp. 185–86.

33. George Winchester Stone, Jr., ed., *The London Stage, 1660–1800*, pt. 4: 1747–1776 (Carbondale: Southern Illinois University Press, 1962), 3:532.

34. "London Concert Rooms and Halls," the *New Grove Dictionary of Music and Musicians*, ed. Stanley Sadie, 20 vols. (London: MacMillan, 1980), 11: 202–3.

35. John Chaloner Smith, *British Mezzotinto Portraits*, 5 vols. (London: British Museum, 1878–83), 3:1319.

36. *The Wildness Pleases: The Origins of Romanticism* (London: Croom Helm, 1983), 144–45.

37. See *Boswell's Life of Johnson, Together with Boswell's Journal of a Tour to the Hebrides, and Johnson's Diary of a Journey into North Wales*, ed. George Birkbeck Hill, revised L. F. Powell, 6 vols. (Oxford: Clarendon Press, 1934–64), vol. 5, 2d ed. (1964), 433–34.

38. See Donald D. Eddy, *A Bibliography of John Brown* (New York: Bibliographical Society of America, 1971), Nos. 97A–100.

39. *Voyage Into Substance: Art, Science, Nature, and the Illustrated Travel Account 1760–1840* (Cambridge: MIT Press, 1984).

40. See Jonathan Culler, "Literary Theory in the Graduate Program," *The Pursuit of Signs: Semiotics, Literature, Deconstruction* (Ithaca, N.Y.: Cornell University Press, 1981), and *Structuralist Poetics: Structuralism, Linguistics, and the Study of Literature* (Ithaca, N.Y.: Cornell University Press, 1976), chap. 11; Jerome J. McGann, ed., *Historical Studies and Literary Criticism* (Madison: University of Wisconsin Press, 1985), introd.; *The Beauty of Inflections: Literary Investigations in Historical Method and Theory* (Oxford: Clarendon Press, 1985), esp. introd. and pt. 2, chap. 2 "Shall These Bones Live?"

41. *Metahistory: The Historical Imagination in Nineteenth-Century Europe* (Baltimore: Johns Hopkins University Press, 1973), xii.

42. See Hayden White, "The Absurdist Moment" and two impregnable defenses of "the possibility of knowledge in interpretation": E. D. Hirsch, Jr., *Validity in Interpretation* (New Haven: Yale University Press, 1967) and *The Aims of Interpretation* (Chicago and London: University of Chicago Press, 1976).

43. See Frederick Crews' attack on "theoreticist apriorism" "In the Big House of Theory," *New York Review of Books* (29 May 1986), 36–42.

44. Quoted by James Sutherland, ed., the *Dunciad*, The Twickenham Edition of the Poems of Alexander Pope, vol. 5, 3d ed. rev. (London: Methuen, 1963), xliv.

45. "The Weak Sister's View of the Sister Arts," in *Articulate Images: The Sister Arts from Hogarth to Tennyson*, ed. Richard Wendorf (Minneapolis: University of Minnesota Press, 1983), 35.

46. "'Quick Poetic Eyes': Another Look at Literary Pictorialism," in *Articulate Images*, 4.

47. See Erwin Panofsky, "The History of Art as a Humanistic Discipline," in *The Meaning of the Humanities: Five Essays*, ed. Theodore Meyer Greene (Princeton: Princeton University Press, 1938), 92. Reprinted in *Meaning in the Visual Arts: Papers in and on Art History* (1955; New York: Doubleday-Anchor, 1957), introd.

3

Johnson's Voluntary Agents

RICHARD B. SCHWARTZ

FIFTEEN YEARS ago the English Institute conducted the first of two conferences on New Approaches to Eighteenth-Century Literature. The American Society for Eighteenth-Century Studies was then in its infancy, and a series of major projects—for example, biographies of Swift, Pope, Boswell, and Johnson—had not yet come to fruition. Paulson's *Hogarth* had recently appeared, and Mack's *Garden and the City;* Johnson's *Rambler* and *Journey to the Western Islands of Scotland* had issued from the Yale press. Harth's study of Dryden had been published a few years earlier, a succession of books on Johnson's religion and moral thought were being discussed, and the controversy over Boswell the biographer was smoldering.

Little more than a decade later the world has changed a great deal. In the fall 1985 number of *The Eighteenth Century: Theory and Interpretation* (once termed *Studies in Burke and His Time*), Laura Brown argued that eighteenth-century studies are now all but dead and that the age of giants has passed (she mentions Crane, Wasserman, Wimsatt, Brower, and Watt, the latter no doubt startled at the news of his own demise). She suggests that this process—rivaling perhaps the vision of the close of *Dunciad IV*—might be reversed if the eighteenth-centuryists could only be persuaded to embrace the opportunities provided by what she terms "the new movements in contemporary theory."[1]

Those who study our work some time in the future will have to reconcile Brown's statement with the recent judgment of Jack Stillinger in *JEGP*. He proclaims that deconstructionism—certainly a dominant movement among those celebrated by Brown—is, to anyone in touch with the state of contemporary scholarship in America, as dead as the parrot in the Monty Python pet shop sketch.[2]

The truth lies somewhere in between. If deconstructionism is dead, its ghost is appearing more frequently than Banquo's or Hamlet's father's, and though the fads, fancies, and new vocabularies pass quickly—quickly enough for Stanley Fish to publicly counsel aspiring authors of books on theory to strike before the market shrinks to nothing—the market remains sufficiently bullish to force us to confront the position and role of theory as we assess the state of period studies such as our own. That students of the eighteenth century have not, in Brown's words, "been open to contemporary theory" strikes me as undeniable. The reason for that posture is of some interest and importance, but I must say something of the trend itself before looking at the resistance it has met.

It should be made clear at the outset that *theory* in the current debate does not refer to the theoretical underpinnings of different practitioners' methodologies. Of course we are all guided by theory, even if that theory is little more than a combination of simple empiricism and trained intuition. As René Wellek has recently written, "There can be no literary theory without concrete criticism and without history; there is no criticism without some theory and history; and no literary history is possible without theoretical assumptions and without criticism."[3] Rather, it is what David H. Hirsch has called the "new doctrine of metadecadence," "theory for theory's sake," "theory in place of literature," that the eighteenth-centuryists have avoided.[4] It is not system, but the spirit of system; not theory, but the exclusive practice of theory, the elevation of theory over literature, theorists over poets, of abstraction over art and life.

Certainly students of the eighteenth century have profited from the thought of contemporary theorists. They have neither closed their minds nor raised a banner of know-nothingism. They have, however, seen the work of theorists as a potential source of insight, not as the grist for an all-consuming activity. They have absorbed it (when it has proven useful) without succumbing to it. I can hardly speak for eighteenth-centuryists as a group, but I believe that they share Wellek's concerns for the place of literature within our lives and the challenges posed by theory. "The abolition of aesthetics, the blurring of the distinction between poetry and critical prose, the rejection of the very ideal of correct interpretation in favor of misreading, the denial to all literature of any reference to reality are all symptoms of a profound *malaise*. If literature has nothing to say about our minds and the cosmos, about love and death, about humanity in other times and other countries, literature loses its meaning."[5] Wellek's comments are particularly welcome, for few can lay claim to a wider knowledge of the subject, and no one can accuse him of enmity toward either theory or Continental thought.[6] I am interested in the malaise to which Wellek refers and would like to discuss it further before turning to the place of theory among the eighteenth-centuryists.

Some have seen the promotion of theory as a political act, an attempt by the disaffected and "marginalized" to change the nature of discourse when they are powerless to change the conditions of literary, academic, and political society. In depriving language and texts of determinate meaning, life can be irreparably altered. In its offshoot forms such as critical legal studies, direct assaults on the very fabric of society can be contemplated.

While some have seen these currents as instances of rupture and disjunction, others have seen them as evidence of continuity. Brian McCrea, for example, has noted that the deconstructors are following precisely in the steps of the New Critics in their overriding desire to further systematize and privatize, to raise the walls protecting our guild from the incursions of journalists and amateurs.[7] The goal is professionalization, the activity careerism. Gerald Graff has argued that although historical research is painstakingly slow, the disparagement of historical approaches enables the new critical theorists to multiply publications, since their only requirement for practice is the mastering of what he terms "certain forms of verbalization."[8] The driving force is the need for market expansion. To meet this need the theorists mimic the capitalists they publicly and stridently despise, even as they overlook the fact that in a capitalist society, tradition (the darling of the humanists and historicists) must give way to fashion. Thus, they introduce the planned obsolescence into our ideas that we have long suffered in our toasters and automobiles.

Reinforcing the stress of continuity rather than rupture, John M. Ellis contends that recent developments in theory simply restore some ground lost to New Criticism a generation earlier. While the New Critics suggested "that extended rational discussion of what texts actually said was possible, and that it was not necessary to restrict oneself to personal responses," deconstructors simply reassert—though in far more obstreperous fashion—the old truism that "response to texts [can] only be a subjective individual matter."[9]

Ellis discusses two types of criticism that he terms the journalistic and the historical. In the first we read the critic, and our primary concern is with his or her point of view. We are reading Leslie Fiedler or Frank Kermode (to use Ellis' examples) rather than reading about Shakespeare or Pope or Dickens. The journalistic critic overshadows the texts while the historical scholar elucidates the personality and art of the authors he or she studies. The journalist is more evaluative; the historicist is more cautious and more factual and is expository rather than judgmental.

Of course, one is permitted to cross the line separating these two approaches, but the manner in which many contemporary theorists straddle it has sometimes gone unnoticed. According to Ellis' categories, their orientation is clearly journalistic. The text (when it exists) is subservient to their reflections on it, and the artistic nature of their own discourse is frequently claimed. Their position is strikingly similar to that of the popular writer / journalist, but with one significant difference. The journalist seeks an ever wider audience, but the theorist often employs a vocabulary designed to narrow that audience. After all, when a scholar and reader of Jean Hagstrum's stature can confess to defeat at their hands,[10] one must wonder whether the language is intensely subtle or simply willfully obscurantist.

This posture, however, gives theorists an enormous advantage because they are able to have things both ways. They can exercise the freedom of journalists or professional writers without facing the pressing responsibility of appealing to a wide audience. They can spin out their own intellectual autobiographies without feeling any pressure to sustain interest or attention, for the smaller the audience, the greater can be the claims of erudition and sophistication. They can indulge in the most blatant forms of impressionistic musing without being accused of late Victorian amateurism. They can, in short, claim to be Kant or Coleridge while actually playing Christopher Morley in devils' costumes.

Those who argue that the current debate is evidence of continuity rather than dislocation may find impressive confirmation of their beliefs in Graff's newest book *Professing Literature: An Institutional History*.[11] Graff argues convincingly that the jeremiads we now hear have been delivered for years. For example, complaints about splintered, absurdly overspecialized MLA sessions were lodged in the early 1900s (110–11). In 1925 Albert Feuillerat argued that the worlds of literary and academic criticism had grown so far apart that to label a literary critic a scholar was sufficient to destroy his or her reputation. The divorce of the academic from the public was, in short, a terrible mistake (143). In 1948 Douglas Bush lamented the fact that critics had separated themselves from the common reader and from human life and were simply writing for one another (186). As moderns criticize theory, previous generations criticized history or New Criticism, often in the same terms.

In some ways the picture is not an edifying one; it suggests that we have trouble learning lessons and relish fighting old battles. That is not, however, the principal lesson of Graff's book, but it is an important one. The principal conclusion is that literature and life are too rich to be subjected to monolithic formulas, that single-minded explanations merely show "'the whole of literature' can all too readily be made to 'respond' to techniques that validate themselves tautologically" (241), and that what we should be doing is exposing students to a plurality of approaches and allowing them to see the precise nature of the debate. Namely, we should be pointing out the assumptions that underlie the variety of positions held instead of shielding students behind administrative devices such as a curriculum based on trade-offs or a field-coverage organizational chart that enables disruptives to simply be added on to a department without facing the clash of opinion or methodology that might have resulted. We institutionalize radicalism instead of confronting it and opt for a frictionless setting that keeps us at peace and our students blissfully ignorant.

I cannot say that I find academic disputation as edifying as Graff does, but I am gratified that he devotes so much space to a commentator who was not as easily taken in by new trends as were his contemporaries. R. S. Crane never tired of stressing that different assumptions yield different and not necessarily inaccurate conclusions, that we must jettison monolithic approaches and remind ourselves constantly of the complexity of our subject, that it is rooted in history and individual humanity, and that it will resist system at every turn. In his work we can find studied anticipations of issues we now treat as if they were discovered yesterday and convincing refutations of notions we currently scorn despite their success in their own time. Graff quotes Crane at length, he says, "because Crane's questions seem to [him] fundamental and because so far as [he knows] they were never answered" (236).

Crane was not only a theorist but a thoroughgoing eighteenth-centuryist, and there are many reasons why students of that period should be as suspicious as they are of contemporary theoretical tendencies. In the first place, intellectual systematizing is the butt of many of the period's major satires. Theory and theorizing are always suspect: to Pope, to Swift, to Johnson, and to Burke, to name but a few. The "High Priori Road" had not yet become a sixteen-lane freeway, but it was already heavily traveled, often by drivers of foreign vehicles, whose English reception was usually as chilly as the reception accorded wearers of foreign clothing in working-class sections of eighteenth-century London. Thus, it is difficult for us to inflict theoretical systems (particularly deductive systems) upon those writers we admire and still retain our admiration for them; not that we need approach their work as settled truth and purest beauty, of course, but their critique of system is so thoroughgoing as to constitute a central concern of their work and the foundation stone of much of their thought.

There is also the question of language. It should trouble us more than it does that the eighteenth century associated dullness with dolt-ishness, while for us the term generally connotes tediousness. A dull person bores us, but he or she is not necessarily a dullard. In the Restoration and eighteenth century, on the other hand, dullness often first suggested stupidity, its opposite being sprightliness, vigor, and alacrity. For example, in *Mac Flecknoe* and the *Dunciad* this is clearly so, and Johnson's *Dictionary* definitions of the relevant terms reinforce the point. I think it is not too strong a statement to suggest that many now associate crabbed, soporific prose with true seriousness. When we wish to appear most learned, we offer density instead of clarity, length instead of precision, cant and nonce words instead of plain English. To be sprightly is somehow to appear less than serious. Now we can hardly lay the exclusive blame for this condition at the feet of literary theorists, for some of them write crisp clear prose, and teutonic histori-cal scholarship (among other things) has played a significant role in restructuring our notions of seriousness. Burke and other eighteenth-century writers associated sublimity with such things as obscurity and difficulty, though the much-praised "Let there be light" that recurs as a model for period commentators upon the sublime could hardly be more straightforward or more clear. The eighteenth-centuryist's imagination will associate heaviness not with profundity but with the Goddess Dulness' using a sheet of Philips' *Thulè* to extinguish Cibber's pyre in the *Dunciad*.

It is not just the weighty jargon-ridden prose that afflicts us but also the prose that seems to have gaps in it: missing words, missing sentences, and missing threads in the argument. Passages must be studied and restudied (as if their authors were Kant or Joyce). Some-times they appear brilliant and at others merely half-baked, but in both cases the reader must fill in the gaps by supplying part of the meaning, an extremely dangerous practice for those writers who value their own argument and seek to convey it directly rather than place themselves at the mercy of those who have presumably come to them for enlightenment. Here are two recent examples, both drawn from important studies by learned people:

> Hume's practice deconstructs the moment of production by exploit-ing the liability to reproduction which is its aboriginal dynamic.[12]

> Thus the traditional genres are conceived not only as impervious struc-ture that is "dragged" from one zone to another by novelistic process but

also as susceptible to their own "unique development," to something like the internalization of process. Indeed, this susceptibility may be signaled by the real difference between the two chosen metaphors, "displacement" and "novelization," and their respectively mechanical and animate suggestiveness.[13]

In reading modern criticism we sometimes see the touch of brilliance, while at others we simply confront muddle. Doubtless this has always been so, but the taste for theory has intensified the urge for generalization and abstraction that aspires to bespeak the presence of great wisdom but often indicates something quite different. The eighteenth century observed the same urges and responded with derision. Even Johnson was ridiculed, though we would have to search far for someone more capable of dealing in generalized statement with skill and genius.

The same can be said of the critical arrogance that places writers beneath their commentators. The eighteenth-centuryist thinks immediately of word-catchers that live on syllables, of small critics whose names are preserved through their association with Milton's or Shakespeare's, or of the commentators at Glubbdubdrib, skulking in distant quarters, hiding in shame and guilt from the authors they study. Aristotle, meeting Scotus and Ramus, considers them dunces, votaries of Pope's goddess. The critic's place here is clear; it is at best secondary.

In short, our cast of mind is necessarily different from that of our romantic or modernist colleagues. From our professional infancy we have been enjoined to clear our minds of cant, and we have met Criticism—in *The Battle of the Books*—as a malignant deity seated between her parents Ignorance and Pride, "Her Eyes turned inward, as if She lookt only upon herself."[14] To systematize, we learn, is to risk the intellectual death that consists of being drawn into a vortex existing only in our own imaginations.

Eighteenth-centuryists will also generally oppose the excessive professionalization of literary study, just as they will oppose its excessive systematization. They deplore the desire to segregate the scholar or critic from the public, to enshrine academic activity in a guildhall where the tainted hands of the amateurs can be kept from their sacred texts. Eighteenth-century writers sought a broad general audience, both in their art and in their criticism. For them, academic study and academic careerism occasioned suspicion (at best) and (more commonly) scorn. That English literature and criticism thrived for centuries prior to the arrival of English literature professors in the nineteenth is clear. Even at its inception, the formal study of English literature was intended to be a bridge between the world of learning and the world of working-class Britain. This is all quite well known now, since the tumult within our profession has driven us to a study of our origins.

The figures we study were professional writers, not professional critics, and as often as not, they were employed in an array of public roles. Newton was Master of the Mint, and Richardson was a printer. Prior was a diplomatist, and Hume was a judge advocate who, like Prior, Addison, Tickell, Rowe, and Sheridan, was also an under secretary of state. Boswell and Scott were lawyers; Defoe was a businessman and a secret agent; Fielding was a justice of the peace; Gibbon was a militiaman and an M. P. Locke, Arbuthnot, Goldsmith, and Smollett were physicians, and Sprat, Berkeley, Percy, Swift, Sterne, Young, Blair, and Crabbe—who also practiced medicine—were churchmen.[15] Johnson, the finest critical mind of at least his century, never tired of depreciating sheltered academic criticism or of praising those in contact with real life and those capable of depicting it.

Thus, the attempt to separate ourselves from the broad reading public and the concerns and activities of our society is a tendency that we as students of the eighteenth century will characteristically resist because we are more at home in an ethos where writers do not shun public roles and where some integration of life and art or art and society is not only thinkable but expected. This is apparent not only in the approach that we take to literature (based, in large measure, on the approach that that literature takes to life) but also in a professional posture that both welcomes nonacademic scholars and benefits from their contributions. We move as easily as might be expected among general readers, book collectors, and literary amateurs, that is, those who study literature because they love it.

What we have seen in literary study is the extension of romanticism from literary practice to literary commentary, and although we are largely powerless to restore the integrated relationship of art and society that existed prior to the nineteenth century, we can certainly resist the attempts to separate criticism from society now. It is, after all, no accident that many of those in the forefront of contemporary theorizing are students of the nineteenth and twentieth centuries.

One point, for example, that eighteenth-centuryists might reinforce is that criticism before the nineteenth century was more often rhetorical than philosophical. The traditions that Johnson associated with such figures as Horace and Quintilian or, later, Vida and Vossius are as foreign to much modern experience as they were useful to practicing writers. How many contemporary critics and theorists would look at something like Bysshe's *Art of English Poetry*, an extremely popular text, manual, and guide, with rules for making verses, collections of singular passages, and a rhyming dictionary? Scolar reproduced it in facsimile twenty years ago; who would do so today? Yet Johnson used Bysshe, just as he used John Walker's more comprehensive rhyming dictionary. Walker's *Elements of Elocution* was in fact dedicated to Johnson.

Such materials are guides for professional writers, not for academic critics. Theorists would ridicule contemporary equivalents, such as guides to fiction or screenplay writing, materials prepared by practitioners, which is to say, professionals, but that only indicates the separation in our lives between the discussion of literature and the writing of literature. It is a situation that we should lament but certainly not one that should occasion any surprise—not at a time when there are literary commentators among us prepared to say that professional writers do not, after all, really know very much about literature anyway.[16]

We have gone from a criticism based in large measure on rhetoric to one that finds its inspiration in philosophy, linguistics, and the systematizing tendencies of the natural and social sciences. However, as Crane pointed out long ago and as experience demonstrates every day,[17] literature is too rich to be encompassed by a single theory (especially, one might say, in a world where the theorists resist the corporate approach of modern science and opt instead for the Blakean approach of fabricating a personal system to avoid being enslaved by the systems of others). As is so often the case, few make the point more effectively than Johnson, here writing about the resolution of the crisis occasioned by the Spanish-English confrontation over Falkland's Islands and the inability of would-be commentators to transfer the rigor of scientific principle to the analysis of human life and human affairs:

> It seems to be almost the universal error of historians to suppose it politically, as it is physically true, that every effect has a proportionate cause. In the inanimate action of matter upon matter, the motion produced can be but equal to the force of the moving power; but the operations of life, whether private or publick, admit no such laws. The caprices of voluntary agents laugh at calculation. It is not always that there is a strong reason for a great event. Obstinacy and flexibility, malignity and kindness, give place alternately to each other, and the reason of these vicissitudes, however important may be the consequences, often escapes the mind in which the charge is made.[18]

As long as writers remain voluntary agents and as long as their works deal with the actions and feelings of other voluntary agents in forms designed to appeal to the tastes and loosen the purse strings of still other voluntary agents, the varieties of discourse and interchange (both intellectual and commercial) will resist explanations and descriptions driven by single-minded theory and system.[19] Our challenge will continue to be the adjustment of a plurality of approaches to specific texts, but our measure must be the extent to which our approach elucidates the text, not the extent to which we can force texts to huddle under the tiny umbrella of a single approach.

A pluralistic approach must still find its underlying unity in history. As Graff, Irving Howe, and others have noted, the historical approach opposed by New Critics and newer critics was vulnerable not because it was historical but because it was, at times, unsophisticated. Methods must be distinguished from their practitioners, particularly methods as broadly conceived as those we generally employ.

We sometimes hear, for example, that literary study changed because traditional methods had become bankrupt, which is to say, dull. It is impossible to see how history itself can be dull, unless one considers reality dull, in which case, following Plato, accounts of it or theoretical approaches to accounts of it or studies of those who develop theoretical approaches to accounts of it can hardly prove to be much more interesting. To say that a historian is dull or that a historical subject is dull is not to say that history is dull. To say that issues or texts are trivialized by a historical approach is really an indictment of the approacher and not the method. An approach or technique might lose some of its interest if it lacks intelligent and skilled practitioners, but again, the approach itself is not affected. One may write about Addison's essays or about his marriage or about his irregular pulse and be more or less cogent and more or less interesting, but the method remains the same.

As we develop an increasing taste for revisionist historiography, we should remember two things. First, there are few fields that can be said to have indulged in more revisionist historiography than eighteenth-century studies. Second, we should remind ourselves that new history is simply history. If the previous account was wrong, it was not history but fiction. So too, if we twist history to fit our ideological preconceptions, we are not looking into the past but into the mirror. Because history is independent of us (no matter how much we would like to deny the fact), we can argue about it, adduce evidence, and reach conclusions that will seldom compel assent but will at least be sufficiently substantive to support and advance the debate. Granted that history is a construct and that the past cannot be fully recaptured,[20] there can still be discussion, and study can proceed. If I give an account that is doomed to partiality, someone else can correct me and show what I have neglected. We will never get to the end point, but neither will we stand still.

It is for this reason, of course, that so-called traditional methods yield revolutionary results while so-called revolutionary methods generally yield predictable results. For all of its disquieting posturing, the conclusions of deconstructionism, for example, are utterly predictable. Vulgar Marxism and ideological feminism are at pains to rock the establishment by showing that class injustice and sexual injustice have occurred in history and are reflected in literature. A few years ago Edward Said stood on the stage at Georgetown inveighing against imperialism and pointing out in some detail what had probably not escaped earlier attention, namely that the British empire grew dramatically through the acquisition of other people's lands. However moving and important these issues may be to us as men and women, they are not interesting to us as scholars because they are apparent to anyone with a good grammar school education and a reasonably well-functioning central nervous system. It is no accident that sophisticated Marxists and sophisticated feminists employ thoroughgoing historical approaches, for dispassionate historical inquiry that is prepared to uncover and promulgate whatever is discovered is far more threatening than any ideologue's harangue and, finally, far more interesting.

At the risk of sounding like one of Swift's narrators, I would say that it is the traditionalists who are really the radicals. The vulgar radicals are really spiritual traditionalists because they repeat only what their followers are prepared to hear, while the methodological traditionalists change things finally. Their work may not be as engaging in its day-to-day development, and publication of that work's results often comes slowly, but if our goal is only to generate debate, conflict, and show without substance, then we are performing less as scholars and more as, say, professional wrestlers with inflated egos, playing a game of bluster while traveling about from forum to forum, carefully staying in character for our followers and demonstrating our power and agility in a dramatic exercise with a predictable ending. This is why we are so subject to parody, as in the novels of David Lodge, but to some of us Lodge's work is often closer to documentary than to comedy or satire.

If that seems harsh I believe it to be quite temperate compared with the notion that texts have no determinable meaning and eminently consistent compared with the injunction to forget the possibility of meaning in literature and trust in the existence of meaning in criticism, criticism that is really literature. Either the critics have overlooked their logical self-entrapment or they are hypocrites. (Hypocritics?)

There is another possibility. Consider, for example, the image of J. Hillis Miller on the cover of the MLA newsletter presenting a plaque to Claiborne Pell with an inscription from Ecclesiastes. Does this text have determinate meaning? If not, is the award ceremony a hoax or sham? If the text has meaning, will it be deconstructed later, if federal aid to education diminishes? Or are the questions unfair, and should we assume that the giver overlooks his own beliefs when operating in his official capacity? My assumption is that this is not really hypocrisy but an acknowledgment that literary criticism is perceived as a kind of game and that it must surely be overshadowed by an activity as serious as the conferring of an honor upon a generous congressional benefactor. Further, the acknowledgment that it is all a game allays serious problems of inconsistency, but it is not an admission that I would want to make staring into the eyes of, let us say, Plato, Sidney, Samuel Johnson, or Ronald Crane.

O. B. Hardison has commented that "deprived of a scenario, poststructuralism is left with a page on which it is impossible to write an incorrect sentence. This freedom can be used to expose contemporary illusions and hypocrisies. It can also become a kind of play in which nothing is serious. Recalling Nietzsche, Foucault calls it 'the explosion of man's face in laughter, and the return of masks.' This is probably valid, but its implications need to be faced. Where nothing is serious, Nothing (with a capital N) becomes the content of discourse."[21] If criticism is play and play alone, can we expect it to compete with play that is a more powerful image of life, world-class chess, for example? Or will it be farther down the continuum, closer to more exaggerated images of life such as professional wrestling? I fear that now, just as in professional wrestling, a majority of the audience for this particular kind of writing consists of believers rather than observers. Indeed, the behavior of the believers is, as a colleague has suggested to me, closer to the behavior of a religious congregation than an audience at a sporting event.

In a certain sense, the fervor over critical theory is encouraging because the terms in which it is praised often point to the empowering of its practitioners. It has made them feel needed, important, and less "marginalized." Whether the final thrust of these movements (many, of course, quite different) will continue to make their followers feel that way is, at this point, an open question. My own concern is that, at base, many of these tendencies do not ultimately speak to human life and experience in the way that more traditional approaches do, but the terms in which the movements are praised are often focused on central human concerns. In other words, the eighteenth century's desire for a criticism rooted in human experience and psychology continues.

In some ways the deflection of literary study from history to theory is based on the belief or unspoken assumption that all of the major questions are already answered. Like Bloom's young poets, young Ph.D.'s are arriving too late. The curtain is falling; there is nothing left for them to do or say. Dwarfed by the achievements of the past, they must strike out in other directions, directions they often believe to actually be new.

To a certain extent they are correct; a great deal has been done. However, when fresh light is shed on historical questions, the results are all the more telling, for everyone is aware of the difficulties involved in making a breakthrough. And it is certainly not impossible. Witness Donald W. Foster's recent use of historical materials in confronting one of the all-time mysteries in literary studies.[22] And even though much has been done, there is more than enough that remains. In 1977 in Victoria Donald Greene organized a session on research desiderata in Johnson studies. The list we compiled was sufficient to keep generations of researchers busy. Paul Korshin provided a list as of 1986, and it remains a very long one.[23] To give but a single example, no one has yet written a book about Johnson's poetry. Contrast that with the amount of book-length attention recently given Swift's verse.

Finally, it is not theory that assures brilliance but insight and experience, good sense and broad reading. This is why we can benefit from the works of commentators whose theories we abhor and be bored by those with whom we share common methodological ground. We can read the most diverse of both creative and critical writers and be the better for it. The important thing is that in acting as Johnson's voluntary agents we remember the riches and complexities both of life and of the works of those who have attempted to capture its mysteries. Crane once said of the New Critics that "they seek simplicity but do not distrust it,"[24] a warning that is always good to keep in mind and one that seeks, as its alternative, an approach to literature that is, to be sure, theoretical, but one grounded in history and in humility.

Notes

1. "Contemporary Theory and the Defense of Eighteenth-Century Studies: Brian McCrea, G. S. Rousseau, and Melvyn New," 281.

2. Review article, *JEGP* 85 (October 1986): 550.

3. Wellek, "Destroying Literary Studies," *The New Criterion* 2 (December 1983): 1.

4. "The New Theoreticism," *Sewanee Review* 91 (Summer 1983): 417.

5. Wellek, 7.

6. As he points out, p. 8.

7. "The Inevitability of Derrida," *The Scriblerian and the Kit-Cats* 18 (1985): 7–9.

8. *Literature Against Itself: Literary Ideas in Modern Society* (Chicago: University of Chicago Press, 1979), 97.

9. "Literary Criticism: Where Next?" in *Proceedings of the Twenty-Fifth Anniversary Meeting,* the Council of Graduate Schools in the United States, ed. Edna M. Khalil (Washington, 1985), 15–17.

10. "Samuel Johnson Among the Deconstructionists," *Georgia Review* 39 (Fall 1985): 544.

11. (Chicago: University of Chicago Press, 1987). Page numbers for subsequent quotations are cited in the text.

12. Jerome Christensen, *Practicing Enlightenment: Hume and the Formation of a Literary Career* (Madison: University of Wisconsin Press, 1987), 12.

13. Michael McKeon, *The Origins of the English Novel, 1600–1740* (Baltimore: Johns Hopkins University Press, 1987), 14.

14. A. C. Guthkelch and D. Nichol Smith, eds., *A Tale of a Tub to which is added the Battle of the Books and the Mechanical Operation of the Spirit,* 2d. ed. (Oxford: Clarendon, 1958), 240.

15. I have discussed this in "The Humanities, the Public, and the 'Public,'" *Washington Quarterly* 5 (1982): 157–60. This tradition continues, to some extent, in Britain. The fact that it does not in America is a cause of many of our problems and predicaments. It could be argued, e.g., that academic criticism further retreats from the public in America because the public has not welcomed it. Rather than bridge the gap we widen it. On Britain see Gary S. Messinger, "The Liberal Arts in Britain: Some Lessons for America," *Academe* 69 (1983): 21–27. Johnson is one of his frequent examples.

16. See the remarkable reference to this effect in Garrett Hongo and Catherine Parke's interview with Sandra Gilbert, in the *Missouri Review* 9 (1986): 89–109. Gilbert refers to a faculty member at the School of Criticism delighting in the "death of the author" and responding to her defense of

poets that "poets are not literary thinkers." One must wonder what such an individual would consider Sidney and Coleridge, Pope and Johnson, Shelley and Arnold, Emerson, Tate, Ransom, Blackmur, and Warren. Such outrageous statements serve to reinforce Graff's point that in the clamor for attention that is modern theory one of the ways to have one's voice heard is to up the ante of outrageousness and take an ever more bizarre position than one's colleagues.

17. Indeed, the constant use of terms such as *foreground* and *privilege* makes clear that different theoretical approaches exclude or radically minimize certain forms, styles, periods, genres, and so on, an acknowledgment that underscores the obvious need for a critical pluralism that responds to the demands of the text rather than a search for that single approach that will inevitably turn out to be procrustean.

18. *Samuel Johnson: Political Writings,* ed. Donald J. Greene (New Haven: Yale University Press, 1977), 365–66. Cf. Crane, *The Language of Criticism and the Structure of Poetry* (Toronto: University of Toronto Press, 1953), 17.

19. I would think that the richness of life and art would be made more manifest by the recent challenges to the traditional canon posed by, e.g., feminist scholars. There has never been a time in modern memory when so many new writers, forms, themes, and national literatures have been advanced for study. At the same time we can observe a passion for theoretical constructs whose tendency is to narrow rather than to open. Similarly, we see approaches that are ahistorical or antihistorical at a time of fervent historical revisionism and far less conflict among the practitioners of all these -isms than one might reasonably expect.

20. The difficulties of writing history and the fictional nature of much that passes for history is, of course, an Enlightenment commonplace. For a serious view of the matter see Martine Watson Brownley, "Samuel Johnson and the Writing of History," in *Johnson After Two Hundred Years,* ed. Paul J. Korshin (Philadelphia: University of Pennsylvania Press, 1986), 97–109.

21. "The De-meaning of Meaning," *Sewanee Review* 91 (Summer 1983): 404.

22. "Master W. H., R.I.P.," *PMLA* 102 (January 1987): 42–54. Those who have not read *PMLA* for years or those who confess to an inability to read any of that journal's articles to their conclusion should see Foster's piece. It suggests that some young Ph.D.'s in English are still being trained to do research.

23. *Johnson After Two Hundred Years,* xvii.

24. "Criticism as Inquiry; or, The Perils of the 'High Priori Road,'" *The Idea of the Humanities* (Chicago: University of Chicago Press, 1967), 2:31.

4

Historical Criticism, Hypotheses, and Eighteenth-Century Studies: The Case for Induction and Neutral Knowledge

HOWARD D. WEINBROT

IN HISTORY as in genealogy, one recreates the past in order to validate the present. Such has been the case with historians of recent critical movements, which often fitfully coexist under a leaky umbrella called the Nouvelle Critique. According to this vision, there once was a staid monolith called the Historicist, who came from nineteenth-century Germany to stultify the American university. The Historicist's shield included compartments portraying the triumph of history over literature, of dates and facts over aesthetic pleasure, of authors over their texts and reader, of courtroom evidence over brilliant speculation, and in general of dry bones over warm and fertile imagination. This sort of scholar, we have been told, proceeded by "interviewing an author's descendants and asking to search their attics."[1] Fortunately, enough authors apparently died without issue or attics to provide a needed escape. Henceforth there arose in the land liberating heroes of native birth—first from the South and, in their richest growth, from the havened soils of Connecticut. These New Critics smote the Historicist hip and thigh and established literature as a thing unto itself, with its own laws, uninfected by history, and committed to universal literary principles shared by all genres.

The American jihad was so successful that the new tyranny required new freedom fighters. A reformed Germany supplied philosophy, and America's spiritual ally France supplied linguistic and philosophic theory and several isms that strengthened the cause. From there came reinforcements of structuralism, then deconstructionism, revived Marxism, and Freudianism. Such volunteer brigades supported the already numerous sympathetic domestic guerilla fighters and others under the standards of feminism and New Historicism.

The Historicist thus fell before the New Critic who, though sometimes transmogrified into a misguided humanist, in turn fell before the Nouvelle Critique and its auxiliaries. They maintained close relations among one another and shared a common dislike for the authoritarian legacy of both deservedly defunct ancestors.

There can be only one objection to this scheme—namely, that it is not true. As anyone educated in the 1950s and early 1960s knows, the realities of the critical wars had very different configurations. The varied critical activity of those years is well illustrated by Frederick Crews' *Pooh Perplex: A Freshman Casebook* (1963), which has sold about 105,000 copies.[2] In it temporarily permanent critical approaches analyze *Winnie the Pooh* with paradox and persona, Marxism, Bloomian bardicism, glum Fiedlerism, happy Christian humanism, Yale Gentleman C chumminess, Harvard autobiographical impressionism, Chicago neo-Aristotelianism, Cambridge Leavis laceration, source study, Freud, and finally, with the school of You Have to Know Everything Before You Can Say Anything. Crews successfully parodied what was widely available to professional students and literate adults. Clearly, the New Criticism was only one choice among many.

The most heated and often most illuminating conflicts, however, were between the Chicago critics, who won some major battles, and the New Critics, who won the war.[3] Neither side had the wit to recognize common ground—an oversight rectified in E. D. Hirsch's admirable *Validity in Interpretation* (1968), dedicated jointly to the Hector and Achilles of this epic contest, R. S. Crane and W. K. Wimsatt, Jr. These two great ancestors also represent one of the continuing strengths of eighteenth-century literary studies. Like many of their colleagues, Crane and Wimsatt practiced close analysis and historical reclamation and mingled those arts with uncommon distinction. They preserved and promulgated models of historical criticism and helped to enlarge the legitimate scope of research into the nonliterary that nonetheless clarified literature. By the early 1970s major and genuinely revolutionary studies would use the visual arts, classics, gardening, lexicography, politics, and theology to make clear the varied intentions, achievements, contexts, and reception of several Restoration and eighteenth-century authors. Historical criticism in a wide signification thus has been a motivating force behind some of the best scholarship of the past two generations. When the interdisciplinary American Society for Eighteenth-Century Studies was founded in 1969, it was both effect and cause, both reflection and encouragement of the continuing generous work that drew upon a rich past to invest in a promising future.[4]

These are some of the reasons that many recent critical modes have not overwhelmed eighteenth-century studies. Students of Pope, for example, long will have studied the Latin poem Pope imitated, its commentary, and its varied generic cousins, and so "intertextuality" seems less than novel.[5] Students of Swift and Sterne long will have known about discontinuity; students of Richardson, sexual and family warfare and history; students of Burke and Longinus, reader response and involvement; students of Johnson and Burke, the mingled determinacy and indeterminacy of language; and students of Dryden, Pope, and Johnson, the interpenetration of economics, literature, and the book trade. Much of the Nouvelle Critique seems *vieux chapeau.*

Recent discoverers of the commonplace thus have badly rewritten the history of modern criticism and have ignored the excellent and well-established historical criticism practiced in eighteenth-century studies.[6] In so doing they have denied themselves the benefit of one of the most learned and rigorous critical theorists in the English-speaking world. Reading R. S. Crane's monographs and essays on literary history and theory stiffens one's resolve to clear the mind of cant. Such reading also tarnishes the new theorists' claims for originality of approach and urges reconsideration of some of their characteristic modes of proceeding.

At varied places Crane anticipates many of the seemingly new discoveries of the present generation. For example, all of us, he says, including those who reject theory, have a theory, and we need to be aware of it and its strengths and weaknesses;[7] we should also be aware of the subjective bases of our judgments; no absolute certainty or demonstration is possible in literary interpretation; we need to determine the audience of a work and its reception; accident and error often take place in a work and need to be considered by the critic, for they can undermine apparent authorial intention; the critic who uses only a form of "historical background" diminishes the value of literary history; since literature may be clarified by contexts far wider than that of traditional history, the critic should have "a constantly increasing set of critical tools" (63). As a consequence, Crane is suspicious of the theory and practice of a historicist like John Livingston Lowes and of historians of ideas like E. M. W. Tillyard on the one hand and of the isolators of art from life like the New Critics on the other. As one extended example of Crane on theory, here are remarks from "History versus Criticism in the Study of Literature":

> Theory, however much it may be denied or neglected, is inescapable: if
> we examine the writings of even the most impressionistic of critics, we

are certain to find, lurking behind the particular characterizations and judgments, a more or less consistent set of general propositions. It is not a question, then, whether principles are essential to criticism or not, but merely what body of principles should be selected and how far it is desirable that they should be explicitly recognized by the critic himself. . . . Theory we must have in any case; but surely much will be gained. . . if the principles with which we operate are given explicit statement and subjected to rational examination before being used in the criticism of individual works. (13)

This statement from 1935 is part of the ample estate Crane left to posterity.

Nevertheless, Crane is not a paradigm for the Nouvelle Critique. To coin a mixed metaphor, if he were alive today he would be spinning in his grave. Crane's disagreements with now dominant schools, however, could teach them even more than his agreements and perhaps help to limit the "methodological dogmatism" (103) that hinders inquiry. Before discussing my own version of Crane's version of historical criticism, though, I must insist upon two absolutes. The first is that invoking history and writing criticism do not make one a historical critic so long as the method is deductive and begins with certainty, rather than inductive and begins with doubt. The deductive critic establishes an omnibus theory and "reads" the work in light of it—as, for example, in the Elizabethan world picture, the *concordia discors,* the age of some worthy or term, Marxist class warfare, discontinuities, or other schemes designed to regulate and shrink an unruly world. The second absolute is that even the best models of historical criticism need not be "right." So long as there is original sin, an important function of the foot will be to put it in one's mouth. Still, the historical critic at his or her best is less likely to be catastrophically wrong or simplistic, and that is a significant advance upon a crooked road.

We may, then, begin with the temperament of historical critics, who so far as is possible hope to avoid imposing themselves upon text, context, and readers. Instead, they prefer to reclaim "only the values held and propagated by the actors in the history; they cannot be the values of the historian. To violate this principle is . . . to risk turning the history into propaganda for a special esthetic creed" (8–9). It also risks preselection of evidence to suit a philosophic, social, or political agenda. Historical critics certainly are free to judge, but they begin by seeking to understand the work on its own terms. A familiar Victorian response to part 4 of *Gulliver's Travels* (1726) illustrates this point. The Victorians often labeled Swift as Gulliver mad because only a madman could be so hostile to humanity. Historical critics, instead, ask why part 4 is the conclusion of *Gulliver's Travels* and how, if at all, it responds to certain issues raised in earlier parts. Unlike the Victorians, they will determine the chronology of composition and will find that in spite of part 4's role as conclusion, it was not written last when Swift, who is not Gulliver, might have been ill (though not mad); instead, it was written earlier when he was healthy. Historical critics may also despise an apparent despiser of humanity, but they will have rendered an independent judgment of a work whose achievement requires decent respect. They of course believe that objectivity in themselves, as in the author studied, is neither possible nor desirable; they also believe that not being a virgin should not make one a whore and that their job includes an effort to understand someone else's subjectivity. Historical criticism urges compartmentalization and self-restraint.

Second, the training of historical critics supports their temperament. It requires historical breadth and depth, scholarly rigor, healthy skepticism, and a reminder that, as Samuel Johnson or Edmund Burke might say, criticism cannot draw its principles from criticism but from nature and art.[8] In Crane's more pedagogical mode, students ought to be "trained with all possible rigor as scholars before they are encouraged to set up as critics"; they ought also "constantly to justify what they say in criticism and to explain how they know, from something other than current theory, that what they say of particular works is true" (44). Breadth of learning is requisite, since specialized critics tend to invoke a single theory or set of causes judged unneedful of competing knowledge and safe from refutation (248). Historical critics are more likely to believe that works may be illumined in a variety of legitimate ways and that the questions they ask direct them to the answers they get. The multi-spoked method, for example, encourages inquiries into the biographical framework of *Tom Jones* (1749) and its relationship between the real Henry Fielding and events or characters in his novel. Such a method also may examine the theological works Fielding might have known that helped to influence his narrator's ethic of forgiveness, or theatrical contexts that structure certain scenes and dialogues. Any of these is legitimate, and when properly managed, several combined will enrich understanding of the text; any one by itself is partial and unable to explain a complex "literary actuality" (191). Expansive pluralist criticism thus consists, in part, of compatible, germane monisms.

A third characteristic of historical critics is a combination of historical research and critical inquiry for the benefit of both. "There can be no adequate criticism that is not solidly based on the history of the art with which it is concerned" (27)—or, I should add, with its history in the more immediate sense of local placement, occasion, and extra literary facets. To better understand Pope's *Epistle to Augustus* (1737) we need to know both what "Augustus" meant and the history of the Horatian epistle as perceived in the earlier eighteenth century; but we also need to know the political value of "Horace" as an author for an apparent administration poet who actually is an opposition poet. And we also need to examine the Horatian parent-poem as represented on the facing page of this imitation of Horace because we then can see the special words and typography Pope selected for our attention and those parts he chose to imitate or expunge.[9]

The fruits of all this are likely to include acceptance of two unfashionable corollaries. One is recognition of the artist as the chief cause of literary creation, to which he or she is necessarily antecedent. "It is only as mediated through him that the general or collective causes of literary change can produce their effects in works, and it is only in him as a continuing substrate of abilities, habits, memories, feelings, interests, and aims, that the immediate particular causes of these effects can operate." As an individual, the author "can never be sufficiently explained as a product of the society or culture in which he acts" (117)—much less in a culture in which he could not act, like that in which proletarian and capitalist or id, ego, and superego collide. The author's mind in the author's own time incorporates and amends external events in the service of art and audience. Faced with, say, needs for plot, character, theme, and language, the author makes certain choices consistent with the idea of the whole and if necessary gives unifying coherence to the work.

Such coherence, though, need not be required, as in a meditative poem like Young's *Night Thoughts* (1742–45), a novelistic memoir like *Tristram Shandy* (1759–67), or loosely related essays like the *Citizen of the World* (1762). In each case the author is as much in control as in the more closely woven *Clarissa* (1747–48) or in *Tom Jones,* but the governing idea includes aperture instead of closure. In the nature of things, he may well unconsciously have considered matters like reading he forgot that he had read, ancillary themes, parents or other relations, and landscapes or buildings he once knew; but he remains in control nevertheless, probably excluding what experienced instinct silently tells him to exclude or, in later revisions of the same work, correcting errors, making the unconscious conscious, and molding the private into public art. We can see such efforts in Pope's revisions of his poems—from manuscript fragment to correction, to further correction, to the combining of fragments, to unified clean copy, to first edition, and then to subsequent editions or even versions. So long as the work remains vital to the artist, it remains unfinished in some way, as Pope's *Dunciad,* begun about mid-1725, was almost until his death in 1744.[10]

Historical critics thus will try to recreate the author's aims and achievement and will not try to substitute their own text for them. If discussing Pope's *Windsor Forest* (1713), for instance, historical critics might ask why the apparent georgic form is useful, how the poem's two parts do or do not relate, what historical events external to the poem help to explain its uses of Ovidian mythology, and why it was contemporaneous with the Treaty of Utrecht in 1713 that ended the War of the Spanish Succession. They will not "show," as a recent Marxist critic thinks she has, that the poem actually subverts its own values and supports the capitalist slavery it pretends to dislike.[11] Historical critics would regard such a deductive effort as critical imperialism that colonizes the poem and refuses to share Europe's relief at the end of a ghastly war whose final great battle at Malplacquet (1709) assembled 250,000 men and left 40,000 of them dead or wounded to pay the butcher's bill.

Another unfashionable corollary of temperament and training is awareness of the individuality of text and context. All of us know the repetitive language of modern critical theory that encapsulates human achievement in a series of formulas. Critics repeat their words like mendicant friars repeating their prayers: antithetical, deconstruct, demystify, desire, difference, discontinuity, discourse, encode, hermeneutic, intertextual, longing, other, power, privilege, self, sign, situate, subtext, valorize. The same secondary sources and critics reappear with comparable regularity to illumine varied texts at varied times through one theory. In most cases, such practitioners belong to the Fido or canine school of criticism. Like the family dog, they visit the same trees and hedges, not because they need to but because others have been there before them. One danger of such uniform rambles is that "the individual and specific traits of . . . literature will be submerged in the abstractions of the unifying scheme" (76); another is that the unique qualities of art works disappear and are replaced by roles as "causes, consequences, instances, or signs of something else" (91); and a third is that the special achievements of art tend to become instead "signs of deeper or larger realities and . . . quasi-Platonic statements" (97). In contrast, historical critics often make it impossible to say what has been said before, as even William Empson found when he spoke nonsense about *Religio Laici* (1682) because he was ignorant of Phillip Harth's contribution to our knowledge of Dryden's skepticism and religious contexts.[12] The uniform or canine critics remove the preserving salt of individuality.

After such preliminaries, historical critics will record their reactions to texts as a series of hypotheses to be tested, modified, or abandoned if necessary. They might proceed in a deductive-hypothetical, as opposed to a deductive-dogmatic, mode. One assumes a guiding hypothesis subject to examination and reconsideration; the other assumes an impregnable hypothesis verified by fiat. Or they might proceed by gathering relevant particulars and formulating a hypothesis from consequent inductions. In either case, their conclusions are a posteriori and a result of inquiry, instead of a priori and an arrest of inquiry. In my own experience, the hypothesis itself is a later rather than an earlier step in a progress from ignorance to education, from a series of questions to a collective statement that embodies a possible answer and becomes a possible explanatory model.

Collins' "Ode to Mercy," for example, seemed to me incomprehensible until I asked myself the following questions. Why in mid-1746 would an ode be written on that subject? Why does it include personifications of Valor, Mercy, the wounded genius of Britain, a savage "*Fiend of Nature*" (15), and the active presence of George II who, by the end of the poem, incorporates Mercy as his queen and bride. Why in its collected volume would it appear after a poem beginning "How sleep the Brave"? Only after I had reasonable answers to these questions could I formulate a modified hypothesis that I then used as the basis for other hypotheses. Namely, Collins' poem seeks mercy for the defeated Jacobite leaders waiting trial for their part in the unsuccessful revolution of 1745; in so doing it takes a dangerous minority position that seemed to ally the poet with traitors, Catholics, and foreigners. I then was able to ask another question: how many other poems in Collins' canon are comparably occasional and engaged? After answering that question, I was able to formulate a consequent hypothesis that, if successful in passing its tests, will mean reconsideration of the conventional wisdom regarding Collins. Namely, his several excellent occasional poems are not consistent with his modern image as an inward-turning self-conscious midcentury poet of sensibility who rejects the verifiable and social world of Pope's generation.[13]

One does not, however, adequately test a hypothesis merely by saying that it accounts for relevant facts, since in most instances of a priori criticism the relevant facts are dictated by the hypothesis—as in the Freudian reading of *Hamlet*, which assumes the existence of an Oedipus complex and therefore discovers it in that drama. In testing hypotheses, then, we need first to have confirming evidence—always easy enough to find or fabricate; then, more important, we need to have justified selection of that hypothesis by showing that competing hypotheses explain fewer of the matters in question than our own; and finally, and most important, we again need to have tested and tried to falsify the remaining hypothesis with relevant variables as independent as possible of the theoretical presuppositions that suggested it.

Within this mode of proceeding, we would not consider the Oedipal theory of *Hamlet* until we had investigated Shakespeare's sources to see whether he adapted a basic plot with or without changing it; had investigated Shakespeare's, not Freud's or Ernest Jones', probable understanding of the family and the relationship between mother and son; had investigated the specific instance of the royal family and the proper conduct of the prince and heir apparent toward his mother; and had investigated as well any comparable tragedies that might have suggested conventions appropriate for Shakespeare's use in *Hamlet*. If there were sufficient information, we should also hope to investigate any differences between the received text and the staged play, since the drama as printed is a radically incomplete record of the drama as performed. Only after these, and no doubt other approaches, were shown insufficient to explain the tense mother-son relationship in the play, could we begin to accept the Oedipal theory. As Crane concludes, we need to start "with the assumption that our hypothesis may very well be false and then permit ourselves to look upon it as fact only when, having impartially considered all the counter possibilities we can think of, we find disbelief in it more difficult to maintain than belief" (268).

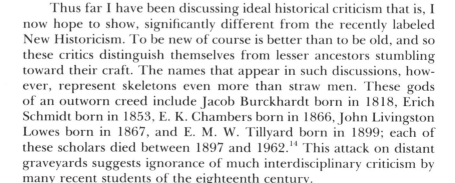

Thus far I have been discussing ideal historical criticism that is, I now hope to show, significantly different from the recently labeled New Historicism. To be new of course is better than to be old, and so these critics distinguish themselves from lesser ancestors stumbling toward their craft. The names that appear in such discussions, however, represent skeletons even more than straw men. These gods of an outworn creed include Jacob Burckhardt born in 1818, Erich Schmidt born in 1853, E. K. Chambers born in 1866, John Livingston Lowes born in 1867, and E. M. W. Tillyard born in 1899; each of these scholars died between 1897 and 1962.[14] This attack on distant graveyards suggests ignorance of much interdisciplinary criticism by many recent students of the eighteenth century.

Such reading and requisite reconsideration might have warped a large plank in the New Historicist's platform—the praised role of the historian as a political intruder upon his materials. Since there is no reliable authority, this argument on authority goes, "even an author's authorized text need have no more authority than we choose to give it." This is hardly "anti-authoritarianism" as claimed, though, since such critics unhesitatingly invade their authors and are remarkably dogmatic and authoritarian.[15]

For example, in the words of the New Historicism's latest apologist, it "must" move in specified directions;[16] in so doing "one must begin" with what is "the nature of Man" (20); "one must acknowledge" certain things (23); "one must enlarge" the scope of textuality (25); there "must be a suspicion" concerning the distinction between history and literature (26); "one must" examine other ancillary fields and "must place literary representations" in larger contexts (27); "one must take" the affective role of literature "more seriously" (28), but one also "must grow increasingly less literature-centered" (42); and one "must increasingly be willing to acknowledge" and even enhance one's "non-objectivity . . . and the inevitably political nature" of one's writings (43). A similar catalog could be made of terms like "can be made to" (15), "appropriated" (16), "only" (19, 27, 29 twice, 42), "mandate" (20), "necessary" (22, 42), "never" (23), "has to" (25), "banishes" (26), "cannot" (27), "no way" (28), and "the best criticism" (31). One is scarcely surprised to find kinship among docile critics following absolutist decrees. The same commentator observes that "the new historical critics so often make the period intelligible by narratives of rupture, tension, and contradiction" (17). Indeed, they are "seeking in . . . texts . . . some articulation of the discontinuities underlying any construction of reality" (15). It has been truly said that once one has a hammer everything becomes a nail. As an alternative to such reductive mechanism, I shall examine the Gypsy episode in *Tom Jones* (12:12) and illustrate both the historical and critical sides of historical criticism and some of the insufficiencies of the New Historicist's approach.

Shortly before Tom and Partridge enter London they take refuge in a barn occupied by Gypsies celebrating "the Wedding of one of their Society."[17] At first Partridge is terrified, but Tom is both polite and ingratiating, engages in dialogue with the Gypsy king, and is educated concerning the differences between Gypsies and Englishmen. "My people rob your People and your People rob one another" (671), his host tells Tom, whose birthright has been hidden or stolen and whose little store of money soon will be demanded by a highwayman. During this exchange the now well-liquored Partridge is caught in flagrante delicto by the husband of a Gypsy woman. "The *Youth*"

(670), as the narrator says of the middle-aged Partridge, is relieved when Tom and the Gypsy husband negotiate a settlement of two guineas. Before money changes hands, though, the Gypsy king determines that the couple had arranged to trap Partridge and profit from the wife's prostitution. The tables are turned, Partridge is exonerated, the Gypsy husband is punished by having to wear a cuckold's horns for one month, and his wife is pointed to and called whore (671). As the narrator says, however, this punishment is possible only in a society, unlike England's, in which shame has moral power. He also warns against temptation by such a royal, unchecked authority that is more appropriate for the devil than for England.

As Martin Battestin has shown, the superficially attractive Gypsies were thought to be descendants of the Egyptians, and their leader was thought to be a model of unchecked authority associated with the Stuarts and France, from whence the Gypsies migrated.[18] In England the Gypsy-Stuart alternative can survive only in a barn or as a simple wandering clan, in which benevolent despotism is possible, as it is not in a constitutional monarchy. A comparable evocation of legal history further enriches the passage. Lawrence Stone has demonstrated that by the middle of the eighteenth century, England had moved from a society in which marital infidelity could be punished by shame to one in which it was punished by claiming Criminal Conversation, or Crim Con, for which substantial monetary damages could be assessed against the offending male.[19] Unscrupulous couples might entrap a would-be Horner and make him pay handsomely for his furtive pleasures; young Wilson pays three hundred pounds (without having been tricked) in Fielding's earlier novel *Joseph Andrews* (3:3; 1742). The Gypsy episode, then, dramatizes part of Fielding the lawyer's and then magistrate's knowledge of the passing of one custom into another and the cynicism and prostitution thereby encouraged. The historical part of our task brings these illuminations to the text and its context.

The critical part asks perhaps the most frightening question in all literary studies—so what? It assumes that Fielding placed the Gypsy episode where he did for a particular purpose and that unless he chose wrongly, as is always possible, we will enhance our pleasure and our understanding of his art if we determine why he uses these historical backdrops at this rather than some other point in his artistic whole.

We see, for example, that Tom is respectful to the Gypsy, on whom others would look down, whereas Partridge views the barn he once thought haunted as an opportunity for sexual adventure. He is indeed an appropriate "hero" of this sexual escapade, for like the Gypsies as evoked, and unlike his master, he himself is a Jacobite. The differences between Tom and Partridge, however, are soon lessened when the drunk *"Youth Partridge"* is caught with a married woman clearly inappropriate for him. Tom had recently left Upton where, after drinking his fill, he was seduced by the presumed captain's wife Mrs. Waters. Like the Gypsy enchantress she is more clever than attractive and in years is to young Tom what Partridge is to the Gypsy. Tom also is discovered and pays the price—of lingering anger and suspicion by Mr. Fitzpatrick and of rejection by his beloved Sophia, who had arrived at the same inn and left when informed of Tom's indiscretion. Partridge, nominally youthful, in his cups, easily seduced, and careless in his selection of partners, reflects Tom's worst traits and comments upon his previous conduct.

As is typical of Fielding's progressive "rounding" of Tom's character, the episode also further shows Tom's good traits. We see that in spite of his poverty he is not tempted by the invaders' political system against which, instead, he was willing to fight. Though he understands the new ethic of Crim Con, he proceeds on the old ethic of restraint by shame and, the later episode with Lady Bellaston notwithstanding, prefers what is right to what is profitable. Had Tom wrongly been given part of Squire Allworthy's estate, he tells lawyer Dowling shortly before this scene, he would at once have returned it to Blifil (12:10). His response to being discovered in Mrs. Waters' bed includes anger, shame, and at least temporary refusal again to engage in such debauchery. Tom thus is made more complex at a key time in the novel, as he is approaching the great fleshpot of England, where all sins are enhanced and available, all men and women are either predator or prey, and the sexual despotism is hardly benevolent. The Gypsy episode and Partridge's Jones-like act are well placed as dual reminders that susceptible Tom needs special diligence to survive but that he is also a young man of largely sound moral, political, and social judgment who is associated with a better time and better motivation. We continue to both care for and worry about him, while also hoping that he will not disappoint us and fearing that he will—all of these are appropriate emotions at the appropriate place.

Here, then, is a text-based criticism that casts a wide historical net while seeking only those fish for which the text seems to ask. The criticism also is reader-centered, to the degree that it tries to recreate responses Fielding apparently wished to create in readers of *Tom Jones*. Though obviously subject to the views of the presenting critic, it essentially is not critic-based, an approach in which critics substitute themselves for author, text, and history and accommodate them to their own creeds. I hope that no one can tell whether I am a Hanoverian or a Jacobite, a republican or a monarchist, am for or against Gypsy rights, or think that shame is any more or less painful or desirable than being separated from a large sum of money. If I had opinions on such matters, I would at least try to keep them to myself. I recognize the dubious commonplace that such a nonideology also is ideological, but I should argue that it is benign because it tolerates more views than absolutist ideologies, extends the self, and assumes that alternative voices and cultures have a right to be heard in their historical particularity.

I would not keep to myself another way in which historical criticism functions—dealing with "discontinuities" in culture. Unlike the New Historicist and others, historical critics will not "seek" these and assume that they pattern "any . . . reality." Instead, they will deal with relevant discontinuities as one among many historical interludes and as one among many events that pose certain artistic questions requiring an answer. The Gypsy episode, for example, offers a potential and an actual discontinuous event. The Jacobite revolution had been over for about three years when *Tom Jones* appeared, but during the action of the novel itself, the '45 becomes backdrop, motivating force, and metaphor. Mrs. Western is a Hanoverian Whig, Squire Western is a nostalgic Tory Jacobite, and their differences contribute to their squabbling. The revolution in the state is mirrored in the revolution in Sophia's family, as she runs away from a bad forced marriage that is being made by a domineering father. Later when she is on the road, she is insulted by being thought the Pretender Charles Edward's mistress Jenny Cameron. The '45 also explains the presence of troops in the countryside, allows several plot complications, and casts light on the machinations in the Allworthy home. Paradise Hall has its false pretender to the estate in Blifil and its true spiritual heir in Tom; he rejects the possibility of destroying Allworthy by refusing to side with the Jacobites. Similarly, the very real discontinuity in the movement from shame to litigation also is important in a novel written by a lawyer and punctuated by legal events, one of which could have been the execution of Tom for murder.

In both potential and actual cases, I suggest, the discontinuity is subsumed under larger patterns or purposes. One such pattern is the conventions of the mingled comic romance genre, in which persons for whom we care undergo varied trials and are rendered happy by a combination of internal growth, external plot events, and clever authorial legerdemain. Our own happiness comes in part from sharing their pleasure and from fulfillment of our expectations. To test this view, try to think of Tom Jones fighting and dying at Culloden on either the royal or Jacobite side, or of Tom actually killing Mr. Fitzpatrick and being hanged at Tyburn. Perhaps even worse, think of Lady Bellaston offering her relation Sophia the protection of her London home while also successfully arranging for Lord Fellamar to rape her, so that Lady Bellaston can keep dandified Tom until she tires of him or until he finds another meal ticket. Any of these dark alternatives so violates the present world of *Tom Jones* that it would become something else. By raising the specter of such ruptures, tensions, and discontinuities, though, Fielding has expanded the emotions roused in a comic romance, has contained them, and has made them continuities in a novel that ends with a return to Paradise Hall, reconciliation, appropriate marriage, and propagation. This does not deny that rupture and discontinuity are present in eighteenth-century and other literature and life. Swift's *Tale of a Tub* and Richardson's *Clarissa* are as powerful in their ways of dramatizing discontinuity as *Tom Jones* is in neutralizing discontinuity. The essential point, however, is that historical critics try to let the text raise its own questions instead of seeking in the text what they predetermine is there, finding it, and using it to support a static, deductive theory that assumes what must be proven.

The New Historicism and historical criticism, then, are both married and divorced—each seeks scholarly breadth but parts on critical method. No hypothesis can be tested if the inquirer decrees that it is true. Such criticism, like other paradigms of the deductive, seems to me timid, a prop for orthodoxy, and therefore insufficiently challenging to the critic or instructive to the audience. Historical criticism is more threatening to orthodoxy and to the historical critic, who is required to accept genuine uncertainty and the risks of being wrong. I shall illustrate this with an example from my own research.

"Augustanism" is one of the notions still informing study of the eighteenth century. This vague term assumes an elevated public pose among writers who were restrained, elegant, witty, polished, and respectful adapters of the best Roman authors. In such a view, the model ruler was Augustus Caesar, who ennobled the throne and was an ideal patron of the arts—as the flourishing of letters in Virgil and Horace demonstrated. These two great poets, the argument goes, were the key literary and political models for the eighteenth century and largely banished the alternatives of the dark, rough, and angry Persius and Juvenal.

I had become progressively more suspicious of the accuracy and prescriptive, often proscriptive, power of the term "Augustan." For example, we would have to ignore much of Dryden, Swift, Pope, and contemporary response to them to believe this concept. We also would have to ignore some of the eighteenth century's most exciting and important novelists—like Defoe and his restless men and women desperately seeking or rejecting middle class comforts; or Richardson and his great cosmic battle of good and evil between the sexes; or Sterne and his mockery of any establishment values including the already growing traditions of the new novel itself.

Not until I had reread the first three chapters of Gibbon's *Decline and Fall* (1776), however, did my method and a long project begin to take shape. Here was a bitter indictment of Augustus as destroyer of the balanced Roman constitution and as father of Rome's decline. I thus needed to determine whether Gibbon's view was singular or representative. After reading numerous Latin, French, and English histories of Rome, I found that Gibbon culminated a large body of anti–Augustan historiography that began as early as Tacitus. In England, Augustus was a norm so long as the divine right of kings was a norm, but after the Glorious Revolution of 1688–89, Augustus was progressively more of an emblem of violent autocracy. His compliant court poets Horace and Virgil soon were regarded as miserable accomplices in their nation's ruin. As the angry author of *Plain Truth or Downright Dunstable* put it in 1740,

> In monstrous times, *such Weeds* thrive best,
> They *ornament a Tyrant's Nest.*
> They serve to *lull and blunt the Pain,*
> Of *vilest Crime*, still hide such Stain,
> In Luxury, they thrive amain.
> Of *Tyranny bear up the Train.*
> Their *Lyes and Flatt'ry,* is good Sense,
> Such Times, it ne'er can give Offence,
> *The Tyrant grants 'em a Licence.*
> More Youth and Men have sure been lost,
> By *Horace'* Book, you so much boast,
> Than any Author you can name,
> Or Strumpet of the *vilest Fame.*[20]

I also found that frequent attacks on Horace brought frequent praise for Persius and, especially, Juvenal. These isolated poets of liberty bravely attacked a corrupt court and protested its incorrigible depravity. As Gibbon said in 1763, "love of liberty, and loftiness of mind, distinguishes Juvenal from all the poets who lived after the establishment of the monarchy. Virgil, Horace, Ovid, Lucan, Martial, Statius, Valerius Flaccus, all sing the ruin of their country, and the triumph of its oppressors. . . . Juvenal alone never prostitutes his muse."[21] Here, it seemed to me, was the satiric voice behind Alexander

Pope's angry resistance to Walpole and George II, a resistance finally crushed in the last book of the *Dunciad,* where Pope's narrator and the remnants of his civilization are buried under Hanoverian rubbish.

In the process of so educating myself, however, a potentially fatal reservation remained—namely, much anti-Augustan rhetoric dating from the mid-1720s was opposition outrage toward the court of George II, or George Augustus. One of the few modern writers on the subject had dealt with some of those attacks; a warm advocate of Augustanism, however, insisted that such crankiness was idiosyncratic and that Pope himself was the archetypal Augustan. There was only one path left—to test, or in Crane's term to try to falsify, the hypothesis that widespread anti–Augustanism was shared by administration and opposition. To do this, I had to read administration propaganda in its own and allied newspapers from about 1726 to 1742, the chief years of enmity toward the prime minister Sir Robert Walpole. If the government-financed *London Journal* and *Daily Gazetteer* regarded Augustus with the same anger that the opposition's *Craftsman* did, my case would be solid. If the *Daily Gazetteer* admired Augustus, then I would have to modify my hypothesis by largely limiting it to the opposition and perhaps abandon some inferences I was ready to draw, like the rejection of Horace as a model for British satire. After sustained work at the British Library, I found that the court's *Daily Gazetteer* indeed claimed that the opposition was Augustan, as well as absolutist, Jacobite, and un-British in violating the balanced constitution.[22] Only after this major hurdle was cleared could I finish a book called *Augustus Caesar in "Augustan" England: The Decline of a Classical Norm*—which changed some minds, infuriated others, and reaffirmed the need genuinely to test hypotheses at whatever risk to one's grand scheme.

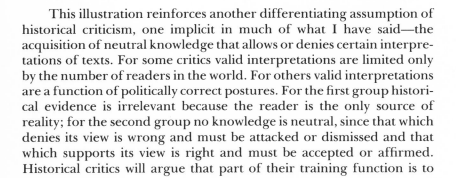

This illustration reinforces another differentiating assumption of historical criticism, one implicit in much of what I have said—the acquisition of neutral knowledge that allows or denies certain interpretations of texts. For some critics valid interpretations are limited only by the number of readers in the world. For others valid interpretations are a function of politically correct postures. For the first group historical evidence is irrelevant because the reader is the only source of reality; for the second group no knowledge is neutral, since that which denies its view is wrong and must be attacked or dismissed and that which supports its view is right and must be accepted or affirmed. Historical critics will argue that part of their training function is to educate the mind to tell the more or less true from the false, or the possible from the impossible, and that to do so one needs neutral information. I shall offer another practical example of such criticism and its consequences.

There long has been a minidebate regarding why Goldsmith's Vicar of Wakefield had to leave his comfortable parsonage with its yearly living of thirty-five pounds and accept a distant humble curacy of fifteen pounds. After all, even though a merchant had absconded with the large fortune the Vicar Mr. Primrose deposited with him, that living, together with some remaining funds, should have been enough for the Primroses and their six children. Two hypotheses reigned: the first, held by Goldsmith's best editor, was that there was an earlier discarded version of chapter 2 explaining this otherwise inexplicable oversight; the other, which had become paramount, was that Primrose published a pamphlet siding with William Whiston in the "famous" Whistonean controversy prohibiting the remarriage of an Anglican clergyman after the death of his wife.[23] Since Primrose's archdeacon, also probably his son's potential father-in-law, had been married three times and was courting a fourth wife, this so angered him that he took ecclesiastical action against Primrose and hounded him from his position. Primrose's foolishness, aggression, and attempt to hide his disgrace, this view holds, are signs that he is the disapproved object of irony, not the approved norm that readers for two centuries thought him.

Though I did not know why Mr. Primrose left his home, I did nothing until a student asked what I should have been able to answer. Thereafter, my equally puzzled colleague Eric Rothstein and I set about illumining our darkness. Our search began by testing each of the available hypotheses. We could find no evidence or mention of a lost chapter and no hint of one until the late nineteenth century. We also determined that since there were five authorized editions of the *Vicar* during Goldsmith's lifetime and since he had carefully revised the second edition, he presumably would have restored the lost or clarified the unclear. In the process of examining textual history, we found that in chapter 2, when the Vicar's financial troubles begin, Goldsmith indeed made a significant change. At first the generous man said that he "gave" all of his redundant salary "to the widows and orphans of the clergy of our diocese"; in the second edition he changed "gave" to "made over." "Gave" his salary denoted a gift that could be retracted when necessary, as his family would expect. To avoid this potential conflict, Goldsmith substituted "made over"—the signing of a legal document that permanently transferred his earnings so that he no longer could claim them. Without either salary or independent

income, Primrose needed another paying job. Our acquired knowledge of changes in the text and of its key new legal term nullified the
hypothesis of an extra chapter.

Although this information also raised doubts concerning the hypothesis of a secretly undercut Vicar, it did not refute it. Here too our
mode of proceeding would spring from an admission of ignorance.
Like Goldsmith's editors, neither of us knew anything about a
Whistonean controversy regarding the remarriage of Anglican
priests, though Whiston himself was a promiscuous controversialist. As
we found after research into Whiston's works, memoirs, biographies of
him, and bibliographies concerning him, that ignorance was inevitable,
for there was no such famous controversy. If it should sometime be
discovered, it was so insignificant that the liberal Church of England
could not use it to dismiss an otherwise acceptable clergyman. But,
we then reasoned, even though such hounding now was at the least
improbable, how would an Anglican clergyman in about 1760 be
removed from office? We found that a traumatic ecclesiastical trial
would have taken so long and would have involved so many statements,
counter statements, and ultimate disgrace for the defeated clergyman,
that it could not go unmentioned and would change the amiable chin-
up tone of the novel. This nullified the reeling hypothesis of a foolish,
satirized Vicar dismissed from his living by ecclesiastical authorities.
Our inquiries thus included both minute particulars of the text and
broader nontextual cultural matters germane to it. The inquiries
shared skeptical but not prejudged examination of previous hypotheses' ability to resolve their problems without introducing improbabil-
ities. When we determined that these were inadequate, we offered our
own hypothesis based upon that acquired relevant neutral information
so that we returned to the text, to which we owed allegiance, and which
our neutral knowledge clarified.

I clearly have reservations regarding the achievements and methods of some recent critical theory and prefer the historical criticism I
have illustrated. When properly practiced, its eclecticism long has
incorporated much of the best of the Nouvelle Critique while avoiding
much of its deductive certainty. Moreover, historical criticism recog-
nizes that however important, it is secondary to the literature it serves.
Many advocates of the newer critical modes see themselves as makers
of a separate discipline and not as illuminating but replacing literature.
Criticism is literature, several theorists have said, as they make them-

selves, their colleagues, or their works primary texts.[24] One such author even claims that the critic is like "a character in a novel," and that criticism has "an esthetic consistency normally reserved for creative literature."[25] Theory's declaration of independence, nonetheless, cannot be a declaration of equality, for in too many cases its exemplars write (badly) about that cherished but limiting subject, themselves. Journals of theory often include articles by critics A, B, and C, with scolding responses by D, E, and F, and counterscolding responses to the responses by A, B, and C. No wonder, we have approvingly been told, such criticism is "a conversation about itself" and that "the study of criticism is necessarily also the study of ourselves as critics."[26] One critic has advanced this process considerably by reviewing his own books and finding them very stimulating indeed.[27]

So much theory is written in the service of the self that historical criticism's role is the more easily seen. As the ally of literary studies, it hopes to offer both pluralist hypotheses and tested inferences regarding literature and history. In so doing, it also hopes to further one of the chief ends of literature, the pleasure that often operates through an expansion and understanding of other responses in other situations, cultures, or ages. As Johnson says about the pleasure of fiction, it allows us to feel, "while the deception lasts," the experience of another human being facing choices to which we might be subject or from which we might learn. Such art can "enchain the heart by irresistible interest"—both in others and for ourselves.[28] Rather than secede from or compete with literature, historical criticism serves its best ends and its readers, engages the critic in respect for and nurturing of alternative points of view, and strengthens the mind's resolve by urging examination of how we know what we say we know and how that knowledge is relevant for human needs. The scope of such studies is both broad and deep. I shall offer but four of the expansionist projects that, I am confident, can be performed by the historical critic on behalf of the larger community.

Clarissa is the greatest tragic novel in the English language, but we still lack a definitive text that includes Richardson's many variations and replies to his own and his correspondents' second and third thoughts. Such an edition would require extensive annotation and, as we might expect from this accumulation of neutral knowledge, probably would limit certain interpretations while encouraging others. I suspect, for example, that the recent bizarre sympathy for the rapist Lovelace must surrender before the line from the *Aeneid* (6.853) that, Lovelace says, should be his motto were he to have one: "parcere subiectis et debellare superbos."[29] Rome will make peace with those who give her what she wants but will make war to the end ("debellare

superbos") with those who resist, as the ravaged Carthage and Clarissa
found.

The relationship between the text as written or first-published
document and text as additive document also remains largely
undiscussed. Once Pope starts to incorporate his many footnotes and
comments to the *Dunciad,* it becomes a work quite different from the
self-contained *Dunciad* of 1728. It even changes its genre, from mock-
epic to Menippean satire that blends prose and poetry. We need a
study of the progress of the *Dunciad,* of Menippean satire in the
eighteenth century, and of the art of the footnote.[30] *A Tale of a Tub,*
the Dunciad, and *Clarissa* are among the important works in which the
footnote is an extension of the text and supplies one or more of the
voices that engage varied parts of the audience.

We also need far more practical reclamation of the contexts of
midcentury poetry. Much has been written about its preromanticism,
anxiety regarding Milton, and retreat to the unverifiable and insub-
stantial. These generalizations are based on few poems and broad
ignorance of historical context. Since William Collins, for example, is
characteristically cited as such a poet, most readers hardly suspect that
about 40 percent of his poetry concerns battles of the War of the
Austrian Succession abroad, the Jacobite revolution at home, and their
consequences. We ought to encourage investigation of such poetry of
the moment and determine whether it can enlarge our view of the
midcentury achievement. I wonder, as well, whether even when that
poetry does turn inward, it is any the less empirical than the more social
and political poetry of the 1720s and 1730s. In one case, Thomson,
let us say, observes externals, orders them, and determines that the
patterns he sees suggest a patterning God. In the other case, could we
not ask whether the Young of *Night Thoughts* and, in some cases, Gray,
Akenside, and Collins are not equally observant but have shifted the
focus of observation from the external to the internal? Could the
workings of the observing patterning eye shift to the workings of the
observing feeling mind or heart? Such questions remain unposed
because of insufficiently tested moribund reigning hypotheses.

Finally we require further study of Anglo-French literary relations. We all know Johnson's *Lives of the Poets* (1779–81), but not
enough of us know the Abbé Antoine Yart's eight-volume *Idée de la
poësie Angloise* (1749–56). He offers new translations, perceptive remarks concerning individual poets, and discussion of similarities and
differences between the French and the British genius. The Abbé
Yart's unapprehended *Idée* is a valuable foreign overview of Britain's
rise from an intellectually insecure offshore island to a confident nation able to rival Greece, Rome, and France. We need to know more

about this work and its possible role as a reflection or formulation of Anglo-French critical thought and poetical practice.[31]

Here then are four among the many possible happy tasks of historical criticism of eighteenth-century literature. Some of its enriching traits include awareness that the inquiry chosen is a part, not the whole, of a text's intellectual milieu; that whatever we think we have learned, we need to show so far as we are able that such a milieu was known or accessible to the author; that even when we can show our knowledge of the author's knowledge, he or she may have used this material in a particular not general way; that before we can claim reasonable accuracy for our hypothesis, we need to show that, unlike its competitors, it explains most of the work's difficulties with the fewest objections and that this hypothesis is not drawn from a self-justifying, deductive, critical system. Such a task is rigorous, challenging, and frightening, not least of all to the historical critic who engages in a contest with uncertainty and often loses. We nonetheless recognize the truth of what Hesiod and Longinus said about Plato's frequent failures to adapt Homer's eloquence. *"Such brave Contentions work the Good of Men."*[32]

Notes

This paper was written during my tenure as a Fellow at the University of Wisconsin's Institute for Research in the Humanities. It is a pleasure to thank the former director Robert M. Kingdon and a permanent member Phillip Harth for the time and invaluable collegial support.

1. Herbert Lindenberger, "Toward a New History in Literary Study," *Profession 84* (New York: Modern Language Association, 1984), 19. Some of the implications of the putative New History have been considered by G. Thomas Tanselle in "Historicism and Critical Editing," *Studies in Bibliography* 39 (l986): l–46.

2. Thanks are due to Mr. William Marshall and his staff at E. P. Dutton for supplying this information.

3. Several of these essays have been collected in *Critics and Criticism Ancient and Modern,* ed. R. S. Crane (Chicago: University of Chicago Press, 1952). See especially R. S. Crane, "I. A. Richards on the Art of Interpretation," 27–44; Elder Olson, "William Empson, Contemporary Criticism and Poetic Diction," 45–82; Crane, "The Critical Monism of Cleanth Brooks," 83–107; W. R. Keast, "The 'New Criticism' and *King Lear,*" 108–37; Olson, "A Symbolic Reading of *The Ancient Mariner,*" 138–44. These brilliant hatchet jobs confirmed the faithful without making converts. David H. Richter has chronicled the later fortunes of such critics and criticism in "The Second Flight of the Phoenix: Neo-Aristotelianism since Crane," *The Eighteenth Century: Theory and Interpretation* 23 (1982): 27–48. Crane's literary principles and pluralism, apparent and real, have been discussed by Donald S. Taylor in "Literary Criticism and Historical Inference," *Clio* 5 (1976): 345–70; Walter A. Davis, *The Act of Interpretation: A Critique of Literary Reason* (Chicago: University of Chicago Press, 1978), 14–23, 53–56, 167–69; Wayne Booth, *Critical Understanding: The Powers and Limits of Pluralism* (Chicago: University of Chicago Press, 1978), 36–97, especially 102–3, 355–56n.8. "Disguised monism" (102) is one term for Crane's pluralism. Most historians of literary criticism, however, write as if immunized from the Chicago flu—as in Frank Lentriccia, *After the New Criticism* (Chicago: University of Chicago Press, 1980). For possible signs of a reinvention of pluralism, however, see Christopher Butler, *Interpretation, Deconstruction, and Ideology: An Introduction to Some Current Issues in Literary Theory* (New York: Oxford University Press, 1984) and Michael McKie, "Criticism as Ideology," *Essays in Criticism* 36 (1986): 75–78, a review of Butler and amplification of annoyance with isolated, muddied dogmatisms.

4. For a fuller discussion of the role of the American Society for Eighteenth-Century Studies, see Phillip Harth, "Clio and the Critics," *Studies in*

Eighteenth-Century Culture, ed. Harry C. Payne (Madison: University of Wisconsin Press, 1981) 10: 3–15.

5. Perhaps the classic statement, or overstatement, of this long-practiced method is in Earl R. Wasserman's "Limits of Allusion in *The Rape of the Lock*" in the *Journal of English and Germanic Philology* 65 (1966):

> The mode of existence of Pope's poetry—and probably of many other neoclassic poems—ought to be defined broadly enough to include a creative act by the reader. For it suggests that the reader is not only to appreciate the poet's invention in finding appropriate allusions but is actively invited by them to exercise, within poetic reason, his own invention by contemplating the relevances of the entire allusive context and its received interpretation. . . . Such literature as this is constituted not only by its own verbal texture but also by the rich interplay between the author's text and the full contexts it allusively arouses, for these allusive resonances are not peripheral but functional to the meaning of the artistic product (443–44).

6. Such turning of oases into mirages is made plain by Laura Brown: eighteenth-century studies, she knows, has not "in the last three decades, been a center of vitality in literary study in general, or a locus of major work with an audience beyond period specialists. For us, as for Dryden, the age of giants—R. S. Crane and the Chicago School, of Earl Wasserman, William Wimsatt, Reuben Brower, and Ian Watt—has passed, leaving the field with only a vestigial place in the undergraduate curriculum." See "Contemporary Theory and the Defense of Eighteenth-Century Studies," *The Eighteenth Century: Theory and Interpretation* 26 (1985): 281. Since all of those distinguished scholars were active during significant parts of "the last three decades," or 1955–1985, one suspects Brown's arithmetic, learning, or lexicon. Given her calendar and catalog, alas, thus have been erased from the Book of Memory, Walter Jackson Bate, Martin Battestin, Wayne Booth, James L. Clifford, Ralph Cohen, Irvin Ehrenpreis, Donald Greene, Jean Hagstrum, Phillip Harth, Robert D. Hume, Louis Landa, Maynard Mack, Marjorie Hope Nicolson, Maximillian Novak, Ronald Paulson, Ricardo Quintana, Claude Rawson, Eric Rothstein, George Sherburn, Patricia Meyer Spacks, and Curt Zimansky, among numerous other important and vital literary critics, literary historians, biographers, and editors.

7. The remarks quoted or referred to within are from "History versus Criticism in the Study of Literature" (1935), "Criticism as Inquiry: or, The Perils of the 'High Priori' Road" (1957), "Critical and Historical Principles of Literary History" (1950), "Questions and Answers in the Teaching of Literary Texts" (1953), "Every Man His Own Critic" (1956), and "On Hypotheses in 'Historical Criticism': Apropos of Certain Contemporary Medievalists" (1961). All are printed in vol. 2 of Crane's *Idea of the Humanities and Other Essays Critical and Historical* (Chicago: University of Chicago Press, 1967). All page numbers are cited parenthetically in the text. Crane's *Languages of Criticism and the Structure of Poetry* (Toronto: University of Toronto Press, 1953) was the Alexan-

der Lectures for 1951–52 and has just been reissued by the University of Chicago Press. Crane's final paragraph includes this unheeded remark: "the greatest obstacle to advance in criticism is not the existence of independent groups of critics each pursuing separate interests, but the spirit of exclusive dogmatism which keeps them from learning what they might from one another" (193).

8. See *Lives of the English Poets*, ed. G. B. Hill (Oxford: Clarendon Press, 1905), "Dryden," 1: 433; "Addison," 2: 148; "West," 3: 333. See also *Rambler* No. 37 (1750) and No. 92 (1751), in the Yale Edition of the Works of Samuel Johnson, *The Rambler*, ed. W. J. Bate and Albrecht B. Strauss (New Haven: Yale University Press, 1969) 3:200–205, 4:122–23. For further discussion of the bases of Johnson's criticism, see W. R. Keast, "The Theoretical Foundations of Johnson's Criticism," *Critics and Criticism*, 398. See also Burke's *Philosophical Enquiry into . . . the Sublime and Beautiful*, ed. J. T. Boulton (Notre Dame, Indiana: University of Notre Dame Press, 1968) 54, pt. 1, sec. 19.

9. For some of these issues, see Howard D. Weinbrot, *Augustus Caesar in "Augustan" England: The Decline of a Classical Norm* (Princeton: Princeton University Press, 1978).

10. The best study of Pope at work is Maynard Mack's essential *Last and Greatest Art: Some Unpublished Manuscripts of Alexander Pope* (Newark: University of Delaware Press, 1984). Of course, a visual or graphic art may be in flux as well, as the several states of many Hogarth engravings make plain.

11. Laura Brown, *Alexander Pope* (Oxford: Basil Blackwell, 1985), 40. This view is seconded by the series' editor Terry Eagleton in the "Editor's Preface," vii. For some further light on the value of traditional Marxist terminology for the eighteenth century, see E. P. Thompson's important "Eighteenth-Century English Society: Class Struggle Without Class?" *Journal of Social History* 3 (1978): 133–65.

12. For this exchange, see Phillip Harth, *Contexts of Dryden's Thought* (Chicago: University of Chicago Press, 1968); William Empson, "Dryden's Apparent Scepticism," *Essays in Criticism* 20 (1970): 172–81; Harth, "Empson's Interpretation of *Religio Laici*" 20 (1970): 446–50; Empson, "A Deist Tract," in his *Using Biography* (Cambridge: Harvard University Press, 1984), 99–122. Empson seemed unable to admit his blunders; but he did not reprint the essay on skepticism, above, claiming instead that its arguments were included and amplified in "A Deist Tract": *Using Biography*, 123.

13. I deal with some of these issues in a forthcoming Clark Library Seminar, "William Collins and the Mid-Century Ode: Poetry, Patriotism, and the Influence of Context." See also the description of the third project for historical criticism, below.

14. Chambers, Lowes, and Schmidt are in Lindenberger, "Toward a New History," 17–18, 21; Tillyard and Burkhardt (from a 1958, New York edition) are in Jean E. Howard, "The New Historicism in Renaissance Studies," *English Literary Renaissance* 16 (1986): 14–15, 18.

15. Lindenberger, 17, 21. He observes, regarding the new historical method: "What is relevant is what seems significant and worth exploring at the moment we are doing it" (9). Compare this with Swift's Modern in *A Tale*

of a Tub (1704): "I profess to *Your Highness* [Prince Posterity], in the Integrity of my Heart, that what I am going to say is literally true this Minute I am writing." Compare also Lindenberger on the subjected author and Swift's Modern again: "I claim an absolute Authority in Right, as the *freshest Modern*, which gives me a Despotic Power over all Authors before me" (*A Tale of a Tub*, ed. Herbert Davis [Oxford: Basil Blackwell, 1965], 22, "Epistle Dedicatory," and p. 81, sec. 5, "A Digression in the Modern Kind"). Much of the literary satire in the *Tale* is germane, including this from sec. 9, "A Digression on Madness": "For, what Man in the natural State, or Course of Thinking, did ever conceive it in his Power to reduce the Notions of all Mankind, exactly to the same Length, and Breadth, and Heighth of his own? Yet this is the first humble and civil Design of all Innovators in the Empire of Reason" (105).

16. Jean Howard, "The New Historicism," 19. Page numbers for subsequent quotations are cited in the text. There are similar constructs of straw and absolutist terminology in Louis Montrose, "Renaissance Literary Studies and the Subject of History," *English Literary Renaissance* 16 (1986): 5–12. Edward Pechter has ably discussed some of the many conceptual problems in this orthodoxy. See his "The New Historicism and Its Discontents: Politicizing Renaissance Drama," *PMLA* 102 (1987): 292–303.

17. *The History of Tom Jones, A Foundling*, ed. Martin C. Battestin (Middletown, Conn.: Wesleyan University Press, 1974), 666. Subsequent citations are given in the text.

18. See Battestin's edition of *Tom Jones*, 664–71 and Battestin, "Tom Jones and 'His *Egyptian* Majesty': Fielding's Parable of Government," *PMLA* 82 (1967): 68–77. To this, one might add the following similarities between the Gypsies and Jacobites: like Charles Edward and his general Lord Murray, who avoided General Wade by entering England from the west, the Gypsies are on the western approach to London; they get close to that city, but do not enter it; they rob the English; they have absolute loyalty to an absolute king they love, who sounds foreign, and who even his enemies admitted was uncommonly ingratiating; they are oddly dressed; they drink and carouse in stereotypical Jacobite ways; their women, as exemplified in the Gypsy wife, are homely, scheming, and sexually licentious. Several numbers of Fielding's *Jacobite's Journal* consider some of these issues.

19. Stone's studies of Crim Con will appear in *Road to Divorce*: England 1530–1987 (forthcoming, Oxford University Press, 1990) and *Broken Lives: Separation and Divorce in England 1660–1857* (forthcoming, Oxford University Press, 1991).

20. (London), 15–16. The work includes "Some Critical THOUGHTS concerning *Horace* and *Virgil*," who were "*flattering, soothing, Tools*," and "Fit to *praise Tyrants* and *gull Fools*" (13).

21. "Extraits de mon Journal," in *Miscellaneous Works*, ed. John Lord Sheffield (London, 1796) 2:103–4.

22. For a record of these findings, see *Augustus Caesar in "Augustan" England*, 108–19. For other texts concerning the matter of Augustanism, see J. W. Johnson, "The Meaning of 'Augustan,'" *Journal of the History of Ideas* 19 (1958): 507–22, and chaps. 1 and 2 of his *Formation of English Neo-Classical*

Thought (Princeton: Princeton University Press, 1967); Ian Watt, "Two Historical Aspects of the Augustan Tradition," in *Studies in the Eighteenth-Century:
Papers Presented at the David Nichol Smith Memorial Seminar, Canberra, 1966,* ed.
R. F. Brissenden (Toronto: University of Toronto Press, 1968), 67–79; Howard Erskine-Hill, "Augustans on Augustanism: England 1655–1759" (a
warmly pro–Augustan essay), *Renaissance and Modern Studies* 11 (1967): 55–
83; Jay Arnold Levine, "Pope's *Epistle to Augustus,* Lines 1–30" (opposition
attacks on Augustus), *Studies in English Literature, 1500–1900* 7 (1967): 427–
51; T. W. Harrison, "English Vergil: The *Aeneid* in the XVIII Century,"
Philologica Pragenisia 10 (1967): 1–11, 80–92; Malcolm Kelsall, "What God,
What Mortal? The *Aeneid* and the English Mock-Heroic," *Arion* 8 (1969): 359–
79; Kelsall, "Augustus and Pope," *Huntington Library Quarterly* 39 (1976): 117–
31 and Kelsall, *Imperious Caesar, Dead and Turned to Clay* (Cardiff: University
of Wales Press, 1977); Donald Greene, "Augustanism and Empiricism: A Note
on Eighteenth-Century English Intellectual History," *Eighteenth-Century Studies*
1 (1967): 37; Greene, reply to Vivian de Sola Pinto, "Augustan or Augustinian?
More Demythologizing Needed?" *Eighteenth-Century Studies* 2 (1969): 293–
300; Greene, "The Study of Eighteenth-Century Literature: Past, Present,
and Future," in *New Approaches to Eighteenth-Century Literature: Selected Papers
from the English Institute,* ed. Phillip Harth (New York: Columbia University
Press, 1974), 26; Weinbrot, "History, Horace, and Augustus Caesar: Some
Implications for Eighteenth-Century Satire," *Eighteenth-Century Studies* 7
(1974): 391–414; Erskine-Hill, *The Augustan Idea in English Literature* (London:
Edward Arnold, 1983); Weinbrot, "The Emperor's Old Toga: Augustanism
and the Scholarship of Nostalgia," *Modern Philology* 83 (1986): 286–97.

23. See *Oliver Goldsmith: Collected Works,* ed. Arthur Friedman (Oxford:
Clarendon Press, 1966) 4:8 for the discarded chapter and Robert H. Hopkins,
The True Genius of Oliver Goldsmith (Baltimore: Johns Hopkins University Press,
1969), 179 for the "clever clue toward an intention of satire." His chap. 5,
"Fortune and the Heavenly Bank: *The Vicar of Wakefield* as Sustained Satire,"
166–230, elaborates on the hypothesis. For the counterview outlined above,
see Eric Rothstein and Howard D. Weinbrot, "The Vicar of Wakefield, Mr.
Wilmot, and the 'Whistonean Controversy,'" *Philological Quarterly* 55 (1976):
225–40.

24. Geoffrey H. Hartman, perhaps recognizing his own subsequent development, observes of Paul de Man's criticism: "He treats critics like Blanchot,
Poulet, and Lukács as if they were primary texts and not commentary—as if
they had the texture and strength of Mallarmé's *La Musique et les Lettres* (de
Man considers it 'more than equal in verbal and thematic complexity . . . to a
page of *Un coup de dés*')." See "Signs of the Times: A Review of Three Books,"
here de Man's *Blindness and Insight* (1972), in *The Fate of Reading and Other
Essays* (Chicago: University of Chicago Press, 1975), 311. For Hartman's own
blending of criticism with "creative literature," see "The Fate of Reading,"
Fate, 270, 271. There are, however, critics who do elevate their prose to the
level of enlarging literature, as Samuel Johnson does, in one example among
many in the *Rambler* No. 86 (1751), introducing his essays on *Paradise Lost.* See
The Yale Edition of the Works of Samuel Johnson, 4:88.

25. Cary Nelson, "Reading Criticism," *PMLA* 91 (1976): 803, 809. See also Nelson's "On Whether Criticism is Literature," in *What is Criticism,* ed. Paul Hernadi (Bloomington: Indiana University Press, 1981), 253–67. Murray Krieger approaches the same subject in the same volume but with different and, in my judgment, superior conclusions: "Criticism as a Secondary Art," 280–95.

26. Nelson, 805, 813. I suspect that this is a consequence of establishing theory as a separate discipline. Wayne Booth's *Rhetoric of Fiction* (1961) was about literature; his *Critical Understanding* (1978) is about his own and others' criticisms and varied responses to them.

27. Harold Bloom reviews Harold Bloom's *Agon: Towards a Theory of Revisionism* and *The Breaking of the Vessels* in *Yale Review* 72 (1982–83): 116–20.

28. *Rambler* No. 60 (1750), in The Yale Edition of the Works of Samuel Johnson, 3:318–19.

29. *Clarissa Or, The History of a Young Lady,* intro. by John Butt (London: Dent and Dutton, 1962) 1:170, letter 34. William Beatty Warner attacks benighted "humanists" and claims that Lovelace has been so maligned by "slanderous" critics who "belong to Clarissa's party" that his shade could "sue . . . for defamation of character." These vexing, annoying, and confused critics fail to recognize that he is "playful" and has his own "categories of selfhood" independent of Clarissa's. See Warner, *Reading Clarissa: The Struggles of Interpretation* (New Haven: Yale University Press, 1979), 268. See also his "Redeeming Interpretation," *The Eighteenth-Century: Theory and Interpretation* 26 (1985): 73–94, especially pp. 86–87, a sustained quarrel with Terry Castle's *Clarissa's Ciphers: Meaning and Disruption in Richardson's Clarissa* (Ithaca: Cornell University Press, 1982). A full and well-annotated edition of *Clarissa* and its variant readings is now underway.

30. A start in this direction has been made by James McLaverty, "The Mode of Existence of Literary Works of Art: The Case of the *Dunciad Variorum,*" *Studies in Bibliography* 37 (1984): 82–105. See also Clive Probyn's important "Swift's *Verses on the Death of Dr. Swift:* the Notes," *Studies in Bibliography* 39 (1986): 7–61.

31. There are copies of Yart's *Idée* at the Illinois, Princeton, Rochester, and Yale libraries. I have made use of his work in *Alexander Pope and the Traditions of Formal Verse Satire* (Princeton: Princeton University Press, 1982), 87, 114–16, 154–55, 191, 240, 242, 270.

32. *Dionysius Longinus on the Sublime,* trans. William Smith, 2d ed. (London, 1742), 38–39, sec. 13, par. 4.

Part 2

Theory and Practice

5

The Discourses of Criticism and the Discourses of History in the Restoration and Early Eighteenth Century

MAXIMILLIAN NOVAK

IN HIS AMUSING academic novel *Small World,* David Lodge has his irrepressible American professor of English literature Morris Zapp inform his fellow theorist, the Italian temptress Fulvia Morgana, that the ideas of one of their fellow practitioners have become passé:

> "Hasn't his moment passed? I mean, ten years ago everybody was into that stuff, actants and functions and mythymes and all that jazz. But now. . . ."

> "Only ten years! Does fashion in scholarship 'ave such a short life?"

> "It is getting shorter all the time. There are people coming back into fashion who never even knew they were out of it."[1]

Although Professor Zapp's observation may be slightly exaggerated, it is not very different from the very real complaint of J. Hillis Miller, who in a recent book states that he has had to learn four different critical discourses in his career and that the method and language of deconstructive criticism have not come easily.[2] If the literary historian feels some pleasure in the disarray of literary theorists, there can be little comfort in hearing those who refer to themselves as theorists of the new literary history attempting to reduce the realm of literary history to text and metaphor and speaking with scorn of the "shame" of the "old" literary history.[3]

If the shame of literary history is a reference to scholars who attempted to break a text upon a procrustean bed of background, it may be argued that while such examples are not difficult to locate, the more common example would be those who continued to work in literary history while attempting to stay informed about new developments in criticism and theory—at least this seems the more typical case of those working in the Restoration and early eighteenth century. Such literary historians would have held fast to their faith in history, but they would have learned, from the very start of their careers, to question all the generalizations about history and literature that had been passed on to them as received truth. They would have recognized in Lévi-Strauss' arguments about the selectiveness of historical discourse—that all history must be a "history for" some particular purpose—one reason why they felt unhappy with the literary history of their teachers,[4] and they would have come to acknowledge the wisdom of Croce's doctrine that all history must inevitably be present history, that only by positioning themselves properly in the present could literary historians succeed in understanding the past at all.[5]

In describing the experiences of these literary historians, I am inevitably thinking of myself. I had the advantage of attending graduate classes first at UCLA and afterward at Oxford. UCLA must have been one of those rare institutions that succeeded in avoiding the almost universal triumph of the New Criticism among academic institutions. Until Ralph Cohen arrived there, the analysis of a text in a classroom for anything but printing variants was a rare occurrence. This meant that I had an excellent training in traditional literary history and in Edward Hooker and H. T. Swedenberg, teachers who encouraged their students to examine literature in its historical contexts. What I learned of the New Criticism was entirely through my own reading.

At Oxford, while working for my D. Phil., I profited from the supervision of F. W. Bateson for a year and from close contact with Claude Rawson and the members of the Critical Club. While I managed to shine in the classes for B.Litt. students that I attended, which were mainly in bibliography and literary history, I came to admire the critical intelligence of Bateson and some of my fellow students. And when I returned to UCLA at the end of two years, I benefited from one of Ralph Cohen's brilliant seminars in which we were asked not only to analyze texts but to question all the received notions of contemporary literary history and the New Criticism. It is a small wonder, then, that I am one of those scholar-critics working in the Restoration and eighteenth century who, without ever abandoning a faith in historical solutions, limped after the New Criticism, phenomenology, structuralism, and deconstructionism, willing to learn anything I could and ready to adapt what I could to my own uses.

But during this period, historical discourse underwent changes as radical as anything in literary criticism and theory. Lily Bess Campbell, in her *Shakespeare's "Histories,"* first published in 1947, thought she could rely on a kind of history that was closer to a true science (and therefore closer to truth itself) than anything she had encountered in literary criticism.[6] Hayden White's *Metahistory* and the many psychohistories that have appeared during the past two decades would have bewildered her. But the uncertainties of history were apparent enough to those of my generation. The inconclusive battles of major historians over the status of the gentry during the seventeenth century seemed to demonstrate that well enough. And the conflicts have continued. Reviewing developments in historical research dealing with the period extending from the reign of Charles I to about 1720, Lawrence Stone weaves his way through the Whig theory of history, Namierism, and the counterattack of J. H. Plumb and his followers to end with the challenge of J. C. D. Clark to all Whiggish theories of change and the view that the debate over "all aspects of early modern English history . . . has yet to reach its climax." He concludes, "The historiographical Battle of Naseby still lies ahead of us."[7] As for political ideas, if J. G. A. Pocock had not already done enough to make us revise our notions, he warns us in a recent book (while discussing a crucial point in the debate over standing armies at the end of William III's reign) that some disagreements must remain unresolved until we have a better understanding of the issues.[8]

The lesson here is clear enough. Anyone depending upon historical models is as likely to err as anyone relying on the latest fad in criticism. This has led some critics to conclude that such uncertainty may free the literary historian to engage in greater play. If literary history can be reduced to a few metaphors, why not substitute other metaphors? But such a substitution would be like taking over the method of the Hack of Swift's *Tale of a Tub,* assuming that where everything is uncertain, the most recent system or image must be the best. I would draw a different conclusion. It should be the task of literary historians to commit themselves to as true a vision of the past as can be achieved even if the attainment of anything like permanent truth is impossible. If this posture sounds a little like the kind of commitment in the face of absurdity popularized by Sartre after World War II, I am ready to live with that.

One of the important journals in eighteenth-century studies is about to run a second issue devoted to the lack of interest in the latest aspects of theory among critics working in the period.[9] Although the premise itself may be wrong, I would like to supply a few answers to whatever truth may be found in it. It should be clear that literary history itself has always enjoyed a higher degree of respect among eighteenth-century scholars than it has had among, for example, those working on the romantics. The relative positions of Maynard Mack among eigh-

teenth-century scholars and of Meyer Abrams among those working
in romantic literature suggests something of this dichotomy. Secondly,
critics working with a single text from the eighteenth century are less
likely to get a favorable hearing, whether among readers of books for
scholarly presses or among readers of articles for journals, than they
might receive from those in other fields. I know that when I read an
article for *Studies in English Literature* or for *Restoration,* my most frequent
rationale for rejecting pieces is a lack of knowledge on the part of the
author, whether it is knowledge of other works by the writer being considered or information about that writer's milieu. In short, the kind
of explication that was popular in the fifties and sixties has not been
replaced by an interest in deconstructing a single text or in surrounding
a work with, for instance, the mechanism of feminist criticism where
that mechanism is not accompanied by considerable knowledge of the
author and the work under consideration.

But there seems to be a third and more important reason for this
comparative neglect of the newer modes of criticism, and that is the
excitement generated by the difficulties of literary history itself. Some
of the most essential problems in the literary history of the period
have yet to be worked out, and what has been going on during the
past twenty or thirty years in the criticism of the novel and of drama
has caused a series of exciting skirmishes. If the crucial historiographical battle has not yet been fought, neither have the central questions
about the novel and the drama been resolved. If the nature of poetry
in the period is less in dispute at this time, the cause may be found in
a canon still dominated by the polite taste that ossified the contents of
that canon at the end of the eighteenth century. Although Roger
Lonsdale has begun raising questions about the nature of the canon,
there will have to be a more insistent reexamination of libertine and
political poetry as well as poems written by women before satisfactory
questions can be formed.[10] Of course there are still questions to be
answered about the canon in the novel and drama, but they appear
less urgent than our sense that, in our concept of the early novel, the
paradigm established by Ian Watt in 1957 has broken down and the
feeling that after the questions raised by Aubrey Williams about the
moral and religious nature of Restoration drama, we are not entirely
sure what these plays are about. The remainder of this paper will
address these two situations—that of a once successful literary historical model that no longer seems workable and of another model that
won only partial acceptance—as examples of how discoveries come
about.

When Ian Watt published *The Rise of the Novel* in 1957, it was rightly hailed as a brilliant solution to a problem in literary history—namely, why prose fiction suddenly emerged as a major literary form during the eighteenth century. He supplied information about literacy, the price of books, the philosophic attitude toward the real and personal identity, and the sociology of economic individualism at the time. He seemed to be raising all the right questions, and most of the solutions he provided seemed plausible. To many, it seemed that his book answered everything we wanted to know about early fiction; yet one reason for its success was its tendency to amplify and reify solutions that were already in place. That it has taken some thirty years for Watt's model to unravel is a tribute to the solidity of his work on questions of literacy and the book trade and to his masterful readings of individual novels.

Small difficulties, however, were apparent from the start. The publication of Bakhtin's criticism, with its broader base in continental literature, now underscores just how provincially British was Watt's vision of the early novel. His dismissal of French fiction seems both chauvinistic and paradoxical, and he clearly had no very good knowledge of the depth and power of Spanish picaresque fiction.[11] A few years after the publication of Watt's book, Diana Spearman, in her study of sociology and fiction, marveled at his refusal to consider Madame de Lafayette's *Princess de Clèves* a novel and hesitated between admiration for the neatness of Watt's judgments and outrage at their narrowness.[12] And his assessment of the nature of the reading audience for fiction, based as it was on the price of new books, failed to take into consideration just how cheap used books might be. We know from various accounts that some members of the lower orders did their first serious reading in volumes that cost little more than a few pence. And a recently discovered journal in the British Library shows that both *Moll Flanders* and *Robinson Crusoe* were serialized right after publication.[13] Publication in parts and in chapbooks gave a wide currency to a writer such as Defoe. These facts of publication are evidence against Watt's contention that there was no real tradition of Defoe to influence fiction in the eighteenth century.

I was a graduate student at Oxford when Watt's book was published. Professor Hooker had suggested that I read Watt's earlier article "Robinson Crusoe as a Myth" as a prelude to a study of the relationship between Defoe's economic thought and his fiction.[14] Watt was influenced by the Weber-Tawney thesis on religion and the rise of capitalism, and his reading of Defoe's fiction was greatly colored by these ideas. My reading had suggested that Defoe addressed the problem directly both in his economic treatises and in his fiction and that while he recognized the relationship between the greed of capitalism and the teachings of religion and morality as a complex issue, he tended to satirize the kind of greed that led to the uncontrolled speculation that produced the South Sea Bubble. I was probably unaware of the degree to which Watt had provided me with the framework for my own investigation, but the solution to the questions raised by his argument lay in a more careful and particular investigation of the historical milieu.

Since I had already started work on Watt's suggestions before the publication of *The Rise of the Novel,* I felt that the fuller development of his ideas had only produced further error. But I also felt thoroughly hampered by the critical theories of the time. If I were to attempt a reconstruction of Defoe's intention as manifested in his fiction, I would be violating the rules laid down by Wimsatt and Beardsley in their discussion of what they called the "intentional fallacy."[15] Fortunately I could fall back on Defoe's tendency to stage such issues in a kind of dramatic debate within the fiction, but I probably never stated these views as forcefully as I might have. Further knowledge of Defoe and additional reading in contemporary polemics simply reinforced my objections to Watt's arguments. Only recently I discovered that Baxter's notion of "works" as a test of justification—a concept which looms large in Weber's arguments—was the occasion of a radical break between the Presbyterians and Congregationalists in 1692. Baxter's attack on the sermons of Samuel Crisp three years earlier was met by a counterattack from Crisp's son and some influential allies. In Defoe's one comment on this matter, he seems to come out on the side of Crisp and the "Antinomians."[16] Contrary, then, to Watt's emphasis, it would appear to be as much of a mistake to overemphasize the importance of worldly success in Defoe's fictions as it has been to read them as if they were merely religious tracts.

Such evidence, if it may be called that, is to be gathered by a process of literary history that attempts to do something quite unfashionable. Instead of leaning on a new critical or historical paradigm, it attempts to get back into the period of an author's life to see just what was happening both in literature and in the flow of events in the age. By the latter, I mean everything from the changing pattern of weather to controversies in fields as remote from literature as theology and medicine. We can never be certain what an author may have been reading. Letters, where they are available, are valuable, but following contemporary newspapers and pamphlets, parliamentary debates, and the kind of gossip that got into newsletters is also helpful.

Watt's reliance on general theories of social and economic development gave him answers that represented the best thinking of his time. They enabled him to construct a model that seemed to be coherent and inclusive. I am not certain that I would have been able to have suggested different models for Defoe's fiction without the foothold that he provided. Its inadequacy for those dealing with early fiction today has to be a lesson in humility. We are bound in by what the prevailing knowledge of our time allows us to see. The prevalent approach to the novel when Watt produced his book was the New Criticism, a system that, in its quest for unity and consistent irony, was better suited to the lyric than to narrative. Fortunately for Watt, he could fall back on Auerbach's *Mimesis,* with its sociological approach and its unquestioning acceptance of realism as the highest value to which the novel could aspire. Backed by the authority of Auerbach, whose close reading of selected passages bore some resemblance to the techniques of the New Criticism, Watt could counter some of the worst notions of F. R. Leavis, but like Leavis, he accepted the high aesthetic line on the novel. And most disastrously of all, he had absorbed the evolutionary concept of the novel that had informed most studies of fiction from the late Victorian period forward.

The doubtful positions into which he was led by such notions are easy enough to enumerate, and I will name just a few. Though Watt clearly admired both Defoe and Richardson, his scheme demanded that they be regarded as primitive, that they be considered the crude but powerful founding fathers. Thus he criticized their vulgar style, and although he noted that the novel might not require a finished style, he certainly did not consider this something in their favor. In so doing, he ignored the significant role both writers played in democratizing the style of fiction and of literature in general. A second element in his criticism that he enunciated as a point of faith was his belief that the critic could not accept anything in the work that went beyond the text, even when the reader was given a signal to understand such absences and silence.[17] Pierre Macherey and others have taught us to read fiction in terms of such absences and silences,[18] but when Watt was writing, such a critical technique would have been regarded as a violation of the limitations imposed on the text by the New Criticism. Interestingly enough, in his novel *Foe,* which, like so much modern fiction, is about the writing of fiction, J. M. Coetzee uses Defoe's characters in a manner that almost illustrates Macherey's argument, creating what may be the reality out of which Defoe shaped his novels.[19]

More briefly, Watt missed the way Defoe developed a sense of the passionate individuality of a given conscience and sought for inconsistencies where none existed. Some of his generalizations about names can be refuted by a glance at the Spanish picaresque. As Martin Battestin has shown so well, he missed much in the morality of Fielding, and his attempted category, the "realism of assessment," has but a tangential relationship to all that he had done in his earlier chapters to give some sense of limitation to our notions of realism. He seems not to have thought very much about the way all forms of fictional representation proceed from a combination of words on the page. And had he operated more in terms of "intertextuality" than direct influence, he would not have read Defoe out of the mainstream of the novel.[20] J. Hillis Miller, in his *Repetition and Fiction,* has recently demonstrated how thoroughly ambiguity and multiple readings can be built into the novelistic text. In the critical manner of the fifties, Watt was still seeking the ideal single reading.

I do not present this litany of lost opportunities as an indictment of Watt's method. That he managed to realize so well the critical ideas of his time is all to the good. If, on the other hand, he had proceeded from the idea that literary history and critical ideas were all relative, all matters of interpretation, and from the notion that such relativism allowed him a full play of the imagination, I doubt if he would have written so valuable a work as *The Rise of the Novel.* The knowledge that history is always, in Lévi-Strauss' terms, for a particular purpose rather than a full record of the truth should make us try to reach for as full a realization of our particular understanding of what seems true to us. It should convey obligation rather than freedom.

One reason I felt dissatisfied with *The Rise of the Novel* on its appearance had to do with my sense that the state of the novel at the time was defiantly out of tune with the criticism. Writers as different as Saul Bellow and Iris Murdoch were producing loosely structured works in reaction to the tightly designed novels that took Flaubert's concept of the form as their model. This return to picaresque randomness seemed the reverse of everything advocated by the New Critics. That Defoe's reputation would rise with such a turn of events seemed inevitable, especially after Watt had shown so many fascinating ways in which he could be approached. Similarly the disjointed technique of the fictional letter suddenly took on a new interest after Watt had shown how susceptible the characters of Richardson were to psychological analysis. And Fielding too emerged stronger both as an artist and as a moralist after Watt's somewhat lukewarm treatment of his lack of adequate circumstantial realism. In short, Watt helped to bring about a complete revaluation of the three great early British novelists even if the critical principles upon which this process took place were almost defiantly opposed to his method.

Curiously enough, the most active rewriting of Watt's script for the rise of the novel is coming from Marxist critics, and those who, like Michael McKeon, have a genuine respect for history have made a significant contribution to our understanding of early fiction.[21] But the more common variety of those influenced by Marxist criticism seem mainly distinguished by the conviction that passive bourgeois readers are dead, or ought to be dead. In their place are readers who prefer a sense of process in which they can participate. Such a criticism is clearly related to the ideals of what may be regarded as the more experimental branch of modern fiction that concurs in such a view. To quote from a manifesto by one writer:

> The contemporary writer—the writer who is acutely in touch with the life of which he is part—is forced to start from scratch. Reality does not exist, time does not exist, personality does not exist. God was the omniscient author, but he died; now no one knows the plot, and since our reality lacks the sanction of a creator, there's no guarantee as to the authenticity of the received version. Time is reduced to presence, the content of a series of discontinuous moments. Time is no longer purposive, and so there is no destiny, only chance. Reality is, simply our experience, and objectivity is, of course, an illusion. Personality, after passing through a phase of awkward self-consciousness, has become, quite minimally, a mere locus for our experience.[22]

A postmodern critic such as Catherine Belsey says much the same thing.[23]

Whatever we may think of such ideas, that they will have some influence on the ways in which we will read Defoe, Fielding and Richardson is inevitable. Some version of this kind of thinking has already had an impact. Terry Eagleton has enshrined *Clarissa* as a work that revolutionized the relations between the sexes and within the family.[24] How the mainstream of literary history will view early fiction through such a set of principles remains to be seen, but one aspect is obvious. Watt stressed the importance of individualism and character in a manner that disturbed no one in 1957 but that may, in fact, represent a reading of early fiction through the expectations set up by the fiction of the next century. The individualism of Defoe's heroes and heroines may well be read as a negative state—the product of a cruel capitalist shaping of character. And Fielding's play with the fictionality of both character and event is likely to stand him in good stead. In short, the shifting process of understanding these writers is likely to continue indefinitely, partly because our own point of view is always changing and partly because of the genius of these writers who gave us never-ending variety in the creation of their fiction.

Whereas critics of the novel have been struggling with a paradigm of literary history that can no longer be considered workable, students of Restoration and eighteenth-century drama have been faced with a number of attempts to refashion literary history. After a brief revival during the 1920s, Restoration drama had come under the lash of the powerful social critic L. C. Knights. Following the demands of F. R. Leavis and the Scrutiny school of criticism for moral seriousness, Knights had condemned Restoration comedy for its lack of social purpose and responsibility. Knights' criticism came during the world-wide depression of the thirties, and it reached deep into the social conscience of that generation. If Restoration comedy was not a depiction of a realm as artificial as the fairy world imagined by nineteenth-century critics such as Lamb and Hazlitt and reified in the drawings of Aubrey Beardsley, it was nevertheless the depiction of shallow, otiose people who were slightly rooted in a real world of labor, pain, and suffering.[25]

Against such a view of these playwrights as essentially unserious came the arguments of Underwood for Etherege's almost philosophic stance, of Zimbardo for Wycherley's power as a satirist, of Fujimura for Restoration comedy's exploitation of a serious form of wit, and of Holland for its sense of psychological truth.[26] I was busy attempting to show that the comedies were serious in another way—as a form of civilized play—when Aubrey Williams unveiled his famous argument for the Christian morality upon which these supposedly wicked comedies were based.[27] Everyone had been working so hard to demonstrate that the plays were not the exercises in triviality Knights had presented that it was difficult to reverse direction in order that although the comedies were to be seen as making significant statements about life and art, they would not be regarded as religious documents.

Williams concentrated his attention on Congreve, but his argument represented a new way of seeing the entire Restoration and eighteenth century. The era was to be viewed as much less secular than had previously been thought. J. Douglas Canfield had no trouble showing that Nicholas Rowe's tragedies were thoroughly sprinkled with appeals to Providence. Indeed, once pointed out, the only problem in proving these plays to be providential tragedies was the tediousness of multiplying instances in play after play. Arguing a Christian basis for the comedies, of course, had to be regarded as more difficult, but the attempt was to be made. Part of the evidence to substantiate this new view of literary history even resulted from enlisting a computer to evaluate the nature of Restoration rakes to provide scientific evidence that they were not really wicked at all.[28]

Replies to these arguments were of uneven effectiveness. Harriet Hawkins' attempt to argue that loading comedy with the burden of a Christian message was foolish because comedy was supposed to be fun was applauded in England but received less enthusiastically in America.[29] She followed this up with a more thoughtful article in which she questioned Williams' method of argument—questioned if he subjected his ideas to the kind of negative evidence that a scientist might use to test radical theories.[30] Whereas Robert Hume moved halfway in Williams' direction in revaluating his own position,[31] Derek Hughes has recently published an article in which, through citing hundreds of sermons, he has shown that there is little contemporary support for Williams' views on the theology of the period and none at all for reading comedy in the manner he suggested.[32]

What Hughes has attempted is to go far outside the texts of the comedies or of the debates over their moral nature in the aftermath of Jeremy Collier's attack to the nature of Christianity itself at the time. One of the weaknesses of Williams' arguments is the attempt to apply a general model of Christian thought to a time when there was much debate over some of its basic tenets. Williams' achievement in attempting to rewrite literary history was to show how important such religious material was to Restoration comedy that, in the hands of Congreve, Vanbrugh, and Southerne, was raising profound social, moral, and religious questions.

In my study of Congreve, I suggested that the use of comedy for such a serious purpose might have been more a reason for Collier's attack than the "profanity and immorality" he saw in these plays. The playhouse was assuming some of the role of the pulpit, and what defender of the Church of England could accept that?[33] I still believe that to be true, but such a view is part of a larger picture that, mainly because of the pressure Williams put upon our construct of both the history and the literature of the Restoration, may now be seen in a clearer light—clearer, at least for our generation.

To show how such a change in literary history may come about, I will concentrate on Congreve's *Double Dealer*. In writing about this play, I treated it as an experiment in satirical comedy. Of its satirical qualities, there can be little doubt, but in stressing its originality, I was surely mistaken. I had followed the lead of F. W. Bateson, who noted that its hypocritical villain Maskwell dominates the action and lends a darker cast to the comedy than was customary at the time. I had read the period of William and Mary through the eyes of Defoe and other Whig historians, and so, it seems, had Bateson. "The Maskwell scenes," he wrote, "may be plausibly excused as an experiment in *serious* melodrama, the kind of melodrama that Strindberg has perfected in 'The Father'; but it must be admitted that it was an experiment that failed."[34] These sections must be ignored, Bateson continued, and our admiration must be focused on the remarkable sense of rhythm that informs the dialogue. If we follow Bateson's advice, the play emerges as a charming failure. Perhaps Williams was right; perhaps there is a larger theme that makes Maskwell central to the play.[35]

That theme may even have something to do with Providence but not quite in the way Williams thought. In the 1979 production of *The Double Dealer* at the National Theatre, every time "Providence" was mentioned, the audience howled with laughter. Was this an indication of historical change? Had the very center of Congreve's serious meaning become an occasion for unintended amusement? Certainly there would have been more of an edge to the laughter in 1693, when the play was first performed, but there can be no doubt about Congreve's intention. The person who finds providential meaning in the action of the play is Sir Paul Plyant, the cuckold whose wife has him swaddled in sheets every night so there is no chance of his yielding to his sexual desires. Lady Plyant has intercourse with him only on such occasions as her affairs create the possibility that she may have become pregnant. He is willing to assign a providential cause for the revelation of what he believes to be the conspiracies that surround him, but no one else is so sure. Maskwell has a few references to Providence, certainly, but they are questioning and even sinister in their implications. What then is the play about, and how can literary history determine the issue?

One element that unites all the characters is a sense of betrayal and conspiracy. Maskwell is the lover of Lady Touchwood and seeks to marry Cynthia, the woman to whom the protagonist Mellefont is engaged. In these actions, he is betraying the trust of his patron and his friend. "Jealous of a plot" against him by Lady Touchwood, whose passionate desire for him he rejected, Mellefont starts a counterplot that includes the seduction of Lady Plyant by his friend Careless.[36] And then, entirely on their own, the aesthete Brisks and the female poet Lady Froth begin an affair and betray the trust of her husband and family, including a baby upon whom Lady Froth pretends to dote. Is it possible that Congreve is making an analogy between the families of Mellefont and Cynthia, who have gathered together on the eve of their wedding, and the nation itself, which is betrayed by various factions? The very use of the word "plot" might have alerted the audience of October 1693 to the possibility that some political application might be required of them. And even the mention of Maskwell's first name, Jack, pronounced by Mellefont in a speech praising his honesty, could have alerted the audience to the possibility that, like the many Jacobites in the population, he would likely prove, as Careless suspects from the start, a person upon whom Mellefont ought not rely. Defoe was to use the same wordplay in the creation of his Jacobite protagonist Colonel Jack some thirty years later.

Congreve wrote his play at a time when William's fortune in England seemed to be sinking. The Tory ministry that had come to power in the spring of 1692 was ineffectual in its attempts to govern but unanimously opposed to William III, particularly to his military involvement. Until Russell's victory at La Hogue, James II was ready to descend upon England. The Jacobites were confident that they could succeed with as little as ten thousand men, but he had gathered twice that number by April. An assassination plot against William by Grandval narrowly failed, and subsequent investigation suggested that Louis XIV and James II were directly involved. The loss of English lives in the battle of Steenkerk caused general dismay, and though this encounter could have been interpreted as a victory, it was advertised as a defeat by the Tories and Jacobites.

And treachery seemed to be everywhere. In the Anglican church, William Sherlock's belated decision to accept William and Mary as God's appointed rulers appeared to many as a complete apostasy.[37] In politics, as rumor had it, Godolphin, first lord of the Treasury, was seen walking with a well-known Jacobite in St. James Park in the early hours of the morning. It was also reported that he had subsequently met with Marlborough and Shrewsbury.[38] Correspondence with the court of James II seemed to amount to simple common sense, since English politicians wanted some insurance against William's possible demise in battle or from sickness.

On the other hand, matters seemed to be going better in 1693. William changed to a Whig ministry that operated efficiently, and the battle of Landen on 29 July 1693, though essentially a standoff like Steenkerk, was interpreted correctly as a victory of a sort. William was not out of the woods yet, but the audience that viewed the play in October 1693 might have felt a little more at ease about the permanence of the political settlement than the audience of a year before, perhaps enough at ease to take some pleasure in a comedy about betrayal but not relaxed enough to enjoy it thoroughly. Even though (as Dryden's poem to him on the occasion of the performance of the play states) Congreve was regarded by many as the young hope of the

Restoration stage, *The Double Dealer* had only a moderate success in its initial run.

If the political environment of the period 1692–93 influenced both the creation and the reception of Congreve's play, then it would surely have had a similar effect on other plays written at the time. Characters such as Maskwell should have been common enough in comedies that were so responsive to contemporary moods, and Bateson's observations on Congreve's "experiment" would be a case of insufficient reading in the comedies of these years. In fact that is precisely what may be discovered. Just as the comedies after the revolution tended to reflect a new spirit of equality and openness, so the comedies written a few years later reflect suspicion and anxiety.

In William Mountfort's *Greenwich Park* (1691), Sir Thomas, described by one character as "an admirable Satyrist," attacks the entire fabric of the society. He explains that he left the court not merely because of its "whoring" but because everywhere "ther's Gaming and Perjury, Murder and Blasphemy, Divinity and Hipocrisie, running in Peoples Debtsd, and borrowing of Money."[39] As for the clergy, Sir Thomas argues that they are all hypocrites and that the wise will believe "none of 'em."[40] At the end of George Powell's *Very Good Wife*, the world is presented as so deceptive that one is lucky just to hold one's own. The main figure tells the audience:

> In short, the whole false World is all Deceit,
> And I have made bold ev'n to retrieve the Cheat,
> Think not of Losses therefore where there's none,
> For all my Care was but to get my own.[41]

Cunnington and Quickwit, in D'Urfey's *Richmond Heiress*, a work performed just six months before Congreve's play, contrive plot upon plot in an effort to outreach each other in the cleverness of their contrivances, revealing their plans to the audience in soliloquies similar to those of Maskwell. The final triumph of Quickwit involved having Cunnington arrested for treason against the government. The connection between private and public betrayal would hardly have been lost upon the audience or upon Congreve. If, as Williams rightly noted, *The Double Dealer* is replete with religious imagery referring to betrayal, the tenor of such imagery is essentially social and, in the larger sense, political.

And what of Providence in the play? There is certainly a debate over whether events may be ascribed to Providence, or to chance, or whether there can be any means of predicting the future. A few years later, Congreve was to deal with a similar subject in *Love for Love*, a comedy in which every character attempts to discover a code by which he or she can read hidden meanings and the future.[42] Although Congreve does not make this idea the central comic concept in *The Double Dealer* as he was to do in his later play, certainly Sir Paul Plyant's faith in Providence has to be seen as part of Congreve's interest in what he portrayed as an obsessive fascination for interpreting what cannot be known. The farcical underside of this obsession is a remarkable inability to see the obvious, and to this fault may be placed the easiness of Maskwell's successful manipulation of his gulls, since, as he notes, "dissimulation is the only Art, not to be known from Nature" (150). It is no accident that Maskwell is allowed to suggest that the idea for his deceptions may come to him from "Providence" (155, 157).

But Maskwell does it maliciously to question whether the universe is not dominated by evil. Sir Paul, on the other hand, thinks that Providence is responsible for uncovering an illicit relationship between Careless and his wife and is equally willing to accept a providential cause for Careless' transparently absurd explanation. His inability to see what is apparent to everyone else emerges in a neat aporia when, having made what he believes to be the discovery of his wife's infidelity, he calls Careless "a Judas Maccabeus and Iscariot both" (178), confusing a betrayal for the sake of evil with rebellion for the triumph of right.

When caught in one of his own plots, Mellefont questions the series of events that have brought him to what appears to be a disastrous fate: "O I could curse my Stars, Fate, and Chance; all Causes and Accidents of Fortune in this Life" (187). The one element conspicuous by its absence is Providence. On the other hand, Sir Paul assigns everything to Providence. If the idea of Providence is used by villains and fools, there must be a reason, and it is revealed in Sir Paul's reaction to the revelations of Maskwell's treachery. Questioned by Lord Froth about where everyone has been while he slept, Sir Paul remarks, "I don't know, my Lord, but here's the strangest Revolution, all turn'd topsie turvy; as I hope for Providence" (200). In the confusion of events, Sir Paul, without understanding anything, supplies Providence as an answer to everything. And in a rapid flash of comprehension, Lord Froth sees that his wife has been turned "topsie turvy" by the foolish literary critic Brisk.

In fact the status of the role of Providence in human history was at a point of change. Among those who brought it about, the revolution of 1688 was considered a good example of the intervention of Providence in the history of England. If the winds had not blown in just the right way, an English fleet might have ventured out to intercept the ships bearing William of Orange to Torbay. And had James II acted with any wisdom at all, the settlement might have been very different even after William's invasion. But among supporters of James II, such an interpretation was unacceptable. Although some retreated to the old idea that the true believers were going through a period of trial, many simply concluded that Providence functioned according to more general laws and that the belief in particular Providence might suit better with the creeds of those who followed a more enthusiastic kind of Christianity than that practiced by the majority of Englishmen.

Nevertheless it remained a standard theme in the preaching of Low Churchmen. Samuel Barton, in a sermon of 1692 preached before the lord mayor, began by pointing out that David had no trouble "so long as he had God and his gracious Providence on his side," and went on to interpret the history of England from 1688 on as evidence that the God of David was also on the side of England and William and Mary.[43] Of course the monarchs preferred being told by Archbishop Tillotson that the victory at La Hogue was a sure sign of God's favor, but even he was somewhat cautious. "Meer Success," he preached before the King and Queen, "is certainly one of the worst Arguments in the World of a good Cause, the most improper to satisfie Conscience: And yet we find by experience, that in the issue it is the most successful of all other Arguments; and do's in a very odd but effectual way satisfie the Consciences of a great many men by shewing them their Interest."[44] But the radical preacher Samuel Johnson argued that it would be slandering Providence to see William as anything but the ruler chosen by the English people under English laws.[45]

Among those wishing for James' return to the throne of England, the rejection of the providential interpretation of history was almost universal.[46] Thus, in a Jacobite utopia published in 1693, the Astreadeans are sceptical about miracles and are certain that one miracle cannot be used to prove another. They also believe that divine inspiration cannot be communicated in a convincing way.[47] Jacobites like Dryden were hardly willing to go as far as that, but they scanned the news and hoped that Louis XIV would win a victory over the confederates led by William III.[48] Ever expecting that William would stumble and that James would soon be returned to the throne, they preferred to think that the Glorious Revolution was an aberration. Providential history was something they simply could not credit.

In *The Double Dealer* cleverness, awareness, a capacity to have good, intelligent friends, and luck are the qualities that are most highly prized. Congreve was a Whig, and the play certainly reads a lesson against the conspirators who would undermine legitimate authority by plots and strategems. But he was also a good friend of the Jacobite playwrights Dryden and Southerne and was a young man still trying to make his way in the world at a time when the survival of William and Mary seemed doubtful to many. Dryden advised William Walsh in May 1693 to avoid committing himself to a public career at a time when he thought that William III might suffer a complete defeat by the French.[49] Congreve's attack on those undermining the legitimate order by plots leaves the notion of legitimacy somewhat open. And the plots of Maskwell are only a slightly more dramatic version of the kinds of betrayals that undermined contemporary domestic life.

The historical milieu that must have given a particular edge to Congreve's play seems to have contained a domestic element as well. The chief complaint about *The Double Dealer* reported by Dryden was that it came too close to the difficulties experienced by the married: "The women thinke he has exposd their Bitchery too much; & the Gentlemen, are offended with him; for the discovery of their follyes: & the way of their Intrigues, under the notion of Friendship to their Ladyes Husbands."[50] Of course Dryden was hardly an unbiased reporter. He had just published his translation of Juvenal's sixth satire with its savage picture of women. Congreve's translation of the eleventh satire also modifies Juvenal's text with the addition of a vivid passage on the wife who comes home to her husband after having had intercourse with nineteen men.[51]

The war over the status of women that raged at the time had some larger political overtones. For the first time since the reign of Elizabeth I, England's real attachment to the throne was through a queen. Mary was not only given equal status with her husband, but with William engaged so deeply in military affairs, she was the monarch who was most before the public. To be profeminist at this time was almost equivalent to being a defender of Mary and the double monarchy. The applications that might be drawn from Dryden's satires were obvious enough. Congreve, on the other hand, creates a genuinely intelligent and warm woman in the character of Cynthia. His cynicism about women is closer to the insecure posture of a young man trying to appear worldly than to a political statement, but he may have been playing into the hands of his Jacobite friends without being entirely aware.

⊏══════⊐

This reading of Congreve's play against a more particular background than that provided by Williams is intended to show that one solution to problems in literary history is reading more intensely in the events and attitudes of given months and weeks in which a work was taking shape and was finished. But that would hardly have been enough to see *The Double Dealer* as I have tried to present it—as a comedy about a historical period in which double-dealing in politics had come to pervade the world of private relations and the family. Theories of history modeled on the belief that marginal groups often embody the real energies of a society and often display more imagination and energy and therefore more sensitivity to change have brought the Jacobites to the forestage of history.[52] And once we begin to see them as active players, they appear to be everywhere, not only in the history of the time but in the literature. And although anyone familiar with the 1690s would have to have encountered a heightened tone as well as a more numerous outpouring of works on the status of women, feminist criticism allows us to see this dicussion in a new light.

The moral to my discussion, then, is that just doing more in the way of literary history is useful but insufficient unless the scholar is sensitized by an understanding of the present. Except when new documents are discovered, the past does not give up its treasures readily. Any out-of-hand rejection of new critical theories will merely result in a repetition of old ideas, and as comforting as such confirmation of our prejudices may be, they can seem less and less right as years pass. Only by keeping ourselves open to new approaches in history, criticism, and theory can we expect to understand the literature of our period. And teaching that understanding in our classrooms and through our writing ought to be what all of us are attempting to do.

I began this paper with the disconcerting prospect that the apparent acceleration in the number of fashions in theory had reached the point that knowing what was in or out was becoming impossible. The prospect does not disturb Morris Zapp because he has arrived at the skeptical conclusion that complete certainty in interpretation is unobtainable. Those who have written extensive notes to editions such as the California Dryden may point out that there are branches of literary history, requiring hard work and (believe it or not) as much ingenuity and imagination as theory, that produce reliable and permanently useful knowledge. Professor Zapp might counter that, theoretically speaking, once these notes are turned into the commentaries that usually accompany such editions, they fall under the same difficulties that accompany all interpretation. And even though such an objection seems to ignore all the original information that may have informed such commentaries, we must admit some truth to it.

Despite the discomfort with such positions among many academics, they are neither new nor suprising. We live in an age of probability, and the absence of such views in theory and criticism is what would be truly odd. This does not mean that we have to adopt such views, but by ignoring them we place our status as literary historians in jeopardy. Listening to a theorist invade the realm of literary history to inform us that the history we have been treating is nothing more than a series of metaphors may require more patience than some of us possess. But even this feckless effort—though having all that characteristic "blight on the mind"[53] that E. P. Thompson has associated with the pursuits of theorists—may at least contain some information about the confluence of modern minds working on literary history at a given moment in time.

Notes

1. (Harmondsworth: Penguin Books, 1985), 34.

2. *Fiction and Repetition* (Cambridge: Harvard University Press, 1982), 18.

3. These comments refer particularly to a talk by Alan Liu, "The Power of Formalism: New History Old Forms" delivered at UCLA 14 November 1986 at a conference titled "Romanticism, Politics, and the New Historicism." For a somewhat more restrained manifesto of the new literary history, see Herbert Lindenberger, "Toward a New History in Literary Study," *Profession 84* (New York: Modern Language Association, 1984), 16–23.

4. Claude Lévi-Strauss, *The Savage Mind* (London: Weidenfeld and Nicolson, 1966), 257.

5. Benedetto Croce, "History and Chronicle," in *Theories of History*, ed. Patrick Gardiner (New York: The Free Press, 1959), 226–33. When the tenth volume of the *California Edition of the Works of John Dryden* was reviewed in the *TLS*, the reviewer argued that in editing this collection of Dryden's comedies, I should have attempted to edit from a standpoint of what might be considered a period of normative sexual mores such as that of Sir Walter Scott. As the editor of this volume, I wrote to the journal to ask if the reviewer actually believed that such an artificial act of achieving a moral norm could be possible. I argued the position that I maintain in this paper—that the historian had to be of his own times if his point of view was to have any validity. I did not hear directly from the reviewer (James Sutherland), but the editor told me that, contrary to what he had said in the review, he agreed with me.

6. *Shakespeare's "Histories"* (San Marino: The Huntington Library, 1947), 3–7. See also her attack on A. C. Bradley in the appendixes to *Shakespeare's Tragic Heroes* (New York: Barnes and Noble, 1952), 241–87. In this diatribe, she speaks contemptuously of the "Old Guard Dinners of the Modern Language Association" as the bastion of the ahistorical approach to literature.

7. *The New York Review of Books* 34 (26 February 1987): 43.

8. J. G. A. Pocock, *Virtue, Commerce, and History* (Cambridge: Cambridge University Press, 1985), 232.

9. See the forthcoming spring 1987 issue of *The Eighteenth Century: Theory and Interpretation*.

10. See Roger Lonsdale, ed., *The New Oxford Book of Eighteenth-Century Verse* (Oxford: Oxford University Press, 1984), xxxv–xl.

11. See M. M. Bakhtin, *The Dialogic Imagination*, trans. Caryl Emerson and Michael Holquist (Austin: University of Texas Press, 1981), esp. 383–422. See also Walter Reed, *An Exemplary History of the Novel* (Chicago: University of Chicago Press, 1981), 1–161.

114

12. *The Novel and Society* (New York: Barnes and Noble, 1966), 50–52.

13. *Factotum*, No. 19 (1984): 22–23.

14. *Essays in Criticism* 1 (1951): 95–119.

15. Although E. D. Hirsch has argued that Wimsatt and Beardsley had not intended to lay down a general rule, the notion was certainly taken in that way. See *Validity in Interpretation* (New Haven: Yale University Press, 1967), 11–14.

16. See *Memoirs of the Life and Eminent Conduct of that Learned and Reverend Divine, Daniel Williams, D.D.* (London, 1718), 81–82.

17. Ian Watt, "The Recent Critical Fortunes of *Moll Flanders*," *Eighteenth-Century Studies* 1 (1967): 109–26.

18. *A Theory of Literary Production* (London: Routledge and Kegan Paul, 1978), esp. 82–95.

19. *Foe* (London: Secker and Warburg, 1986), esp. 114–15.

20. *Robinson Crusoe* quickly, but usually without any acknowledgment of indebtedness, passed into the corpus of fiction from the echoes in *Gulliver's Travels* and its imitations to *Robinsonades* in Fielding's *Jonathan Wild* and the gothic novel.

21. Michael McKeon, *The Origins of the English Novel, 1600–1740* (Baltimore: The Johns Hopkins University Press, 1987).

22. Ronald Sukenick, *The Death of the Novel and Other Stories* (New York: Dial Press, 1969), 41; quoted in "Authorial Presence in American Metafiction," by Aaron Winkelman (Ph.D. diss., UCLA English Department [1986]), 306–7.

23. *Critical Practice* (London: Methuen, 1980), esp. 67–84.

24. *The Rape of Clarissa* (Minneapolis: University of Minnesota Press, 1982).

25. "Restoration Comedy: The Reality and the Myth," *Explorations* (London: Chatto and Windus, 1946), 131–54 (published originally in *Scrutiny* in 1937).

26. See Dale Underwood, *Etherege and the Seventeenth Century Comedy of Manners*, Yale Studies in English 135 (New Haven: Yale University Press, 1957); Thomas Fujimura, *The Restoration Comedy of Wit* (Princeton: Princeton University Press, 1952); Norman Holland, *The First Modern Comedies* (Cambridge: Harvard University Press, 1959); Rose Zimbardo, *Wycherley's Drama*, Yale Studies in English 156 (New Haven: Yale University Press, 1965).

27. See Aubrey Williams, *An Approach to Congreve* (New Haven: Yale University Press, 1979); J. Douglas Canfield, *Nicholas Rowe and Christian Tragedy* (Gainesville: University of Florida Press, 1977).

28. Ben Ross Schneider, *The Ethos of Restoration Comedy* (Urbana: University of Illinois Press, 1971).

29. *Likenesses of Truth in Elizabethan and Restoration Drama* (Oxford: Clarendon Press, 1972), esp. 99–114.

30. "The 'Example Theory' and the Providentialist Approach to Restoration Drama: Some Questions of Validity and Applicability," *The Eighteenth Century: Theory and Interpretation* 24 (1983): 103–14.

31. "The Myth of the Rake in 'Restoration' Comedy," *Studies in the Literary Imagination* 10 (1977): 25–55.

32. "Providential Justice and English Comedy 1660–1700: A Review of the External Evidence," *Modern Language Review* 81 (1986): 273–92. See also the most vehement attack on Williams' theory to date: Arthur Scouten, "Recent Interpretations of Restoration Comedy of Manners," *Du Verbe au Geste* (Nancy: 1986), 100–107.

33. See my "Artist and the Clergyman," *College English* 30 (1969): 555–61.

34. Bateson, ed., *Works*, by William Congreve (London: Peter Davies, 1930), xxii.

35. Williams treats the play as a Christian theodicy. The problem with such an approach is that if one decided that a comedy was actually a tragedy and surrounded it with the critical machinery used in treating that genre, it would naturally begin to appear to be very different.

36. *The Complete Plays of William Congreve,* ed. Herbert Davis (Chicago: University of Chicago Press, 1967), 129. All subsequent citations to this play will be included in parentheses in the body of my paper.

37. See Charles F. Mullet, "A Case of Allegiance: William Sherlock and the Revolution of 1688," *HLQ* 10 (1946): 83–103.

38. See Stephen Baxter, *William III* (New York: Harcourt, Brace and World, 1966), 307.

39. *Greenwich Park* (London, 1691), 9.

40. *Greenwich Park,* 31.

41. *A Very Good Wife* (London, 1693), 47.

42. "Foresight in the Stars and Scandal in London: Reading the Hieroglyphics in Congreve's *Love for Love*" in *From Renaissance to Restoration,* ed. Robert Markley and Laurie Finke (Cleveland: Bellflower Press, 1984), 181–206.

43. "A Sermon Preached before the Right Honourable the Lord Mayor and Aldermen of the City of London," (London, 1692), 8.

44. *A Sermon Preached before the King and Queen at Whitehall, the 27th of October. For Victory at Sea* (London, 1692), 32–33.

45. *An Argument Proving that the Abrogation of King James by the People of England from the Regal Throne and Promotion of the Prince of Orange . . . to the Throne of England in his Stead, Was According to the Constitution of the English Government* (London, 1692), 39–42.

46. See, for example, John Dryden's "Character of a Good Parson": "The senseless Plea of Right by Providence / Was, by a flatt'ring Priest, invented since" (11.117–18). *Poems,* ed. James Kinsley (Oxford: Clarendon Press, 1958) 4:1739. See also G. R. Cragg, *From Puritanism to the Age of Reason* (Cambridge: Cambridge University Press, 1950), 175–85.

47. *Antiquity Reviv'd: or, the Government of a Certain Island Anciently Call'd Astreada* (London, 1693), esp. 31.

48. See, for example, John Dryden, *Letters,* ed. Charles Ward (1942; reprint, New York: AMS Press, 1965), 57. For a more enlarged notion of Jacobite ideas during this period, see MS. Carte 209, 233, Bodleian Library.

49. Dryden, *Letters,* 53.

50. Dryden, *Letters,* 63.

51. *William Congreve,* [*Works*], ed. Bonamy Dobrée (London: Oxford University Press, 1925, 1928) 2:263. Like the *Fables,* Dryden's volume of translations of Juvenal and Persius were used to attack William and Mary. Dryden's introduction to his translation of Persius' fourth satire discusses the work as a veiled attack upon homosexuality in high places, and since the opposition to William III attacked him for being a pathic, the poem must be regarded as a veiled attack upon England's monarch.

52. The emphasis on the importance of marginal groups as often embodying the most energetic and innovative elements in society owes much to the work of the anthropologist Victor Turner. See, for example, Turner, *Dramas, Fields, and Metaphors* (Ithaca: Cornell University Press, 1974), 231–70.

53. The passage is worth quoting in full: "In its present incarnation as 'theoretical practice,' this notion of Theory is like a blight that has settled on the mind. The empirical senses are occluded, the moral and aesthetic organs are repressed, the curiosity is sedated, all the 'manifest' evidence of life or of art is distrusted as 'ideology,' the theoretical ego enlarges (for everyone else is mystified by 'appearances')" (*The Poverty of Theory* [New York: Monthly Review Press, 1978], 165).

6

The Novel and the Contexts of Discourse

J. PAUL HUNTER

I BEGIN WITH four vignettes of readers reading. The first is reading on a beach, stretched out on a chaise longue, surrounded by white sand, blue water, and hundreds of other vacationers. She is an attractive woman in her late twenties or early thirties, wearing a stylish, efficient, and (for this French West Indies beach) modest bathing suit. When she speaks (as she does reluctantly and matter-of-factly) to passersby who try to distract her, she does so with an unmistakable Parisian accent, but the book she is reading is in English, the Penguin edition of *Jane Eyre*. She is alone, thoroughly absorbed in her book— a shopkeeper perhaps, an engineer, or a journalist; it is hard to tell, but she is certainly not a student: she does not pause or mark as she goes. From time to time, every hour or so, she rises from her book and swims far out into the deep blue Caribbean water, returns, covers herself again with tanning lotion and reenters the English language a century and a half away. It is not the wide Sargasso Sea, exactly, that surrounds her, but it is close enough. She seems altogether comfortable in a world of sun and water and laughter and tropical drinks, but she is also very much at home in the pages of a novel.

The setting for the second reader is a baseball field. In the home-team dugout of Atlanta Stadium before the game has begun, the starting shortstop, wearing thick glasses, is reading a thick paperback. The "color man" on Braves television has taken to calling him "The Little Professor" for the camera once caught him during a rain delay at a moment like this, and he is often seen in the clubhouse, uniformed and ready to go when it is time to go but, meanwhile, reading, concentrating as fully on pages now as he will later on the well-paid rituals of his game. He is a professional

118

athlete, the best at his position that his team has had in years; he is also a reader. He is sometimes teased by his teammates who, with two or three interesting exceptions, are not so much puzzled by his reading as by what he chooses to read—not *Playboy* or *The Sporting News* or junk reading on politics or fishing. He disappears into novels. On this particular day, it is *Gravity's Rainbow;* on another it will be *Giles Goat-Boy* or *Middlemarch* or *Tristram Shandy*.

The third reader is on a ship at sea, some years ago. Deep inside, a member of the crew, a boatswain's mate, a hulk of a man-boy in his twenties, slouches on his bunk in a cramped, sunless, and cheerless cabin, laboriously working his slow way through *Tom Jones*. He had discovered and claimed it because another sailor, drafted out of graduate school, had been reading it and laughing immoderately, and he had gotten dibs on it. It takes him a long time and he never smiles, but he stays with it faithfully to the end, altogether oblivious to his surroundings, having moved himself into the eighteenth century. And when at last he finishes, a narrow but observant pilgrim to far off places and times, he heaves it across the cabin to the friend from whom he had borrowed it. "Anybody," he says soberly but firmly, perhaps even defiantly, "anybody tells you that ain't the best goddam book ever written has got me to deal with."[1]

The fourth reader is in an international airport in a better-than-ordinary airport bookshop. Among the selections there is an unlikely paperback, published by Airmont Press, called *The Augustan Age*, a collection of essays by various hands. A dignified businesswoman has picked it off the rack and is intensely reading its opening essay by Ian Watt, reading about publishing practices, the reading habits of another age, the rise of the novel. After five minutes of deep browsing, she buys the volume and disappears toward the gates with the book that will be her companion for the afternoon.

These are not readers from Wolfgang Iser, Stanley Fish, or Norman Holland. They are from life, real readers in real places, and they stand for many thousands of others, people who read in general and people who in particular are attracted to novels and to the novel's concerns. But they do not stand for us, critics and scholars of eighteenth-century literature attending a conference that self-consciously probes what we do and how well we do it. There is nothing wrong with the fact that they do not stand for us. Although we often concern ourselves greatly with readers these days, putative readers and sometimes with real ones, we are seldom conscious of vacationers, baseball players, boatswain's mates, and executives in airports, and we ask few questions about their habits and needs. The readers we are concerned with are readers we construct, literary readers who play by some kind of rules that if we do not make up, we at least describe and codify. They usually read in libraries, sometimes in the abstract.

Now I am not going to attack *rezeptionsästhetik* or other recent tendencies in criticism and theory for passing lay readers by, nor am I going to berate these readers for not knowing or caring about our rules or our concerns. I do wish to note how odd it seems to mention actual historic readers like these in this context, note how uncomfortable such readers may make us, and return at the end to the question of what they have to do with us. But in the meanwhile I want them simply to be visible and before us, a reminder of readers we do not touch, opportunities not fully met. For that is what I want to address, opportunities not yet fully met by historicist approaches to eighteenth-century fiction.

My interest is in the fortunes and misfortunes of historicism over the past half century, in what it has and has not done for the study of the novel. I emphasize things not done because I want to show what can be done now. It would be easy to praise the many accomplishments of historicism, but I want to emphasize instead those factors, choices, and contexts that have prevented historicism from realizing its full potential. Of all the approaches to literature, historicism is perhaps the most often mentioned, the least understood, the most variously defined, and both the most readily dismissed and tenaciously clung to. There are, in fact, many historicisms, but few of them in recent years have gotten much respect, and the question is whether historicism, in any form, can now have much to do with the reading of literature, specifically with eighteenth-century novels. I think it can and that the immediate future is quite promising, but first I want to review the past.

In the mid-1950s the publication of three important books within a narrow three-year span suggests rather definitively both what has been done and what is yet to do in studies of eighteenth-century English fiction. In 1954, Walter Allen brought forward his powerful and influential book *The English Novel,* not so much making a myth as codifying a then-familiar one. He claimed a high and stable place for the novel in academic criticism, and (although his book did not sweep aside all the objections that once and still put novels lowest among major literary modes) it established the field and made it seem legitimate and academically serious. No longer were studies of the novel merely journeys into popular culture and amateur social history or students of the novel merely journalists and pretenders to high culture; now scholar-critics were putting together a significant piece of literary history.

But no gain comes without concomitant losses: Allen raised the literary status of the novel in general while relegating eighteenth-century fiction to a decidedly ancillary place. Allen's English novel was a nineteenth-century structure; the eighteenth-century novel became a preface or a porch to the real thing that was massive, mansionlike, and lasting. There were four lengthy chapters on nineteenth-century English fiction but only a single introductory one on the eighteenth century. Allen did not invent this view, in which there are Victorian novels, modern novels, and "others," but he cast it impressively and he made it respectable. As the English novel arrived in literary history, eighteenth-century fiction became literature and minor at the same time. Two books in effect responded to that view, and together they rather fully stand for what happened in the study of eighteenth-century English fiction over the next quarter of a century.

Ian Watt's *Rise of the Novel* is one of those books; the other, less obvious perhaps but equally important in its own way, is Alan McKillop's *Early Masters of English Fiction*. McKillop's book appeared first in 1956, just two years after Allen, and a year later Watt flashed on the scene, suddenly bathing the eighteenth-century novel in a flood of unaccustomed attention, raising deep questions about the nature of the relationship between literary forms and cultural change, and offering an attractive theory of origins.

Now it may be true, as Watt's critics have sometimes ruefully insisted, that for most people who are not specifically students of the eighteenth-century novel, Watt is all they know on the subject, a common substitute even among graduate students for reading the novels themselves, but it is certainly true that *The Rise of the Novel* became one of the most talked-about scholarly books of its time. Certainly, it made eighteenth-century novels interesting to a great many people; a wide variety of people—specialists and nonspecialists, academics and browsers in airports—can talk of the Watt thesis in a larger context of interest in major historical and sociological issues. Watt's name has become shorthand for the view that literature is, consciously or not, a product of social and cultural forces. Watt's book, or the theoretical section of it anyway, is even better than the legend it created, but its influence has been both less and greater than its substance.

The Rise of the Novel, in spite of its centrality to almost all subsequent discussion, did not set the directions of study and did not much influence the methodology of criticism and scholarship for the sixties and seventies. Its emphasis on social history, literacy, cultural change, and the nature of literary forms points more to questions that pique interest now than to the most pressing issues in the decades that followed its first appearance. Although Watt has been mentioned, quoted, debated, and sometimes regarded not only as the founder of the field but as its cartographer and lawmaker as well, his work did not really set an agenda. He was honored but not followed; he became a quick reference for definition or historical explanation but not a guide for labor in the field.

McKillop's work comes closer to predicting the main thrusts of activity in the sixties and the seventies, because in *Early Masters* he concentrates his attention on the novels themselves—their texts, their individual features, the characteristics that distinguish them or their authors from others' works or consciousness—and his attention is only secondarily on history or sociology. McKillop did not set the agenda for the next twenty-five years either; things happening elsewhere in literary history and in the postwar cultures of England and America (for the Continental winds had not yet blown westward) had more to do with the slew of individual new critical readings of novels than did any one book, any one author, or any one school. But McKillop's reading skills, especially because he was an old-fashioned, unreconstructed scholar trained in old historicist ways to say more about all kinds of contexts—historical, biographical, political, social—than about texts, were a model of what could be done and an indication of where unsuspected interests in texts might lie. His book is really an extraordinary one; many things that now seem commonplace about the major novels and novelists have their first articulation or their still-best explanation there. Those who have not reread McKillop in thirty years are challenged to do so; they will be astonished at the crisp, fresh insights and the cool perspective that few later students of the novel have matched. He is a testimony to what solid learning, independence of mind and spirit, and a receptivity to emerging approaches and methods can do. McKillop is as much a monument as Watt, although just as fully dated, as lacking in direct progeny, and as sad a symbol of opportunities missed.

McKillop and Watt present, in the mid-1950s, diverging and nearly opposite directions of historicism. McKillop's historicism, which had led him earlier to do a biography of Richardson as a printer, a study of the background of Thomson's *Seasons*, a ranging and eclectic period anthology, a wonderfully factual handbook to eighteenth-century literary study, and a long list of articles on materials he came across as he devoured eighteenth-century items of all sorts, was of an ancient and declining kind. His kind of historicism did not, of course, disappear, but it slipped into the shadow of criticism. His was a historicism rich in anecdote, devoted to isolated facts, and curious about the lives of authors. It was interested in tracing how something (an image, a device, an idea) got from place to place, in life or in a text, and it was curious about parallels that had no apparent causal relationship—hence its devotion to sources on the one hand and analogues on the other.

History in those years tended to get defined, by literary historians, in terms of political events or some broad cultural definition or tag. Basil Willey was yet a name to be conjured with; "the eighteenth century believed that. . . " was a common formula; the history of ideas was pursued like the passing-on of material goods; and a public figure, a Walpole or a Locke, might be used to explain literary direction more simply than a broader analysis of process or cultural conflict. Insofar as there was an intellectual history it was a history of discrete ideas that moved from great man to great man and finally trickled down, and "society" was a governing concept more than "culture."

The historicism of McKillop's early years was sometimes indiscriminate in its interests but wonderfully aggressive. Often it was vacuum-cleaner historicism—eager, hungry, voracious, anxious to suck up everything lying around in history, curious about facts for their own sake if they had anything at all to do with literature or anyone who was involved in writing or producing it. Such historicism did not always know what to do with what it picked up, but it picked up everything it could find: crumbs from the coffee house, scraps of biography, threads of history, fingernail parings not only of authors but of their companions and hangers-on, whatever there was. And out of that sense of what history was and what it had to offer as "backgrounds" to literature, a very great deal of useful scholarship developed in the early twentieth century, before the professionalization of English studies and a belletrization of literature that "purified" and narrowed literary study.

Not all the scholarship that grew out of these years is first rate. Methods tended to be rather unself-conscious and even unmethodical, materials were unevenly available, and interests often naively antiquarian, but curiosity (perhaps because backgrounds could include anything) cast a wide net. Not only novelists like Fielding and Sterne and Defoe but booksellers like Curll and Tonson and journalists and hacks like Ned Ward had their own biographers and even their scholarly champions.

McKillop by no means abandoned his historicism in *Early Masters*—the critical skills he showed there were a clear overlay on his historicist career—and the old historicism did not end abruptly in 1956 or even go into retreat. Good historicist work continued to be done, but the energies of the old historicism did begin to lose some of their thrust, and the self-conscious directions of Watt's historicism did not take over from McKillop's.

At thirty years distance, it now seems rather bizarre that there was so little profit from Watt's example. He was attacked often enough to suggest that a lot of people were wrestling with his theory, but many of the attacks were provincial, or even local, carping about his misreading of a single book or author. Many, too, simply rejected the whole notion that readers could have such major effects on literary form and the creative process. But there were precious few emendations or suggested recastings of his thesis and very little follow-through among either his critics or his supporters. Those who saw the theoretical and ideological implications of his work were content to have them unnoticed by others, and most readers in those days did not care to notice. For a sophisticated book with complex theoretical implications, *The Rise of the Novel* got a surprisingly easy reception, either a blanket acceptance of almost all points or a total rejection of its approach. In either case, that was that. Watt did not lead to better or even more historical studies. It is not that he did not offer leadership. But nobody followed him over the hill. It was not until the eighties that the issues he opened up began again to be addressed in any but a perfunctory way.[2]

Why were the times so unready for that kind of social, almost cultural, history? Much, of course, had to do with the ahistoricism (often having become antihistoricism) that went with New Criticism.[3] It was not just that readings tended to avoid biographical, contextual, and other historical issues because they violated formalist principles and assumptions; those interested in readings were rebellious, anxious to establish credentials as critics by denying any interest at all in the issues raised by older historicists; they were eager to get out of their fathers' house. To raise a historical question at all, except to evoke a quick formula that would characterize an age or broadly summarize a development, was to risk derision among one's peers. Readings seldom had room for history; critics were interested in temporality only if it could be safely controlled within a formal structure. Watt was a good shibboleth but no Moses. Besides, the other disciplines that Watt depended on—social history, sociology, and anthropology in particular—were not themselves, in the Anglo-American academic world, surging forward in notable ways, and what advances there were, if any, were unlikely to be noticed in contexts that discouraged real interdisciplinarity. English departments in the sixties, heady with their own successes and full of a sense of destiny, wanted little to do with anyone else. Departments could be as closed as texts, and the discipline itself was as much characterized by formalism as were its scholarly outlets. Comparative literature, in all but a few nonconforming places, was in retreat or disarray, for it seemed enough to know one language, one literature, and often one text. Thus there were likely to be no extensions of Watt's thesis and no incursion of his issues into other languages and cultures in which novels had also "risen." And given the biases against interdisciplinarity more generally, whatever came to be known in other literatures or in other disciplines was destined to find few readers among students of the eighteenth-century English novel or among students of English literature more generally.

At least three other factors may have impeded the following up of Watt's version of historicism. One simply has to do with difficulty and practicality: why should one do the hard digging implied in Watt's thesis or think through complex cultural interrelationships when there was easier and more highly respected work to be found? A second involves the issue of a tree falling in the forest: some isolated discussions of these cultural issues in fact do exist, but they did not get crucially absorbed in mainstream discourse and were left to expire, or at least to lie quietly in repose, in the desert air of library quarterlies or old-fashioned historical journals. Graduate students and young professors in the sixties and seventies, my generation and just after, did not read them much. Still a third factor involves the reluctance of students of the novel to rock the boat. Uncertainties about the novel's status as literature used to be a problem for novelists ambitious for their reputations, and now it is still an issue, though a seldom talked-about one, for critics. A recent MLA forum on fiction transcribed in the journal *Novel* triumphantly reported that in the academy old biases against novels had disappeared or at least seriously dissipated, and the number of recent Ph.D. dissertations on Victorian fiction was cited as evidence.[4] But throughout the discussion one could repeatedly hear anxieties about academic status, suspicions that all this heady parvenu talk was taking place somehow in an anteroom at the club. No doubt, as civil rights leaders like to say, great strides have been made. Most graduate schools now feature specialists in the novel on their faculties, something that was not true at many of the most prestigious universities in England or America a generation ago, and fiction may now attract at least its fair share of dissertations. (It has long attracted a disproportionate number at newer, less prestigious institutions where library holdings are less deep.) And perhaps the locker-room jokes about the fringes of literature are now less often turned against novel study and novel students, for there are newer and more threatening targets.

My point is not about the actual place of the novel in the academy or in hierarchies of literary kinds of whatever origin, but rather about

perceptions of status among students of the novel themselves. Students
of eighteenth-century English fiction seem collectively, with individual
exceptions of course, to be a rather insecure lot about their subject,
worrying about whether it is taken as seriously as French fiction,
or nineteenth- and twentieth-century fiction, or as the poets of the
eighteenth century. Anxious about their place, students of the novel,
rather like Fielding in his muddy quest for formal lineage, tend to be
more concerned to establish the novel's relationship to prestigious
established forms than its popular roots and relationships. During the
sixties and seventies especially, when a mixture of professional high
hopes and personal insecurities was at its most volatile, students of the
eighteenth-century novel shied away from compromising or contro-
versial topics, especially those involving low life or popular taste. Thus
the affinities between the novel and religious dissent and methodism
have been consistently understated. Similarly, the close relationship to
personal forms such as autobiography, meditation, and letters has
been handled most delicately with more emphasis than is strictly justified on the gentility of these forms and with an exaggeratedly abstract
sense of subjectivity and epistolarity. And (until quite recently) the
close connection between the novel and female readership and authorship has been skewed, explained ashamedly away, or even denied,
sometimes by distorting actual literacy evidence.[5] Despite some bold
historical work grounding the novel firmly in aliterary or even antiliter-
ary traditions, the tendency has been to associate the novel with its
betters rather than its poor relations and grubby ancestors. Thus we
find the emphasis on the novel and the epic (Tillyard and Maresca),
on the novel and literary biography or formal history (Passler and
Braudy), and the ubiquitous readings of novels on the model of well-
wrought urn burials, despite the obvious wrench in assumptions and
method.

    As scholars we like to think of ourselves as above politics and
jealousies and human insecurities, but the role that individual and
group psychology play in the history of the academy and in the story of
literary history and criticism remains an important, largely unstudied
issue. Now that the history of the profession is beginning to engage
serious attention,[6] and now that ideology is beginning to be regarded
correctly as a determinant of literary and critical directions, it is high
time that we admit practical social factors of ambition, disappointment,
and personal security as well, for what we do depends upon some
murky desires and drives as well as upon high-minded ideals and
commitments. Academic directions are as much a matter of personality
and personal insecurity as politics, although it is a good bit more

dignified to consider such matters within the confines of intellectual history.

There were, of course, other historicisms between McKillop and Watt (speaking spatially not temporally), and many of them survived the relative quietude of the sixties and seventies. Much of the literary criticism that I have described as readings was in fact historically curious and based upon materials unearthed by historical scholarship. Not all New Criticism was know-nothingism, and a historical consciousness was not altogether absent from many of the readings; some of the best critics, in fact, actively sought it. The best academic writing from that era can be found in the work of scholar-critics who found a fruitful collaboration between the skills of close reading and the scholarly habits of historical research. And even the most doctrinaire of the New Critics usually subscribed, at least theoretically, to the old historical assumption that the best reading was the one that most closely approximated that possible at the historical present of the work, an ancient truism only quite recently questioned with any lingering seriousness.

And of course the work of many good historical scholars continued during the triumphant period for critical interpretation. The Bodleian, the Huntington, and the Newberry continued to have their devoted visitors, and rare books rose in price and prestige; antiquarianism thrived even when historicism was imperfectly grasped. Biographies were written, editions produced, and purely historical articles continued to appear. But the triumph of criticism was so nearly complete in graduate schools, in the founding of new journals such as *Novel, Studies in the Novel,* or *Genre,* and in the radically altered contexts of journals like *ELH* or *Modern Language Notes* that no one could doubt where values lay. The major energies did not go into projects founded, or even grounded, in history.

I do not wish to minimize the importance of truly major historical projects, works such as the Wesleyan edition of Fielding or studies of the social and intellectual backgrounds of Defoe and Richardson, but given the number of laborers in the vineyards, the harvest seems astonishingly small. Adequate modern biographies of Smollett, Sterne, and Richardson have come forward, and ambitious ones of Defoe and Fielding are in progress; in addition, most of the "major" novels now have acceptable texts available. but after decades of hopes, promises, and projects, we have only a partially completed standard edition of Sterne and a barely begun one of Smollett, with little hope in our lifetimes of seeing similar projects completed for Richardson or Defoe. And for other novelists—the one-book novelists, those who have never been accorded major status or those dismissed as popular or out of the common road—there are not only few available editions, reliable or not, but there has been (until very recently) little attention of any sort, historical, critical, or otherwise.

The narrowing of attention (not only to a smaller number of reading issues but to a smaller number of "major" authors and privileged texts) is probably the most important development in eighteenth-century studies of the past half century, and it may turn out to be the most serious deficiency in the legacy of the New Criticism for literary studies more generally. In the bad old days of unbridled and unfocused historicism, when the novel was not a field and had no more status in literary study than periodicals and other self-conscious extensions of the idea of what literature was, books like *The Female Quixote* and *The Man of Feeling* attracted scholarly attention and had readers, at least among graduate students. And authors like Charlotte Smith, Delariviere Manley, and Eliza Haywood got substantial if often pedestrian press; they were acknowledged if not revered or read much. Lots of novelists, like lots of journalists, actors, and booksellers (and for the same reasons), got lots of historical attention. To look at the *PMLA* bibliographies for the thirties and compare those of the seventies is a revelation. While the bulk of material increased severalfold, the amount of attention to less-than-major figures actually decreased. Defoe and Richardson had up to ten times as much attention bestowed on them annually by 1980, but the likes of Frances Brooke and Sarah Fielding actually had less.

Watt and McKillop are themselves no more responsible for the narrowed attention to major figures and "classic" works over the past thirty years than for the waning of historicism more generally, but their focus, in establishing (as a codicil to Allen) eighteenth-century fiction as a field of its own, is indicative of how the territory has been identified, mapped, and subdivided. McKillop was actually daring in his claims; to call Defoe, Richardson, Fielding, Smollett, and Sterne "masters" was to make an extraordinary assertion in 1956, even though he made them "early masters" and not "old masters." Watt, except for omitting Smollett, featured the same figures, and subsequent study— critical and historical—has rallied round them as equivalent to *the* eighteenth-century novel. When there has been debate about the propriety of figures for study, it has usually involved tighter exclusion and narrowing of taste, not greater inclusivity or comprehension.

Finding Sterne too unusual, Defoe too primitive or episodic, and Richardson too unself-conscious and authoritarian always presents itself as an application of high standards and rigorous discrimination, but it is often simple snobbishness. The dismissing of "Smellfungus" or the distrust of "earless Daniel" often has the air of kicking Stinky out of the club. But the club itself stands. Liberal outreachers may include Burney in a discussion or even a course, and some may gather in a token Gothicist or treat someone like Jane Barker or Elizabeth Singer or Clara Reeve as an associate member or visitor with a temporary pass, but the eighteenth-century novel has essentially been seen increasingly as the extended shadow of five great men (some say four or three, but few say six or admit a second sex).

This has meant that no richness of context has emerged for the years in midcentury, that little knowledge of the formative process before Defoe (or even Richardson) has entered critical or historical discourse, and that virtually nothing after the 1770s until Jane Austen appears in academic courses or has become a part of the definition of the eighteenth-century English novel. There have, of course, been admirable exceptions—John Richetti's account of the novel before Richardson, Jerry Beasley's contextual review of the 1740s, and some extended treatments of Gothicism and the Jacobin novel—but mainstream attention has centered almost exclusively on five men. Until quite recently, that is, and I turn now to the very recent past to suggest that radical change is in the air and that there are extraordinary historicist possibilities in the present scholarly, critical, and theoretical contexts.

As historicists know only too well, nothing can happen without appropriate contexts. The question of what historicist tasks lie before us depends at least as much on conditions in the field, in the profession, and in the larger intellectual community as it does on the identification of things that need to be done. Before outlining some of the tasks worthy of pursuit, I want to note four things about present conditions.

In the first place, historic materials are now more readily available to a wider variety of students than ever before. The Eighteenth-Century Short Title Catalogue (ESTC) project, unprecedented in its scope, already has begun to affect the kinds of historical study fit to be undertaken. Information now available by computer makes infinitely easier many journeys into historical materials—searches for titles, publishers, key words, topics—and rare items can now be traced quickly to many locations. Already, long before printed catalogues are available, we have for the years after 1701 more and better data than in the STCs for earlier ages. So many previously unknown or unlocated editions have been turned up by the process that the British Library now estimates that only 40 percent of the relevant titles are available there. They had previously assumed that they held up to 75 percent of published titles,[7] so that in sheer newly found items alone the project has made available work for generations to come. More important though, the simple presence of the project richly suggests historical work to be done. Much of what is now possible—in editions, in seeing chronological and possible causal or reflective relationships of texts, and in knowledge of booksellers, publishers, and bookmaking—simply could not have been done before. Similarly, the technology that made this tool available can perform many other tasks that make historical study easier and more efficient. Computers are likely to change radically the nature of the projects students set for themselves in the next generation; we have not yet begun to explore their potential to store, sort, match up, and reorder information that not even the best human brain can handle. Materials and technical tools available now stand as a kind of measure of our creativity.

Second, the backlog of energy and interest in matters historical is enormous. Much of that potential lay dormant during the years when criticism dominated so fully, and the frustration of a large number of scholars in older generations runs very deep. Frustration may blunt or even kill, of course, and no doubt many uncompleted projects planned long ago will never see the light of day, but there are now about to be available far more hands to do the work than have been available for some time. Historicism is a labor-intensive approach to literature; to be efficient, especially in editorial, bibliographical, and stylistic projects, research teams seem necessary. For the past decade and a half, for good reasons, graduate students have not been available, and younger faculty members have seldom had time to engage in long-term projects or in those deeply dependent on others. Eighteenth-century studies will have to be appealing enough to attract and challenge the numbers of students now beginning to be available, but the pool is there. People for the task are now as readily available as materials.

Third, developments in related disciplines have serious implications for the subject, and it is becoming harder to disregard their findings. In the past decade, what has happened in social history has profoundly changed notions of what the eighteenth century was like, and we have barely begun to absorb those implications into studies of the novel. Demographic studies now have told us much more about literacy and related developments than Ian Watt could know thirty years ago, and conceptual developments in anthropology suggest that much more sophisticated cultural history, abetted by developments in intellectual history, lies not far ahead. Too, the deep distrust of interdisciplinarity, much of it inspired by some brand or other of historicism, now seems abated, and even those afraid of engaging in interdisciplinary work themselves boldly borrow conclusions from other disciplines.

Fourth, recent developments in critical theory suggest a sharply rising interest in history and point to directions that historicism may take. In the past three years, claims for a New Historicism (capital *N*, capital *H*) have been growing more vocal, and they have often come from those who associated themselves with the forefront of critical theory over the past fifteen years. The New Historicism announced itself formally—or appropriated that name for itself—in 1982, and primarily its results have been visible in Renaissance studies. But the basis for New Historicism is broad, and its interests and methods apply just as readily to other eras, especially perhaps to concerns about historical interpretation in eighteenth-century fiction. Already the New Historicism, whatever its own impact, is visible and open enough to attract other historicisms and older historicists to its banner. To those other historicists who wish it, it offers a flag good for safe passage in seas that have recently been quite perilous. Whether the New Historicism, as presently focused, becomes the historical alternative to literary theory remains to be seen, but it has already uncovered a broad interest in historicism more generally, and its recognition paves the way for a renewed pursuit of historicist methods and objectives. History has become, in recent months, the single most often heard call to arms in literary discussion.

In October of last year, a reviewer in the *TLS* noted that a major publishing house had headed its new list with a statement that "literary history is back" and went on to note that for many intelligent scholars and observers, it has never really been away.[8] To those for whom history has always been important, the stark, simplistic, and unresonant announcement that history is back may seem merely funny, and sometimes it is hard for old-line historicists whose commitments have stayed constant for decades even to find humor in the trends and fashions of study or in announcements of what is in or out, up or down, gone or back. Those whose commitments have not changed substantially in a lifetime are apt to be understandably impatient with others who seem too responsive to the shifting rhythms of popularity, and they are apt to feel cynical about literary study that subjects itself to fashions and popular trends.

The spectacle of bandwagon riding or of switching vehicles in midcareer is not one of the more attractive pictures of academic literary study or of intellectual history more generally. Where there is no center, no commitment to principles, and no interest in a subject beyond its ability to generate personal attention, popularity, partisanship, and promotion, abrupt changes in method and approach are indeed suspect and probably deserve to be ignored. But human growth, development, and enrichment are not sad spectacles, and basic and genuine changes in sensibility and commitment are significant, an aspect of the temporality historicism itself depends on. Poll taking or applause meters are obviously inappropriate measures of truth, but paying attention to what readers pay attention to is an important part of cultural observation. I presume that no self-respecting historicist would wish to set his or her compass by the blinking lights of journalism or academic fads, but knowing what students care about, what stimulates new thoughts and hard work, what factors drive the intellectual marketplace, and how to get the attention of readers seem to me necessary if somewhat precarious. I confess that I do not understand the anger and fear that some historicists feel toward some of the new approaches to literature. I will not like every use that history is put to, but historicism (or historicisms) now has more friends than at any time in the past half century.

The New Historicism is not, of course, altogether new. Fifteen years ago Wesley Morris wrote a book called *Toward a New Historicism,* and at about the same time the journal *New Literary History* was born. Many historicists of the sixties and seventies in fact thought of themselves as (and some called themselves) new historicists or new contextualists because they saw a need to distance themselves from some of the older directions and methods (or at least from naïveté and professed lack of ideology or theoretical grounding) while continuing to set their agendas in history. Today's New Historicism has, of course, its own distinctive emphases and preoccupations, as did each of the previous would-be new historicisms, but the particular politics of New Historicism seems to me less important than the sense of enthusiasm it has uncovered for historical issues generally. Any major return to historical considerations now, however motivated, seems likely to provide a platform for many who felt silenced or at least outshouted during the past three decades, and whatever form any historicism takes now, it seems certain to feature an arena for all sorts of historical issues.

The New Historicism did not, of course, develop in a contextual vacuum. Both Marxism and feminism, although not often regarded as friends by traditional historicists, have helped to get the spotlight back onto history; they have been, in fact, more effective in doing so

than have traditional historicisms. It is probably the open and aggressive ideologies that traditional historicists find offensive, the more so
because traditional historicisms have usually refused to name their
own ideological underpinnings and sometimes have even denied that
they had any. But for the past thirty years, Marxists have been more
fun to fight with than anybody, largely because they take history
seriously, have a deep engagement with patterns, and love to fight. In
recent years, feminism has even more effectively opened historical
issues, and the impact of that on historicist projects of all stamps seems
likely to be extensive. If the New Historicism promises to sponsor
a renewed historical interpretation of texts, feminism and Marxism
promise renewed literary history. Marxism and feminism do not always ride the same rails, but they have in common the fact that the
routes back to historicism in theory were through ideology, not in
opposition to it, and they both have eager audiences. Perhaps there is
a moral there somewhere.

Three different kinds of challenges are offered by the present
contexts of study. All of them involve earlier roads not taken or not
traversed very far by traditional historicisms, and all involve special
opportunities now because of a concatenation of circumstances. These
challenges involve the canon and the "minor" novelists, the relationship between novels and popular literature, and the question of the
eighteenth-century English novel's place in the larger novelistic
tradition.

A minor industry involving the study of the lesser-known novelists
has already begun, largely under the aegis of feminist studies, and its
implications may be far-reaching indeed. At stake is nothing less than
the definition of the novel; at the moment this definition means a taste
only for the fiction of Defoe, Richardson, Fielding, Smollett, and
Sterne. One does not have to subscribe to the lost-masterpiece theory
of historical digging to believe that the revaluation of the canon is
long, long overdue, for the narrowing of the sense of what is there to
be read has ramified from undergraduate syllabuses and graduate
seminars to the full practice of scholarship. But in the past few years,
in the wake of Gilbert and Gubar and as prophecy of what is to come,
several books have begun to try to put lesser-known women writers in
perspective,[9] and just now there begin to be more detailed major
reconsiderations in full-length articles and in serious revisionary studies, the first visible tip of an iceberg that reaches into scores of dissertation projects.

And the texts of writers like Barker and Manley, Lennox and Haywood—most of them out of print since the eighteenth century—are beginning to be available. Some years ago, a number of expensive and cumbersome facsimiles of a few once-popular but since neglected novels were printed by Garland Press, usefully making available in libraries what had, except in rare book rooms, been impossible to find; now a new Mothers of the Novel series is making fifty previously hard-to-find titles available in paperback, and Penguin has also begun to introduce some pleasant surprises. Not all the less-read titles are gems, and the Early Masters boys are not likely to fade away. But the effect of having many additional texts available at reasonable prices is bound to have an impact on syllabi and ultimately on our entire sense of what the eighteenth-century English novel is. Familiarity has a lot to do with taste, perhaps nearly as much as quality itself. And definitions of quality are once again open to discussion, if not up for grabs, as more readers have more examples to draw upon.

So far most of the texts newly made available and much of the historical scholarship on "minor" figures is on women novelists. They have been disproportionately neglected, and (besides) female writers and readers had a disproportionate amount to do with fiction at most points in the eighteenth century. But reconsideration is a hard thing to control once begun; once a canon is opened it is difficult to put the lid on again. Paul Salzburg's book on seventeenth-century fiction begins to suggest some of the figures left out or underrecognized early on—for example, Bunyan and John Dunton—and a host of figures at the end of the eighteenth century deserve reconsideration just as fully. Just how altered the canon of eighteenth-century novels will be by the wholesale revaluation remains to be seen, but even if the most revered novels turn out to be, in fifteen years, the same ones admired by McKillop and Watt (an unlikely outcome), the sense of what the eighteenth-century novel is (what its range and variations are) will never again be the same after such an expansion of considered texts. And it is impossible to predict what will be the result of concentrated historical research on a greatly expanded number of lives and literary relationships. Valuable new information should emerge about literary influences, interactions, and the motivation and stimulation for writing and reading novels.

A second potential arena for historicism involves materials that used to be dismissed as subliterary and paraliterary or offered secondary status as background, milieu, or popular culture. Separating "literature" from popular culture has always been more difficult and arbitrary than literary history has liked to pretend, and too often classification has been made on the basis of grand claims on the one hand and commercial motivations or mass reception on the other. Eighteenth-century studies have been especially plagued with distinctions artificially bifurcated because of the tendency of early-century traditionalists, especially Pope, to dismiss their antagonists as unserious, untalented, and unworthy of readers, and postwar studies have been far readier to support that bifurcation than were earlier scholars in a more broadly friendly historical context. The novel does not fare well generally in a literary universe mapped by traditionalists because its own credentials are too uncertain and its ancestry too blurred, but the next cut of reading materials—those "below" novels that fit no literary category at all—loses out altogether when privileged categories are honored.

It is difficult to sort out the novel's relationship to other reading materials and particularly to discover its origins or emergence when other materials, generally regarded as lesser, are not fully studied and well known. The novel in its early years, throughout all of the eighteenth century and well into the nineteenth, competed for its audience not primarily with established literary kinds but with other materials not canonized but widely read: journalistic materials, didactic materials, travel books, popular histories and biographies, anthologies of anecdotes—materials that share with novels common structural features or common rhetorical appeals. Because the novel had no categorical status during most of the eighteenth century—not only no name but no agreed upon set of features and not even agreement as to whether it was factual or fictional, primarily narrative or not—its authors no more than its readers had any place to go for analogues or models. Practicing novelists took from a variety of sources what they could—facts, devices, strategies, structures, precedents, and routes to readers—and much of what they took came from popular, not literary, sources.

Studying the history of the novel only by reading other novels makes very little sense in an era when definitions were, at best, provisional and when novelists themselves were finding their way among readers and making their choices of subject matter, story, and mode more by instinct than by calculation, more by sorting among possible competitors (fictional and nonfictional) than by following tradition or convention. It was not a prescription or even a series of predispositions that determined what or how they wrote so much as a desire to reach readers who wanted to understand the actual choices of contemporary life. A commitment to delight and instruct in storytelling (but with a lot of nonnarrative parts intermixed) brought together a great and unlikely variety of writers—women and men, authors traditionally prepared and those who came to writing by accident or necessity, those with conventional moral and social attitudes to further and those whose values were new, unorthodox, radical, and rebellious.

Many wrote novels because novels quickly became the readiest route to readers, not because of a commitment to form, to fiction as a system, or even to narrative as a mode. And the influences on their craft could come from the unlikeliest places—all kinds of written material intended for all kinds of audiences and uses, the materials (published or not) of daily life, oral tradition, stories, anecdotes, conversations, the sounds of the road and of the London street. Because most novelists were only secondarily (at most) conscious of the traditions of previous fictions like romances, they did not set their aims or define their limits according to specifiable forms and traditions, and it is not possible to say by reading just fiction or just narrative that one has hold of all the relevant things for an eighteenth-century novelist of any stripe, even so traditional and self-conscious a writer as Fielding, let alone for the species. Novelists often make a show of comprehension by including, as Sterne does, narrative insets, variations on oral tropes, minispecies, and passing habits not even named. Such matters are not background at all in the usual sense, or even foreground; they are the materials of novelistic life, and if we want to know either how to read individual novels or how to account for the beginning and developments of the tradition, we cannot ignore such matters. The appropriate contexts for the novel are not just the contexts of fiction itself but the contexts of discourse defined broadly.

The potential to do such work has, in a sense, always existed, but developments in critical theory make it much more attractive now, largely because recent work, especially poststructuralist work, has broken the sense of privileged texts and has suggested that materials traditionally regarded as nonliterary can be treated in the same terms as belletristic texts. Literary history can now be seen—must be seen— as a history of all kinds of texts and writing, at whatever level, for whomever intended, and of whatever quality. And literary history also has to be part of a larger cultural history that includes not just the intentions of the high culture but the everyday life of the low. There had better be, by the next generation, something in literary history to match E. P. Thompson, Braudel, and Foucault. Already in a title like *The Rise of the Woman Novelist,* a fine 1986 book by Jane Spencer, one can begin to see at once the deepening and widening of Watt's historicist agenda and the enlarged understanding of its implications. *Rise* means something different when one is discussing novelists instead of novels. It implies careers and culture, not etherealized teleological forms, and in the social and cultural resonance of the Spencer book, there is the start of much enhanced historicist possibility.

A third contemporary arena for historicism involves the place of the eighteenth-century English novel in the novel species more generally. That place needs to be defined more precisely, both relative to the traditions of English culture (and thus to the later English novel of the nineteenth and twentieth centuries) and in relation to the Continental novels and their contexts. Although these activities will inevitably compete conceptually, they both need to be pursued. Both are implicitly historicist activities.

Ultimately the relationship between eighteenth-century and Victorian or modern fiction will only be clearer to those who cross period lines and undertake detailed developmental (but not teleological) history. Stricter periodization, which is another product of field creation and emphasis, has been a serious handicap to better understanding of continuity, influence, and innovation, not only because Victorian novel people tend to slight eighteenth-century forebears but also because eighteenth-century specialists pay so little attention to nineteenth- and twentieth-century examples. Synchronic programs such as those of the dix-huitièmiste societies, good for interdisciplinarity in general, have been bad for serious historical studies of genres and modes. The English novel is a real, definable, and in some ways continuous phenomenon, but its Englishness needs to be demonstrated in deep cultural study of a long historical section.

But speaking of an English novel has its problems because there is also a novelistic stratum that cuts across countries, cultures, and languages. That too is now easier to study, not only because there is good work in the French, Spanish, Russian, and German traditions separately but also because genuine comparative study has begun to transcend the thematic and structural and to be historically sophisticated. To know more about international and interlinguistic interaction, we shall ultimately have to know a great deal about the comparative cultural circumstances in different places where the novel emerged. It is not enough to trace readings, borrowings, and influences and know only where the Cervantic exists and when the Richardsonian flowers in a new climate.

It is my prejudice that cultural studies for each national tradition will have to be done thoroughly first, for I see the origins question to be deeply cultural and temperamental, but of course the national interactions must be paid attention to as well. In comparative studies on the one hand and in cultural ones on the other, some deep disagreements and mighty conflicts are sure to spring. Those who seek to study novelistic origins in the habits, popular outlets, and consciousness of a single culture—people like Watt, Spacks, McKeon, and myself—will have to fight it out with those who see form beyond culture and ultimately beyond history—for example, Robert, ter Horst, Doody, and Reed. That part of the battle that can be fought on historical ground is ready right now.

Finally, I return to the four readers seen at the start. I have wanted them to haunt all our proceedings, for their very existence is at once a challenge and a chastisement to us all, a reminder that countless readers outside academia seem to have little to do with what we do inside. A few times I have glanced at them again passingly, but perhaps they have been most present in their absence, in the self-conscious talk of how much we write for each other and in response to priestly trends, not the needs of the laity.

About two of these readers I know nothing beyond what I observed physically, not what formed their taste or what brought them initially to novels and novelistic interest at all. About the other two I know only a little more—that one, formally unschooled himself, came to read his novel because a college-stimulated friend had enjoyed it and that the other later decided, for purely avocational reasons, to take a couple of literature seminars. Perhaps most modern readers read novels because they got hooked as undergraduates by good teachers or in well-conceived or well-baited courses. Or perhaps they were self-taught or self-motivated. I would like to think that novel reading results from what we do as scholars and teachers, but I do not know whether we deserve even indirect credit for these four.

Whatever its conceptual limits, the New Criticism did recruit a lot of readers, turning them into lifelong word watchers; some of them no doubt turn to novels now in whatever workaday places they find themselves, and some are, like Oedipa Maas, "just a whiz" at deciphering verbal signs and have therefore become obsessed pursuers of texts. The older historicisms did little for general readers, however, giving them no method for new materials and often little motivation to pick up the unfamiliar. Critical theory has done somewhat better, infecting some with fashion and ultimately perhaps many more with intriguing puzzles and complicated reasonings and posing large ultimately philosophical challenges. Semiotics, psychoanalytic criticism, and deconstructionism have powerful and surprisingly wide intellectual appeals. The question now is twofold: can an enlightened cultural historicism create amateur readers of novels, and can contemporary historicism—the New, or another new, or a renewed old one—have anything to say to readers who read for fun?

I maintain in both cases that it can. Anyone interested in a novel is interested in outcomes and ultimately in referentiality and the nature of the world that novels reflect. Real readers who read novels now are a lot like readers of novels in the eighteenth century; they read with deep needs and epistemological interests in mind, not for form and aesthetic values. This does not mean that novels lack formal beauties but that more mundane concerns drive readers. We need to know about these needs (real modern readers can help us to be good historicists), and we need to be honest about mundane motivations and curious to seek them out historically. Ordinary human needs put people to reading novels, and ideologies drive curiosity, taste, and behavior. I doubt that a lot of women readers will have to be urged much to pick up some of the new Mothers of the Novel paperbacks, and I bet that serious conversations will result from those readings, literature actually affecting reality in a substantial way.

If historicism becomes allied with cultural analysis, it could have a great deal to say, at least indirectly, to "common" readers and their contemporary descendants. Scholarly writing need not be written for beaches and airports or directly for common readers, although writing in a jargonistic way so as specifically to exclude them seems perverse, a function of the silly pride our profession has long taken in difficult, bad writing, just as bad in the old days as now. Few historicist works may end up on beaches or in stadia, though with a little luck we might make the boats and the airports. But the desire of novel readers to know the world is a translatable need for scholars; it is an issue in time and culture, ours and ones past. It is a mistake to underrate or undervalue common readers whose very commonness contains the essence of our task. They too should help form the contexts of discourse now.

Notes

1. For this anecdote, I am indebted to the oral tradition. It is said to be based upon a youthful Navy experience of Henry Knight Miller.

2. The most significant follow-up on Watt, published just after the Georgetown conference, is Michael McKeon, *The Origins of the English Novel* (Baltimore: Johns Hopkins University Press, 1987).

3. Many matters that seem to derive from the New Criticism are, of course, indebted instead to the larger contexts that produced the New Criticism. For a recent account of those contexts, see Daniel R. Schwarz, *The Humanistic Heritage: Critical Theories of the English Novel from James to Hillis Miller* (Philadelphia: University of Pennsylvania Press, 1986). Quite beyond its roots in European formalism, the New Criticism as practiced in England and the United States takes some of its bluster and much of its insularity from a powerful cultural desire to remain separate from the political turmoil of Europe between the world wars, and that desire had powerful implications in shunting aside history more generally.

4. See Marianna Torgovnick, "'The Present and Future States of Novel Criticism': A Hopeful Overview," *Novel* 18 (Spring 1985): 199–202.

5. For example, Lawrence Stone, whose judgments about studies of male literacy are among the most reliable that we have, seems to abandon plentiful quantitative evidence about female literacy and rely totally on anecdote and opinion. For solid conclusions about male literacy, still for the most part valid after almost two decades of intense research on the subject, see "Literacy and Education in England 1640–1900," *Past and Present* 42 (1969): 69–139. For his jovial and offhand conclusions about female literacy, see *The Family, Sex, and Marriage in England, 1500–1800* (New York: Harper and Row, 1977).

6. See, for example, Gerald Graff, *Professing Literature: An Institutional History* (Chicago: University of Chicago Press, 1987).

7. These estimates were given to me orally by Michael Crump, a member of the ESTC team at the British Library.

8. John Lucas, "Textual Preferences," *TLS*, 10 Oct. 1986, 1141.

9. Despite the early tendency of feminism to engage primarily nineteenth- and twentieth-century texts, the revaluation had begun by the mid-1970s and is illustrated by such studies as Anthea Zeman, *Presumptuous Girls* (London: Weidenfeld and Nicolson, 1977); Ellen Moers, *Literary Women* (Garden City, N.Y.: Doubleday, 1976); and Patricia Meyer Spacks, *The Female Imagination* (London: Allen and Unwin, 1976). The most recent examples include Dale Spender, *Mothers of the Novel* (London: Pandora, 1986) and Jane Spencer, *The Rise of the Woman Novelist* (London: Basil Blackwell, 1986).

Part 3

Challenges and Accomplishments

7

Scholarly Texts: An Unapologetic Defense

JOHN H. MIDDENDORF

IN HIS INITIAL letter suggesting the idea of this conference, Dick Schwartz wrote: "I would encourage presentations that would be more personal than usual." Before turning to more serious major concerns, I would like, briefly, to respond to this invitation in a most obvious way, if only perhaps to hint at some of the sources from which my remarks emanate. I begin with a few anecdotes, the latter two of which will be familiar to you in versions from your own experience.

For a number of years in the mid-1960s I had corresponded with the late Bud Bronson about his introduction to volumes 7 and 8 of the Yale Johnson, but it was not until a few years later that I had the pleasure of meeting him for lunch, in London as it happened. We got along well from the beginning, and it was not long before we were reminiscing about our earliest encounters with the eighteenth century. "I remember mine very well," I said. "I was about thirteen or fourteen and was reading through whatever novels were available in our local library. Being not as imaginative, perhaps, as I should have been, after I had read all of the Scott novels I could find, I moved along the shelves to the next S—Smollett, as it turned out (more precisely, *Roderick Random*). And after about an hour or so of reading I knew I had found my home." Bronson looked at me meditatively for a few moments and then remarked, "Oh my, but you must have been a bloody-minded little bastard." Now this was not the first time I had been misread. Or had I been read correctly? In any event, it was a reading that has always lingered in my mind. Was it my earliest encounter with reader-response criticism? Surprisingly, I think not.

My second and third anecdotes are not as superficially dramatic, but they point to common attitudes still held by many of my profes-

143

sional colleagues toward the branch of our scholarly enterprise to which I have devoted the past twenty-five years—textual editing—and the main topic of this paper. During the discussion following a dissertation defense, after the candidate had clearly demonstrated that he should have been told years before to try a different profession, and after he had left the room, a colleague observed, "It is too bad we cannot catch students like this early on, and steer them to some sort of editing job." I should add that this colleague is still a good friend and that he respects me (I think) for the work I have done. My third anecdote: recently I met a well-known new New Critic, who after a few drinks looked at me and sighed, "How I envy you, John, working on something solid, like your edition." Now this came from a man who has made a great reputation insisting that a text has reality only in the eye of the beholder, and then only for a moment.

The morals are obvious. Scholarly editing does not require the powers of critical imagination and thought that other scholarly activities require. The scholarly editor lives in a world of certain certainties, although, of course, it is nowadays often thought to be a world with no certainty apart from the editor's own need for certainty. This latter state is, indeed, I would think (borrowing from Swift), "the sublime and refined point of felicity, called the possession of being well deceived; the serene peaceful state of being" an editor among critics. Alas for morals. The moral of neither of these last two anecdotes is true.

When I began graduate work in 1945, the old New Criticism was alluring to some, frightening and threatening to others. I myself found it immensely useful in the classroom, especially in courses designed to give the student a sense of the complexities and delights of discovery that poetry can generate. I found the New Criticism less useful in courses based on certain assumptions that I respected, felt quite at home with, but knew were limited and to be taken as guides or acted upon only with great caution. In other words, I found the New Criticism less useful in teaching survey or period courses based on assumptions that there is a "history" of literature—that knowing something about authors' lives, philosophy, psychology, and culture can help to provide frames and matrices enabling a more finely tuned reading and understanding of the poems, novels, essays, and plays of the time. The New Critics drew attention to intrinsic values and problems, the older historians to extrinsic values and problems. But everyone knew that essentially these were distinctions without a difference. Since I respected both the new and the old but settled exclusively for neither, obviously I say *everyone*. The past few decades—judging by the amount of talk, attention, and publicity—have been decades of critical theory, rather than of criticism. And most recently we have heard talk of the new historicism.

One of the objections of the recent theorists of literary history to the old literary historians is that the old were so tightly in the grip of notions of literary periods, influences, and evolution that they were blinded to the realities of the literature they professed. Literature, in other words, became secondary, of interest and importance primarily as the means or evidence by which a history of the evolution of literature might be constructed. These were objections, needless to add, that were leveled by the old New Critics against *their* predecessors. Presumably, as someone who began teaching in 1946 and still has a few years to go, I am counted by the theorists of the new literary history as a member of the old generation of literary scholars. I say *scholars* because I think of myself as neither theorist, critic, nor historian, but as time and occasion require, a little bit of each. I do know that I have never thought of the eighteenth century as a "period" in the "development" of English literature. I have always thought more of Pope, Swift, Addison, Johnson, the novelists, Collins, Gray, and others as writers who flourished at a certain time, who were aware of and responsive to, yet independent of, their literary heritage and of their time each in his own way. Who among us, opening a course in eighteenth-century literature, does not begin by warning his or her students of the arbitrariness of the traditional terminal dates given for the eighteenth century and of the dangers of accepting the clichéd definitions and implications offered so confidently by the handbook guides and, more cautiously, by the older overviews like Baugh's *Literary History* or McKillop's *English Literature from Dryden to Burns?* My point is, simply, that with respect to these matters at any rate, a good part of the attitude of the new historians, as I understand it, may well be defined as a negative response to the worst of the old. Until a mode of approach is discovered or devised that manages somehow to consider literature simultaneously as both within and outside of time, which of course it is, I am content to retain traditional chronological frames with a full awareness of their limitations and of the traps they set.

As an aside, in my experience, from the very first appearance of the old New Criticism it was apparent to all but the dimmest of us that the most skilled readers of the poem qua poem were also the most knowledgeable about the context and environment in which it was conceived and born, that is, about its author and his or her times. Happily, this is also true of the most impressive professors of the new theory and history (of whatever persuasion) when they turn their attention more strictly to criticism. Too frequently, it appears to me, the theorists tend to think of intellectual differences as real differences. But fortunately (to put Matthew Arnold's observations on religion to a different use) this is of no great real importance, for while theorists imagine themselves to live by their theory, they really live by their true practice. At their best—that is, when they are being most useful to others—they confront literature unencumbered by theory and are governed by their knowledge, their imagination, and their taste.

A few years ago in his article "Toward a New History in Literary Study," Herbert Lindenberger described the old literary history in terms that were too simple, as if the scholars of the past three to five decades accepted without question notions of chronology, development, causality and the like; as if the old historians were concerned only with facts, dates, and other quantifiable data; and as if they were against interpretation in any form, of whatever sort.[1] Who, then, can disagree when Lindenberger asserts, "It is no wonder that the scholarship we now pursue cannot take the forms or speak the language of the older literary history"? (16). Of course it is no wonder. The wonder is that the new theorists of literary history, if Lindenberger may be taken as a spokesman, have failed to recognize that the best of the old historians—and surely we must judge by the best— were not shackled by rigidities that presented literature solely in terms of chronology, evolution, causality, author, source, and influence. "Bring out rule and measure in a year of dearth." But was 1946 a year of dearth because it saw the publication of Marjorie Nicolson's *Newton Demands the Muse*, or 1955 because it saw the publication of Walter Jackson Bate's *Achievement of Samuel Johnson*, or 1959 because it saw Reuben Brower's *Poetry of Allusion?* The list could be extended. Has there ever been a time when the line between criticism and history has not been blurred, as is the line between critical theory and critical practice? The old literary history has been badly misunderstood and far too narrowly defined if it is not recognized that it encouraged and easily accommodated the likes of these.

What my remarks so far come down to is that I see no sharp break between old and new. Much of what we discover about literature or how we respond to it, it goes without saying, may appear to us to be new. But often it is just that—appearance. Or perhaps it is new to its discoverer. It is almost too obvious to repeat that what is a discovery or a new perception for one may not be for another, and certainly will not be for one who made the discovery decades earlier.

I am not arguing against the need and value of seeing the old in a new way, or even against the possibility that there are new ways to be discovered (though I think it is the slimmest of possibilities). But I am arguing against the insistence that all discovery is necessarily dis-

covery of the new. A hard-fought-for truth, once accepted and established, becomes old and tends to harden into dogma. Certainly the old
must constantly be questioned, reexamined, and not allowed to govern
our understanding or critical response out of habit or because of
inertia. Every generation must find the vocabulary that best expresses
its sense of the world of literature it inhabits. But there is a danger in
assuming that a different vocabulary is a different truth. *Problematic* is
a word defining conditions or situations we encounter every day. But
how often is it used nowadays by professors of literature to cover
conditions or situations doubtful, questionable, and unpredictable and
used in such a way as to suggest that its user is somehow in possession
of a truth well outside the grasp of ordinary blokes? *Text, enabling,
diachronic,* and *synchronic*—we can all make our own list of buzzwords.
In the *Tale of a Tub* Swift recognized clothes for what they are and
pointed to the dangers of overclaiming:

> And whereas the mind of Man, when he gives the spur and bridle to his
> thoughts, doth never stop, but naturally sallies out into both extremes of
> high and low, of good and evil; his first flight of fancy commonly trans-
> ports him to ideas of what is most perfect, finished, and exalted; till
> having soared out of his own reach and sight, not well perceiving how
> near the frontiers of height and depth border upon each other; with the
> same course and wing, he falls down plumb into the lowest bottom of
> things, like one who travels the east into the west, or like a straight line
> drawn by its own length into a circle (section 8).

In recognizing the inevitability and value of every generation's
finding received ways of talking about literature inadequate, but in
cautioning against allowing a different critical vocabulary to seduce us
into thinking we have discovered a different "thing in itself," I realize
that I have walked into the trap set by many of the new critical theorists—of assuming that there is a world independent of the word, of
assuming that life is not simply a process of reading and being read,
significant though this process may be. But I see no way out of this
trap. At some point one must say stop and, like Blake's Milton, "cast
off the idiot questioner who is always questioning / But [is] never
capable of answering . . . / Who publishes doubt and calls it knowledge, whose Science is Despair" (plate 41, ll. 12–13, 15), though, I
should add, despair of a particular sort, the sort that some students
(and some faculty) during the Columbia troubles in 1968 sang about
with enormous gusto and with obvious pleasure.

Johnson kicked the stone for many reasons. At least one of them
was not because he did not understand Berkeley, but because he
understood him all too well and symbolically insisted that he at least

had to get on with the business of living. The world would be a poorer place had Berkeley never lived. And our world would be poorer without the recent developments in critical theory and speculations about literary history, though I suspect—this is obviously wildly exaggerated, self-serving, self-indulgent, and unfair—that in only one way do I envy those who dematerialize the text: they have solved the problem of shelf space.

By now it must be clear that I see the state of the scholarly-critical world during recent years as not having undergone a radical transformation from old to new unless one defines old and new solely in terms of their outer edges, where the sin of the old might be said to have been oversimplification and naïveté and the sin of the new, overcomplication and shamanism. Now it may well be (again, Lindenberger) that the "practitioners of the old and new histories . . . see themselves playing . . . sharply divergent roles" (16). But words like *seamless* and *continuity* seem more appropriate to describe the scholarly-critical world as I have experienced it. The center has held. Just as what once seemed threatening about the old New Criticism has long been assimilated into our ways of experiencing and teaching literature, so too, I suspect, will scholars twenty years hence lay heavier stress— notice I use the comparative *heavier*—on the role played by the reader, for example, than by the author in the long-recognized, traditional trinitarian relationship of author, work, and reader.

Before leaving the matter, at least for the moment, I am reminded of Johnson's observation on Young's *Conjectures*. Johnson, reports Boswell, was "surprized to find Young receive as novelties, what he thought very common maxims."[2] Johnson was right, but in a sense, Johnson was not quite right. There is a tone, and emphasis, a slight tipping of the balance in Young's observations on originality that to me do not signal anything radically new, as the old historians who invented and accepted the notion of preromanticism used to think, but a different way of apprehending and feeling the old concept and term. If forced to define this difference, I would invoke phrases like "a sense of growing isolation," "a loss of faith in a community of endeavor," and "a dissatisfaction with the Popian/Swiftian cautions against allowing a hard-mouthed imagination to shake off that light rider reason." But to accept the invitation of such phrases might push me uncomfortably close to relinquishing my view that the newness generated by perception and feeling is not newness in any essential sense. And this relinquishment might, in turn, force me to the point of contradicting my earlier position. And that would never do. Lindenberger speaks of playfulness as a characteristic of the new historicism, and here I am on the giddy brink of play. But are there any among us who have not always recognized the element of play in our work? Perhaps we old scholars should have allowed our recognition to show more clearly. The best scholarship of the old has always been offered as tentative, however vigorously and even dogmatically its advocates may have presented and fought for it. But if by *playfulness* is meant some quality of joy, the solemnity and portentousness of much modern theorizing has overwhelmed it. Swiftians, Johnsonians, Sternians of the world unite! You have nothing to lose but your solemnity.

Now I shall try to show more explicitly how a few of the "new" ways of seeing literature are, from my point of view as a textual editor, not so new after all.

A common element in much of the new theory is the insistence upon the fluidity, the instability of the text. Hillis Miller expresses this insistence very well: "The new turn in criticism involves an interrogation of the notion of the self-enclosed literary work and of the idea that any work has a fixed, identifiable meaning. The literary work is seen in various ways as open and unpredictably productive. The reading of a poem is part of the poem. It produces multiple interpretations, further language about the poem's language, in an interminable activity without necessary closure."[3] The tip-off here is the phrase "the notion of the self-enclosed literary work and of the idea that any work has a fixed, identifiable meaning." Down with Brooks, Ransom, Wimsatt, and their ilk. But even if one assumes that Brooks, Ransom, and Wimsatt were so simpleminded, what is the value of an equally limited alternative? "The literary work is seen in various ways as open and unpredictably productive." But the old New Critics also recognized this. "The reading of a poem is part of the poem." Obviously, when we read Pope's *Epistle to Arbuthnot*, we have somewhere in our minds Mack's reading and the various rebuttals it spawned. But in what sense is our/their reading a part of the poem to a sophomore who reads it for the first time and has never heard of Mack and his rebutters—indeed, who may think of them as a rock group? "It produces multiple interpretations, further language about the poem's language, in an interminable activity without necessary closure." Putting aside the obscurity of "an interminable activity [that is, presumably, an endless activity] without necessary closure," need we be reminded of what we already know? Of course. And in saying this I am echoing Johnson, who was echoing generations of his predecessors: we need not be taught anything new, simply be reminded of what we already know. Johnson was speaking of moral truths. But his thought applies equally well to matters of literary enquiry. Those who remind us of what we already know are to be commended, but let them spare us the implication that we do not already know it.

In a paper on Pope's *Epistle to Arbuthnot* recently submitted to me a student writes: "No one takes Pope at his word anymore." This was written after the student had read through the last ten or so years' crop of articles on the poem. The remark admittedly reflects a low level of critical sophistication, but the student nevertheless had a point. All literary experience begins with the word on the page. The text is anterior to all criticism. And yet it too is the result of a critical process. It is in this sense that the work of the textual editor involves the reader in processes followed through by the interpretative critic.

Before considering what the editorial process is, we might first consider what result is sought. What, in other words, is a scholarly-critical text, or edition? And here I should emphasize that just as in my previous remarks I spoke not as a theorist but solely as a teacher, so now I speak not as a theorist of textual editing or as a bibliographer in any way on the level of Fredson Bowers or Thomas Tanselle but rather as a practicing editor, and that only on one edition, the Yale Johnson.

Back to the question. We can at least say what a scholarly edition is not. It is not definitive in any sense of bringing to an end. Though I am proud to be associated with the Johnson edition and believe that it will be considered as the most reliable text of Johnson available for a very long time, I have no doubt that sometime in the future another edition of Johnson will be urged and—optimist that I am—that money will be found to pay for its production.

If one thinks for a moment of some of the major scholarly editions of the past thirty or so years in our field (some complete, some still in process), there come to mind the California Dryden, the Twickenham Pope, the Wesleyan Fielding, Donald Bond's *Spectator,* and Arthur Friedman's Goldsmith, to mention only a few. But if one considers the diversity of their textual policies, how many definitive texts of each could be produced if the policy of one were to govern another? Think of the possible number of versions of any of these texts lying somewhere between diplomatic editions, regularized editions, and modernized editions. Depending upon the work (or works) to be edited and the audience for whom the edition is intended, the modern editor is faced with a cornucopia of possibilities to create. He or she must create, for that matter, a text from an early printed source that in itself (from initial conception to first printed edition) was the product not only of the author but of (perhaps) a copyist or copyists, a compositor or compositors, an editor or editors, and a printer or printers.

If the stability of the eighteenth-century text can legitimately be questioned, and the stability of the twentieth-century version can also be questioned, it follows naturally enough that the same conditions will govern in the future. No responsible editor, in my generation at least, has ever been foolish enough to believe that the text ever was, or ever can be, forever fixed in amber. Anyone who argues that this has not been known for years is ignorant of textual theory and practice. Allen Hazen, my textual mentor, a scholar of formidable learning and critical imagination, was the greatest ad hoc textual editor I shall ever meet. Time and again he resolved cruxes by drawing upon whatever evidence, local or distant, was relevant, reversing or contradicting previous similar decisions with a blithe indifference to what textual quantifiers might say. A true Johnsonian, he understood in its deepest sense what Johnson meant when, in his preface to his edition of Shakespeare, he said of Shakespeare's mingling of tragedy and comedy: "That this is a practice contrary to the rules of criticism will be readily allowed; but there is always an appeal open from criticism to nature."[4] If the text cannot be fixed in amber, how can the meaning?

Even if there ever could be universal agreement upon a uniform textual policy, MSS or other printed versions might well be discovered, and evidence might well be forthcoming to establish hitherto unknown authorial or compositorial emendations or tampering. The most that can be said is that today's definitive edition represents a stage in the evolution of the text. It is *a* text, not *the* text. Indeed, some so-called definitive multivolume editions—and here I have in mind both textual and critical apparatus—may be more accurately defined as a series of texts, as candidly admitted by George Sherburn in the introduction to his edition of Pope's correspondence, on which he began work in 1934 and which he completed in 1956: "The results of this prolongation of effort [he wrote] have been to allow . . . some confusions to arise. . . . It is hoped that the footnotes of 1935 may still sing more or less in the same key with those of 1955."[5] Sherburn's experience has been repeated by other editors of multivolume editions. Since every edition is the product of the editor's reading of the text, or of an editorial committee's reading of the text, every critical edition, despite the suggestions of objectivity and finality generated by the apparatus, is the product of an individual mind and eye, perhaps modified by the minds and eyes of a committee. Hence each volume is individual in its particular way. All critical editions, whether or not their editors have followed the lead of Greg and Bowers, are the result of countless judgments, assessments, and critical decisions. In the best criticism, as George Steiner has correctly observed, interpretation does not translate the object but multiplies its aspects. The object—the novel, poem, essay, or play—to use Lionel Trilling's phrase, has a history of meaning. This is also true of the best editions, which stabilize the text, but only to the extent warranted by the words available from manuscript or page. The fact of textual instability has long been recognized.

Where old and new literary historians differ is that only a new historian, after discovering for himself or herself what the old historians already knew—that authorial authority is not always authoritative—could say that "even an author's authorized text [what is that?] need have no more authority than we choose to give it" (Lindenberger, 17). The old historian would not say this, for the same reason that Johnson kicked the stone. Surely some limitations must be admitted. Would a pirated Irish edition carry no more authority than an edition for which there is evidence its author read proof? No text can be final, though admittedly some can be more final than others. And those critical editions that are more final than others are so because they enjoy a measure of independence from their readers and interpreters. It is the hope of discovering that measure of independence that motivates the textual editor.

There are parallels here between the problems faced by the textual editor and those faced by the biographer. The biographer is limited in presenting his or her subject, unlike the novelist. Johnson may have been slothful or inhibited, a sufferer of existential angst or an eighteenth-century melancholic Christian, but he can never be presented as a Scotsman. The editor is equally limited. A line of poetry may exist in different versions, and it is the editor's task to accept, reject, or modify one or the other or to conflate them in some way. But unless or until a third version is found, the uncertainty stops there. We do have the need to choose, but we cannot choose outside the limits of our manuscript or printed page.

Every responsible scholar-critic has always been aware of the mysteries uniting author and work and work and reader and has always known that each reader responds to the mysteries in (if not radically different ways) ways different enough to have spawned—to use only one obvious example—judgments of *Tristram Shandy* that range from sentimental to satiric, with countless shades and permutations between. But if in a sense all judgments are arbitrary and solipsistic, the fact remains that the text has a tangible solidity. Words are printed with ink (or photographed or laser beamed) on flat sheets collated and gathered into books. The book is there. It can be hefted, opened, and smelled. If the opening words of the book we are reading are "Ye who listen with credulity to the whispers of fancy, and pursue with eagerness the phantoms of hope; who expect that age will perform the promises of youth, and that the deficiencies of the present day will be supplied by the morrow," these words will still be there when we have read the conclusion in which nothing is concluded, and they will be there next week and next month when next we pick up *Rasselas*. The word *concluded* will be there, regardless of whether we read it as "determined," "settled," or "ended." It is easy, and not necessarily unimportant, to be reminded, and to remind ourselves, that readers will respond to these words in both predictable and unpredictable ways. It is not always so easy, but just as important, to remind ourselves that the scholarly-critical edition, until it may be superseded, is one of the few stabilities in an unstable world and to remember that if new information casts doubt on the text now recognized and accepted as authoritative and forces a new text, that new text becomes our new stability.

In an article entitled "The Reading Process: A Phenomenological Approach," Wolfgang Iser asserts that "the act of recreation [by which he means the reader's recreation of the writer's creation] is not a smooth or continuous process, but one which, in its essence, relies on interruptions of the flow to render it efficacious. We look forward, we look back, we decide, we change our decisions, we form expectations, we are shocked by their non-fulfillment, we question, we muse, we accept, we reject; this is the dynamic process of recreation." Without an act of recreation, he further states, "the object is not perceived as a work of art."[6] Leaving aside the rather surprising reference to the work of art as the "object" rather than, as we might have expected, the "reading experience" or the "event," the process of recreation that the reader experiences, as explained by Iser, is analogous, within the limits permitted by the words on manuscript or printed page, to the editorial process leading to the recreation of a text.

Lines 23–24 of canto 2 of the first edition of *The Rape of the Lock* (in later editions, lines 104–5 of canto 4) read: "Honor forbid! at whose unrival'd Shrine / Ease, Pleasure, Virtue, All, our Sex Resign." In five editions (three in 1714, 1715, and 1717), "All" is followed by a comma: "Ease, Pleasure, Virtue, All, our Sex Resign." In the editions of 1736, 1740, 1743, and 1751, the comma is omitted: "Ease, Pleasure, Virtue, All our Sex Resign."

The Twickenham editor Geoffrey Tillotson chose to print the line with a comma, following accepted modern practice regarding accidentals. But no editor blindly accepts general textual practice, especially in a case like the above, in which the presence or absence of the comma can result in crucially different meanings. Obviously Tillotson's inclusion of the comma was a choice, a decision, the result of the process of recreation—if not in every exact detail—that Iser describes. Tillotson's note to the line justifies the comma by referring to parallel lines and expressions of similar import in Racine and Boileau. The note is the result of, presumably, what Iser goes on to describe as a "main structural component[s] within the text" that steers the process of recreation. This steering component, he tells us, is a "repertoire of familiar literary patterns and recurrent literary themes, together with allusions to familiar social and historical contexts" (293).

Examples of editorial "recreation," to apply Iser's useful term to the familiar process leading to a textual decision, could be multiplied. One, pointed to many years ago by Donald Greene, may be found in one of Johnson's political pieces. Says Johnson: "I have not in general a favourable opinion of restraints, which always produce discontent and an habitual violation of laws." Greene points out that the eighteenth-century writer tended to set off all subordinate clauses by commas, making no distinction, as we would, between restrictive and nonrestrictive elements.[7] No comma after "restraints" limits Johnson's unfavorable opinion only to restraints that always produce discontent and a violation of laws. Insert a comma, and Johnson is saying that he disapproves of all restraints. At the least, a decision about how to print this line requires knowledge of what Iser calls "familiar literary patterns and recurrent literary themes, together with allusions to familiar social and historical contexts"—and, I should add, biographical contexts.

The last volume of the Yale Johnson to appear—volume 15, Johnson's translation of LeGrand's translation of Father Jeronimo Lobo's *Voyage to Abyssinia*—contains numberless references to "checs," or (as we would say) sheiks. The Yale edition modernizes capitals. A straightforward reference to a particular sheik poses no difficulty. But many, if not the majority, of the references are not of this sort. Is a reference to a sheik made to a particular one or to sheiks in general, as a class? An answer can be found only by an appeal to context. But here we encounter a familiar dilemma, about which much theoretical ink has been spilled. Does a context exist before we have created it? Again we can call upon Iser's words about the reader and apply them to the editor: "As we read, we oscillate to a greater or lesser degree between the building and the breaking of illusions. In a process of trial and error, we organize and reorganize the various data offered us by the text" (293). The text is therefore the product of countless recreations. It is, in a sense, the editor's "reading." It is a text that never before existed, and never again will exist except in its present form. I admire and am grateful for Iser's detailed restatement of what presumably goes on in a reader's mind. But as an editor I emphasize *restatement,* and as a skeptical "old" scholar I emphasize *presumably.*

The editions of eighteenth-century writers bequeathed to us by the nineteenth century were too often produced without benefit of modern textual knowledge and theory and were notable as well for a kind of cavalier inattention to modern ideals of fullness and accuracy. Little or no attempt was made to collate successive editions of the same work, and a new edition was usually based on its predecessor. The genealogy of the so-called standard edition of Johnson, for example, the 1825 Oxford edition, can be traced back through the editions of 1823, 1816, 1806, and 1792, to the Hawkins edition of 1781–89. Pope was represented by the Elwin-Courthope edition, Swift by Scott's, and Dryden by Scott-Saintsbury. (I will not bother to run through the list.) Reliable nineteenth-century editions of the correspondence of eighteenth-century writers are nonexistent. Letters were rearranged, bowdlerized, conflated, cut, improved, and omitted. To be sure, there were occasional exceptions, like the Hill edition of Boswell's *Life*, but by and large the nineteenth-century editions of major eighteenth-century writers left much to be improved, both in reliability of text and extent and in usefulness of explanatory annotation. This says nothing about the works of those dwelling on the Olympian slopes—Prior, Gay, Cowper, Smart, and others—all presented poorly if at all. (All of this is well known.)

Saintsbury's descriptive phrase for the eighteenth century, the Peace of the Augustans, was long ago laid to rest as in any serious way true of the period. But the condescending resonances of the phrase—Oh, our indispensable eighteenth century!—may be said to have determined the editions I have mentioned (in other words, not to be taken very seriously). Thus, the Reverend George Gilfillan, together with Charles Cowden Clarke, could "edit" thirty-one of the British poets without leaving his Dundee parsonage. The combination of textual ignorance and a sense of cultural superiority guaranteed, at best, dubious results.

Turning to our own century, Donald Greene's description of our period—the Age of Exuberance—might be equally well applied to the activity and ferment of our own age of critical editing. It seems entirely likely to me that the past four or five decades will be remembered by scholars in our field primarily for the enormous effort, and the impressive results of that effort, in producing reliable texts of works and correspondence. (I say this realizing that I have laid myself open to the charge of self-puffery.) If texts are indeed anterior to criticism, we have given much to the critics to work with: editions (some in process or only in part) of Addison, Boswell, Burke, Chatterton, Collins, Cowper, Dryden, Garrick, Gay, Goldsmith, Gray, Johnson, Lady Mary Wortley Montagu, Percy, Pope, Prior, Savage, Smart, Steele, Swift, Walpole, and Young. (I am certain that I have forgotten a few.)

Of the major novelists we have seen volumes of the Wesleyan Fielding and the Florida Sterne. After a slow start, the Smollett edition is at last underway. We await Defoe, especially the vast amount of his work that has never received any serious textual attention. But I despair of ever seeing a complete correspondence and works of Richardson, though he has been well served by the likes of Jocelyn Harris' edition of *Grandison*. The 1985 Viking edition of the complete *Clarissa,* edited by Angus Ross, contains no textual apparatus and simply reprints, with alterations, the first edition. Anyone hoping to find the evidence of Richardson's emendations and additions, which tell us much about his conception—and changing conception—of his own work will be disappointed. Ross' explanation of how he handled the text (31) is instructive, however, as an illustration of my earlier remarks about textual instability and as an illustration of how the editor creates a new text. He tells us that his aim was to "give a smooth readable text without unduly distorting possible nuances in the old pages." "Unduly" and "possible" are beguilingly vague, and is it unfair to wonder about the implications of the "old pages"? Without going into details—Ross modernized, more or less, what he calls Richardson's "use of the contemporary printers' heavy and intrusive punctuation" (without giving any evidence in support of his put-down of the printers), and makes the punctuation much "lighter" (his word) by dividing "very long sentences" into "two or three units." That Ross is interpreting Richardson with a vengeance is made even more evident when he tells us, with reference to Richardson's use of dashes to suggest emotional stress, that since "modern readers are perhaps more receptive of authorial experimentation than audiences of the past, and less hung-up on 'correctness,'" he will retain the dashes, while at the same time rejecting—or at least altering—his text's "correct" syntactical punctuation. The result, he concludes, is a "livelier and more direct text." The result, I conclude, is a reading of *Clarissa* that may inspire—given the fact that a reasonably priced complete edition of *Clarissa* is now available—interpretations as off the mark as Ross' text.

The picture of the age generated by the responsibly edited editions of our time, taken together—if only by calling attention to the extent and variety of eighteenth-century literary production—is a kind of multivolumed exemplification of the richly textured age brought to life by Roger Lonsdale in his *New Oxford Book of Eighteenth-Century Verse,* a life more indecorous, less certain, with greater imaginative range and curiosity than previous such collections have suggested.

The task that remains is to continue to enlarge and enrich this picture by, first and most obviously, completing the editions already underway. For even though the traditional roster of the major and minor writers of the period is today being challenged (How did it come into being? What forces—cultural, social, economic, and political—may have helped to determine it?), to my knowledge no one has so far suggested that the likes of Dryden, Fielding, Johnson, and Sterne are to be excluded.

But not only do we need to see the completion of critical editions now at some stage of forwardness. We also need to supply sound texts for the many others—Akenside, Arbuthnot, Beattie, Warburton, the Wartons, and Young, to name but a few at the start and end of the alphabet of those who have long been recognized, by my generation at any rate, as belonging among those considered by their contemporaries as worthy of serious attention.

I have little hope that this will be done, however, given the realities of academic life, where recognition, promotion, and rewards seldom if ever follow textual work (and here I emphasize again texts, textual and explanatory apparatus). The brightest of our students quickly pick up the attitude of their teachers ("Too bad we did not steer this fellow into editing something."), quickly learn where the jobs are, and rarely receive from their teachers a sense of the challenging critical demands made by editing or a sense of the importance of textual reliability, however subject that reliability may be to revision in the near or distant future. And even if these conditions were altered, where would the publishers and money come from in support of unprofitable publications?

If the possibility of producing editions of these traditional writers is all but nonexistent, the possibility of producing editions of writers outside the recognized realm is, I would think, totally nonexistent. And yet are not editions of this sort precisely what we need if we are to provide materials to those who are unhappy with the tradition they have inherited? I shall return to this a bit later, but now I add to the gloom. I suspect, talking with younger colleagues at Columbia and elsewhere, that many or all of them have little knowledge of or interest in the likes of those I have just mentioned—Akenside, Arbuthnot, Beattie, and others, not to mention those still to be brought to life.

To summarize for a moment, I believe that we need vigorously to continue our production of critical editions, including many writers in the tradition and others without. Yet such an effort now receives only tepid encouragement from within the profession, partly because of our own condescending attitude toward textual and editorial work, and this in turn continues to affect the attitudes of other main groups in our world (graduate students and administrators), so much so that our younger colleagues are ignorant of or indifferent to masses of literary materials the importance of which my generation took for granted. It is not a happy picture.

Lest it seem that I am simply pleading for the continuation and enlargement of the world I have grown up in, I suggest that the conditions I have alluded to bear directly upon what the new critical theorists and speculators about literary history have been saying. The older scholars went mainly to science, economics, history, and philosophy to illuminate or open up literature. The new literary historians, we are told, are more inclined to draw upon the methodologies, speculations, hypotheses, and conclusions of other disciplines—most notably anthropology and social theory and history—in their attempts to place literary works within contexts that acknowledge no disciplinary boundaries. A possible danger for the practitioner of the new history, given these interests, goals, and methodological assumptions, is that he or she may lose sight of literature altogether, a criticism leveled at the history-of-ideas approach fifty years ago. Presumably no one wishes to turn the world back to the time when literature was pronounced "litrachure," with the implications of exclusivity and the invitation to swoon and gush. But I think we should attend seriously to whether we really wish to become second-rate anthropologists or third-rate philosophers. Obviously, from what I have said so far, I am quite content to hear that scholars in eighteenth-century studies have been, as a group, reluctant to embrace new critical theories and methodologies. This is not simply scholarly ludditism. We have had the enormous advantage of having been nourished on a sound diet of Swift, Johnson, and (dare I add?) Blake. Having had the benefit of that diet for fifty years, I welcome the new history, but I ask, what are the materials with which the new historians will work?

Are we to assume that the new historians, so skeptical of the old, will be willing to work only with what the old have given them? And if they are, will not this reliance in an important sense narrow rather than broaden their, and therefore our, understanding of eighteenth-century literature and culture? For example, a serious study of analogues, parallels, and linkages (say, the interplay between the language of eighteenth-century literature and the language employed by eighteenth-century political and economic power brokers) would certainly contribute additional density to our sense and understanding of the period. Putting aside the question of newness—analogues, parallels, and the like were long ago recognized, for example, linking the language of agrarian poetry and the propaganda of agricultural improvers—we might find that such a study would provide new insight into the interconnectedness of literature and the culture at large, but I for one would be made uneasy by implications of narrowness. What literary materials will the new historians work with? Or, as I have already hinted, are they really anthropologists and sociologists manqué?

It has been argued against the now-scattered Yale school that the theories once emanating from New Haven lacked the possibilities of broad application. One of the great scholarly accomplishments of our time has been the Eighteenth-Century Short Title Catalogue (ESTC). Will the new historians avail themselves of its resources? It is to be hoped they will. But so far only the old historians seem to have welcomed it. With so much honey available, may we hope for an increase of bees?

We have literary theorists, critics, and historians. The lines separating them are blurred, if indeed they exist in any real sense. The theorists have been with us now for quite a while. The critics have tended to be mute. The old historians—in the broad sense of the term that I have tried to suggest—have kept on working. Theory must be translated into practice, must in some way energize the mind and imagination into productivity, and must—most importantly to me— make clear that it can contribute to our sense of the relationship between literature and life, of what Johnson says comes closest to a person.

In *Rambler* No. 154 Johnson wrote: "Fame cannot spread wide or endure long that is not rooted in nature, and manured by art." In some copies of the 1825 edition "manured" is printed as "matured." Johnson defines "manured" in the *Dictionary* as "to cultivate by manual labor" and illustrates with a quotation from Milton: "They mock our scant manuring, and require / More hands than ours to lop their wanton growth." The *OED* tells us that the last use of the word in Johnson's sense was in 1791. Does it matter that 1825 prints "mature"? It does. Let the new history flourish, but let us continue to nourish and practice the old.

As an editor I find two aspects of the new history encouraging: its emphasis on the embedment of literature in the culture as a whole; and its emphasis on the need to think our way back into time. Perhaps I am encouraged by these aspects because they remind me of how I was trained. Regardless, all of our critical editions would benefit by a greater attention to, and knowledge of, the language of the eighteenth century. In my work with Johnson I am reminded again and again of my ignorance of the resonances, the echoes, and the implications of Johnson's language that I dimly sense are different from the resonances, echoes, and implications awakened by the same words as I use them now. We are fortunate to have the *Dictionary*. But more studies of eighteenth-century words in use are needed. Editors should, I think, do more to elucidate usage. Here there is the possibility of a fruitful union with the new historians, whose interests in the culture at large could conceivably encourage a greater editorial sensitivity to the words we are editing.

Are we, as a recent commentator in the *Boston Review* said, apropos the modern world of critical theory, now between an exhausted humanism and an institutionalized avant-garde? I have forgotten his answer, but I know my own, and it is a decided no. I and those of my vintage in my discipline have lived through the old New Criticism, the new new theory in all its varieties, the old history, and the theoretically presented new history and, in another, closely related discipline, through Butterfield, Namier, Plumb, Holmes, Speck, Williams, and Stone. No one of these has entirely supplanted the other.

I close with a well-known (slightly altered) quotation from Johnson's preface to his edition of Shakespeare, with a due appreciation of Johnsonian irony and a due recognition of the mock-heroic distance between high and low: "Perhaps, what I have here not dogmatically but deliberatively [delivered], may recal the principles of [literary study] to a new examination. I am almost frighted at my own temerity; and when I estimate the fame and the strength of those that maintain the contrary opinion, am ready to sink down in reverential silence" (7:80–81).

Notes

1. *Profession 84* (Modern Language Association, 1984), 16–23. Further citations will be given by page number in the text.

2. Boswell's *Life,* ed. G. B. Hill, revised and enlarged by L. F. Powell (Oxford: Clarendon Press, 1934–50; vols. 5–6 revised 1964), 5:269.

3. "Stevens' Rock and Criticism as Cure, II," *Georgia Review* 30 (Summer 1976): 333.

4. *Johnson on Shakespeare,* The Yale Edition of the Works of Samuel Johnson, ed. Arthur Sherbo (New Haven: Yale University Press), 7:67. Further citations will be given by volume and page number in the text.

5. *The Correspondence of Alexander Pope* (Oxford: Clarendon Press, 1956), 1:v.

6. *New Literary History* 3 (Winter 1972): 293. Further citations will be given by page number in the text.

7. "No Dull Duty: The Yale Edition of the Works of Samuel Johnson," in *Editing Eighteenth-Century Texts: Papers Given at the Editorial Conference, University of Toronto, October 1967,* ed. D. I. B. Smith (Toronto: University of Toronto Press, 1968), 104.

8

Reading Eighteenth-Century Plays

SHIRLEY STRUM KENNY

FOR SCHOLARS of eighteenth-century drama, this is an incredibly fertile period. We have a field burgeoning with research opportunities, and we have newly available to us resources and technology to make possible research far more extensive than ever before.

The eighteenth-century theatre that we inherited was rather narrowly defined. A few plays were still performed in the nineteenth century, and the plays of a very few authors were printed now and again, with commentary on their relative amounts of wit and bawdry. The plays of the most popular of these playwrights, heralded as the best, continued to be published in the twentieth century. Critics considered and reconsidered them; literary historians grounded their perception of a whole theatrical era on the few plays that continued to be printed. Even by midcentury, when Emmett L. Avery began compiling a record of performances, the world of eighteenth-century theatre seemed neat, compact, and orderly. By the 1960s our view became somewhat more expansive. We began to examine the entire canons of the chosen playwrights; occasionally someone would stray out, perhaps for a dissertation, to edit the works of a playwright not on the traditional list. The dramas of favorite eighteenth-century authors, Dr. Johnson's *Irene,* for example, were occasionally mentioned if not necessarily read.

That is still true, of course. The Restoration and eighteenth-century canon, as defined by the conversation of literate people, even eighteenth-century scholars, is still limited to a dozen or so plays, and there are still those who have not read *Irene.* Our familiarity with these works tends to be closely correlated with which ones appeared on the reading list for comprehensives when we got our degrees. Those reading lists were directly related to what was in print when the senior faculty who made the lists studied for their comprehensives or to what appeared in inexpensive editions in our own student days. Those two sources provided identical lists then, lists remarkably close to the ones we give our students now.

But by the 1960s our theatrical world view began to change in other ways. With the publication of *The London Stage,* that remarkable calendar of London performances that provides us a comprehensive and complicated compendium of information about what actually occurred in the London theatres, we were thrust into a very different realm of possibilities. Even now we have not begun to mine these volumes. Indeed they have presented so many opportunities for enriched research that our ranks do not have enough scholars to carry them out. Because the possibilities are so abundant, we have some difficulty in ascertaining what is important to pursue and what is not. Now we have *The London Stage* in computerized form. But the instant availability of knowledge from *The London Stage*—a great boon to those of us who have trudged through it time and again by hand, realizing that in some volumes the indexes are so bad we have to turn every page—still leaves us the obligation of determining the right questions to ask because the choices are so plentiful.

As the volumes of *A Biographical Dictionary of Actors, Actresses, Musicians, Dancers, Managers, and Other Stage Personnel in London, 1660– 1800* emerge, we have another rich and complex resource. Between these two works we can learn a great deal about a play. We can ascertain its popularity on stage as measured not only by first run but by continuity in the repertory, selection for benefits, box office receipts, evolving casts, need for afterpieces, and other information. We can investigate its actors, measuring them by other roles, published reviews, and personal history. As an avid user of these materials, I know that before *The London Stage* was published, no one would have even considered trying to trace the performance history as a regular consideration in editing or studying a play. Before the *Biographical Dictionary* appeared, I personally used to leaf my way through *The London Stage* in order to learn which other roles had been played by individual actors so that I could understand audience expectations for their characters in the plays I was editing.

Other important primary research followed. Some editions of great merit appeared—Arthur Friedman's meticulous work on Wycherley, for example, or Cecil Price's Sheridan. We looked at our tasks through the eyes of the great editors of Renaissance texts, led by Greg and McKerrow and Bowers, and approached the texts of these plays more seriously than they had ever before been considered. (On the other hand, irresponsible editors continued and still continue to publish texts without much knowledge of textual scholarship.) Growing interest in theatrical machinery elicited books and articles on how stagecraft actually worked. Scholars began to read plays that had not been studied before and studied them in terms of broadened contexts. And we came to realize how much work could be done.

This efflorescence of research on Restoration and eighteenth-century drama had two defining characteristics: (1) it was based on newly acquired historical knowledge, a factual base that had not marked the study of these plays in the past, and (2) it was interdisciplinary. During the midtwentieth century Restoration and eighteenth-century plays were seldom performed; we knew them primarily as literary texts, flat on the page. The tragedies were approached as dramatic poetry, and the comedies sometimes for their verbal wit, sometimes merely as interesting fictions in dramatic form. We never examined them in the context of the original performances. But when the new research resources became available, we felt that we could no longer talk about these plays without understanding something of their music, costuming, sets, actors, audience reception, and similarities to other plays, because all that information was now available. This yoking of the historical and the interdisciplinary in our study of eighteenth-century drama has radically changed our perception of the field.

New technologies have facilitated and accelerated the retrieval of an extraordinary amount of information. I suppose we could start with the airplane and particularly with bargain fares that have made frequent trips to England or to major repositories in this country such a common part of scholars' lives. And then there is Xerox, which easily and inexpensively furnished primary materials, at least in those early days when any library seemed willing to copy anything. Computers have been put to many tasks, from collating editions to counting performances, and of course they assure greater accuracy in newly edited texts.

At the same time, obviously, these materials are related to the twentieth-century reading of plays only in terms of historical perspective and authorial intention. Because a play was popular does not mean it is good and therefore should be studied. Because its plot and characterization are traditional does not mean they are shopworn or unoriginal. Because a dramatic formula is commonplace does not mean that a remarkable artistic creation cannot develop from it. So the relationship of traditional scholarship and today's criticism requires establishing the proper relationship between the play in its early run and the play now as considered by the scholar who will probably never see it performed.

The way is open, the tools at hand, the research topics abundant. Why, then, have we seen so little really important research and criticism of Restoration and eighteenth-century drama in the last decade or so? Given the truly exciting potential of our field, why has so little happened in terms of new work? Why are there still so few good editions of plays? And, more strikingly, why do so many of the new articles and works on drama of this period lack any cognizance of the pioneer work that has been done? I have been astonished at the number of critical articles that follow the old fashion of discussing eighteenth-century plays in terms of wit and morality or other well-worn critical frameworks, as though the scholarship never happened or had no relationship to criticism of the plays. I am not talking about critics who turn to the new historicism or literary theory (postmodernists have tended to ignore eighteenth-century drama almost altogether) but about those who have continued in the old modes without revealing any awareness that all this scholarship might affect how we interpret plays. In short, the new availability of hard facts about the theatre of the period has not seemed to have strongly affected general understanding of the drama.

A glance at the 1985 MLA bibliography of eighteenth-century work gives what I suppose is a fairly usual picture: of 342 items for the period 1700–1799, a total of 17 (or about 5 percent) were on drama. This included 6 listings under the rubric "theatre," which do not actually concern plays, bringing the total that deal with plays to 3 percent. Two were on drama in general and 9 on individual authors— Fielding (2 items out of 30 on his works), Goldsmith, Lillo, the authors of *The Merry Loungers*, Rowe, Sheridan, and Townley. This productivity can be compared with 43 items on Blake, 17 on Defoe, 42 on Johnson, and 26 on Pope. The Restoration fared a little better, with 22 items on individual authors. At the national convention of the MLA in December 1986, of 709 sessions (or about 2,000 papers) I found 2 on Restoration and eighteenth-century English drama—1 on *The Rover* and 1 on the replacement of drama by the novel.

Research in our field, despite the incredible potential, is not occurring extensively for several reasons: market considerations, the lack of trained researchers, and the revolution in theory and criticism.

The embarrassingly practical side of all this is, of course, market considerations that affect our quest for knowledge. Discussion of such issues may be unseemly, but the sad fact is that undergraduate students do not yearn to read eighteenth-century plays—or even some other eighteenth-century literature. They like Swift very much, they can be persuaded to try Pope, and Fielding would be fine if he did not meander so often from the tale at hand. And of course everyone, I must assume, still loves Dr. Johnson. But Congreve? Farquhar? If twentieth-century pens are those preferred and both youthful love of the romantics and a growing interest in the Victorians bolster nineteenth-century studies, we have yet to stir the passions of our young to plead for more Steele, more Cibber. One result of this regrettable lack of enthusiasm is that colleges and universities do not have a lot of positions begging for eighteenth-century drama specialists. And one result of the dearth of eighteenth-century positions is that we do not find graduate students clamoring to get into the field, and rightly so, if they choose to teach. As a result, we are not overrun with young Ph.D.'s wishing to carry on our work—or wishing to order texts of *The Conscious Lovers* for their undergraduate surveys, which will be the only place that groups of other young students will encounter our glorious century.

If, then, we have few eighteenth-century Ph.D.'s new to the field, we can scarcely wonder that there has not been more exciting new research within the last decade or so. But the matter is worse. Suppose the profession needs, as it badly does, editions of more plays. Surely all of us are aware that for those who do not edit texts there is often the misapprehension that editions are not real books, that they are not a matter of significant original research comparable to a book-length monograph. Indeed, there is often the misperception that factual research, for example biography or literary history, is not important in the way criticism is, that it somehow betrays pedestrian minds capable only of hacking and hewing. Young Ph.D.'s, even those who have persisted in eighteenth-century studies and found jobs in the academy, must face the tenure decisions of their colleagues, who are often not at all sympathetic to the intellectual complexities of research projects. They simply cannot afford to focus on such complex research—much of which involves major commitments of time—at least until they have achieved tenure.

That means that when they, like their older colleagues, feel compelled to include a play or two in their eighteenth-century survey, they are going to ask for ones they know: *The Way of the World* or *School for Scandal*. And of course that means that publishers will continue to publish multiple editions of the same big sellers, preventing us from broadening the range of choices available for courses. Only very few scholarly presses will publish editions of other eighteenth-century plays, and that will mean, of course, that the prices of editions will be prohibitive. And to take things one step further, if students, graduate students, and professors have so little available to them in the way of texts of plays, where will we find the market for the kind of scholarship and criticism that these new materials cry for? We have a problem.

Second, I fear for the number of trained researchers we are producing. Despite the richness of research possibilities, we are not emphasizing in doctoral programs how to mine research materials, particularly primary sources. The doctoral curriculum is taught at many institutions strictly within the confines of the English department, without requirements of complementary courses even in history, philosophy, or the arts. I do not know how many universities still require courses in research methods, but I know many Ph.D.'s who have never taken one. I suspect it is possible to get through course work without serious research and to do one's dissertation by consulting only secondary sources. If doctoral study does not instill both a love of research and an understanding of how to do it, few people will acquire that love and skill later. If it does not give students a sense of history and an interdisciplinary understanding of the eighteenth-century context, they will not necessarily know the questions to ask. Scholars catapult from the doctoral dissertation to the tenure decision so rapidly, even as they begin their full-time teaching experience, that they usually begin by publishing from their dissertation work, and that tends to set their publication patterns for the future. I suspect that unless we begin training them as they work on research papers and dissertations, few will pursue major research later.

Third, the postmodernist movement has, of course, affected us dramatically. Even as it has revitalized and energized our profession, it has discouraged graduate students and faculty alike from research pursuits. Again if one looks at the market considerations, why should publishers choose texts that readers will not purchase, such as studies of the works of long-forgotten playwrights, if the demand is for deconstruction or poststructuralism? Although I welcome the stimulation of the new approaches to literature, I confess to some fears for the continuity of the training of scholars who will ferret out new knowledge and continue the vitality of my own field of research.

I wonder, as I complain, if fogyism is creeping up on me. I do sound as though I deplore the fact that academic pursuits are not as good as they were in the old days. But they were not so remarkable when I was young. I reiterate my initial recognition that rigorous scholarly work is a new phenomenon in my research field—only a few decades old—and it never was an enterprise that engaged hordes of people. So I should not expect many younger scholars now. Nevertheless, I believe it is important for those of us in the field to continue developing new researchers with agile and tenacious minds. For there is much to be done.

We are in a period when we will continue to discover facts not previously known both through investigation of primary materials in the major repositories and through new access to smaller collections. We also have a major agenda ahead in significant linkage of facts that have already been discovered.

The need for editors of many plays not yet readily available in print is great. We need both scholarly editions and inexpensive texts that can be used in the classroom. But regardless of the amount of scholarly apparatus, I hope we will begin to acknowledge that editors ought to know something about textual criticism and about the theatrical practices of the period before making textual decisions. These do not seem to be prerequisites at this point. Editing texts should not be an amateur-hour activity. It should not engage the untutored novice, and it certainly should not be considered lightly as a means to fast or easy publication. Moreover, we have to reconsider our rationale of copy text after reexamining what exactly it is that we are trying to encapsulate. We should take the texts of our plays as seriously as our colleagues in Renaissance studies do; that will, in fact, necessitate treating the plays in a manner different from Renaissance editors with procedures particular to our own set of problems. But that is a topic to be considered at another juncture.

We can learn a great deal about the plays from examining their performances and publication and combining this information. For example, I have personally worked with two questions of authorship, the first concerning which parts of Steele's *Tender Husband* were written by Addison and the second involving which parts of Farquhar's *Stagecoach* were created by Motteux. In the first, the solution lay in the printed text only, wherein clues could be found through such details as variations in abbreviations of speech prefixes not attributable to the compositors. But in the second, an integration of theatrical, biographical, and publication details provided the answer. First of all, there were three distinct versions: a Dublin edition of 1704 and a London edition of 1705, as well as a London edition of 1735—twenty-eight years after Farquhar died—with a totally unexpected alternate text. No notice of the first performance appears in *The London Stage*. I was able first to narrow the possibilities for dating the premiere to no earlier than fall 1700 and no later than February 1702, although scholars had believed that it opened shortly before the text was printed.

To do so, I coordinated some clouded references in Farquhar's other works and letters, references in prologues of contemporary plays by other playwrights, and internal evidence (for example, a soldier speaks "in the King's name" rather than the queen's, indicating the play appeared before William died). I also determined that the play opened at Lincoln's Inn Fields rather than at Farquhar's usual Drury Lane. Biographical and textual data led to the conclusion that the

Dublin edition derived from Farquhar's manuscript (biographical information shows that he was in Dublin when it was published and that his brother was a bookseller there), that the London 1705 edition was attributable to Motteux, and that the 1735 edition was taken from the Drury Lane promptbook. Information on Motteux's usual activities in the theatre and his habits and quirks in the publication of his own plays added further evidence. Finally, with all this information, the division of labor could be identified. In other words, theatrical, biographical, and textual information had to be combined to provide the answers.

Similarly, other linkages of various kinds of available data will solve other problems, as illustrated by another example from Farquhar. The 1728 edition of *The Beaux Stratagem* produces interesting information not in the editions of 1707. The full words of the songs are printed, and Count Bellair's scene is italicized. A note explains that the scene and the Count's entire part were deleted after the first night, with his lines in act 5, scene 4 assigned to Foigard. By linking information from a text printed twenty-one years after Farquhar died, the cast lists and theatrical calendar in *The London Stage,* and biographical data on the actor, I determined that John Boman, who played the count, left the company the following season for Smock Alley in Dublin and was not replaced. Then I had the information to base a decision on which version to reproduce.

I mention these inordinately complicated research problems only to suggest how the facts of performance and publication when combined can lead to information we could not find otherwise. In studies of authorship problems, such a combination can be invaluable and similarly can affect textual decisions. When we can learn of discrepancies between printed texts and performances, we obviously have very important information. The more we know of the day-to-day life in the theatre, the more we understand about the plays themselves.

The surprising thing—the altogether wonderful fact—is that by putting together the information we can garner from various available resources, such as *The London Stage,* the *Biographical Dictionary,* newspapers on microfilm, original and new editions, pamphlets, biographical data, manuscript collections, theatrical daybooks and other records, we can piece together a remarkably full picture of theatrical history, and we can answer questions we could not answer thirty years ago.

I hope we will concentrate efforts on important problems. For example, I believe we need more work that involves intensive reading of many plays and play-related materials. In fact, I would recommend reading plays seriatim, a practice I have found enormously helpful. One gains intimate detail about the day-to-day life of the theatre and thereby has a more knowledgeable context into which to put the works being considered. By reading plays in the order they premiered, I have worked with questions of theatrical history, such as the war between the theatres at the turn of the eighteenth century, and on critical pieces, such as the identification and definition of humane comedy. An accompanying awareness of daily events as reported in the newspapers and other publications can be of great service when viewed with the plays. And of course full knowledge of the total repertory, as opposed to just new plays, gives a much more particular understanding of the taste of the times.

I hope there will be more study of the relationships between theatre and the other arts. Historians of music and theatre need to, and have begun to, work closely together. One example is the annual symposium at the Maryland Handel Festival, which has looked to theatrical topics in order better to understand Handel's operas. Not only have dramatic and musical textual editors sat together, but one symposium focused on Handel's heroines, naturally in the context of the dramatic heroine of his time. Those of us in literature have almost ignored the music in the plays until recently, although obviously it was a very important part of the performance in a time in which opera and theatre sometimes inhabited the same stage and usually appealed to the same audiences.

There are still major discoveries to be made in terms of music for the theatre. I have found research on music essential for editing. For example, I discovered three songs that had been sung in the first production of Farquhar's first play *Love and a Bottle* but had never been printed with the play or identified after initial publication as related to the comedy. As I have pored over the collections of half-sheet broadside songs in the British Library, the Bodleian, and the Folger, I have speculated on how many other unidentified theatrical songs exist; surely I did not stumble upon the only three. One can also discover act tunes for these plays. Our printed texts, printed when the plays were new, usually give only words (which often differ from those on the broadsides) or sometimes only a snatch of the lyrics. We are frequently left without information on the full lyrics or on which version is correct or on who wrote the music and perhaps the words. We do not know whether the songs were added for adornment or considered integral to the text. But we have the capability to learn much more through integrated research.

The relationship of the drama and the novel is a vital area for scholars and critics in both fields. The intimate relationship between the two genres is fundamental. Eighteenth-century drama became increasingly realistic, not only in characterization, plot, and dialogue but also in scene painting, more elaborate machinery, costuming, and acting styles. Comedies were very strong on the eighteenth-century stage, and they, unlike tragedies or operas, presented realistic situations. They also dealt with subjects appropriate to the novel. Usually, these subjects were treated on stage as they became topics of social interest, so that the theatre provided opportunities for avant-garde examination of social issues of importance.

For example, the questions of courtship, marriage, and even divorce were central focuses of comedy when there were strong social and economic determinants, as opposed to emotional ones, for marriage and virtually no possibilities for divorce. These issues became central to novels as well, many of them written by men with some professional interest in the theatre. The scenic quality of many comic novels—the drawing room scenes, courtship scenes, and so on—is heavily influenced by stage traditions. The author may describe the setting and costuming, as well as providing adverbial indications of how lines were delivered. Novels were read by viewers and readers of plays; the connections are significant. I propose that what we know about actual performances in the theatre can enlarge our understanding of the novels, their readership, and the expectations they fulfilled.

Although I could mention many other areas of particular need, let me address only one, the need for criticism by those cognizant of our expanded information base. Critics still often address drama of this period purely from twentieth-century cultural biases unaffected by awareness of eighteenth-century facts. Knowledge of theatrical practices, the contemporary social context, and the author's canon will temper that propensity by offering more information to be considered. For example, Steele was long honored as the father of sentimental comedy because he was not read in context. Actually he was by no means alone in his directions, and his plays should be considered in a more complex fashion. Because readers had only had Restoration comedy of wit and manners with which to contrast Steele, the sentimental aspects appeared much more dominant than is appropriate. We focused on sentimentalism in comedy because of its contrast with the few plays we knew when in fact there are many sentimental attempts before Steele. We called Farquhar a Restoration writer and Steele a sentimentalist, although their work is contemporaneous and their directions very similar. We were just not familiar with the entire canon. Or let us look at the ending of *The Beaux Stratagem*. A little digging in social history of the period verifies that there is no way Mrs. Sullen could get a "divorce" such as the one in act 5 or indeed any divorce. How then are we to understand the ending of the play? What does the adaptation of *The Inconstant*—the omissions, additions, revisions—tell us about that play? I could cite many examples; the intimate interaction of critics and scholars simply must occur.

I seem to be ending where I began, with a belief in the importance of scholarship that is historical and interdisciplinary and with considerable pleasure that a plenitude of interesting problems remain to be solved. Scholars have available so many short cuts to information that could not be easily garnered before the 1960s that they have new opportunities for both adding to the information available and connecting what is published to provide linkages that answer complicated questions. The pool of scholars is small, and the productivity is modest compared to that in other fields. There will be enough to do for many years to come. Those of us long entranced by the field will do our bit. I hope we will also bring along new generations of scholars to continue to investigate this remarkable time and its fascinating stage.

9

Causes and Consequences in Historical Scholarship

GWIN J. KOLB

AT THE TIME Richard Schwartz invited me to participate in this conference, I was putting the final touches on an edition of *Rasselas* that had been many years—but only intermittently, I told myself defensively—in the making. So, even before Professor Schwartz's letter arrived, having reached the age when most people have retired, I was casting backward glances over a conventional academic career checkered with the ordinary segments of teaching, administration, and research, the last including fewer squares than I would have liked. But the invitation, encouraging me to be autobiographical, focused my retrospective musings on the character and causes of my scholarly production from its start to the present; I do not say *finish* because I hope to add to my bibliography before succumbing to the lure of the so-called golden years. The invitation's emphasis on the personal also helped to ensure my appearance, for I promptly remembered that, according to the Great Moralist, "there has rarely passed a life of which a judicious and faithful narrative would not be useful."[1] In the following remarks, I shall do my best to be both a judicious and faithful reporter on that part of my life pertinent to the concerns of this gathering.

My first article was a source study of a chapter of *Rasselas;* my most recent piece deals with Dr. Johnson and his circle as book reviewers. Between these two items lie a group of books and essays that exemplify very familiar modes of investigation: bibliographies; editions; attributions; histories of ideas; biographical, textual, and reception studies; and so on. For many members, especially younger members, of our profession today, such inquiries may seem quaintly passé, often untenable, the relics of naive assumptions and procedures. Without repudiating for a moment either my past writings or my future ventures, I freely assent to the description of my work as traditional historical scholarship.

I propose to discuss two questions. First, why did I undertake this sort of scholarship? Second, what, in my obviously biased opinion, has been the import for eighteenth-century studies of the kind of investigations to which I and many more productive, more important researchers have devoted substantial portions of our lives?

My parents never brought me up to be a researcher of any kind. A high school graduate, my father was a fireman for the Mississippi District of the Illinois Central Railroad Company. My mother, also a high school graduate, was a housewife. They understood the virtues of school teaching; formal education was something they coveted for their children. So they approved my decision to enter the academic profession. But, until the day they died, they remained rather puzzled by the lightness of my teaching load and the long periods I spent in the library and my study. "Son," my mother would ask, "tell me again how many hours a week do you teach?" Then, always looking perplexed, my father would follow up, "And how many people will look at that article you're writing?"

On the other hand, my parents, especially my mother, began reading to me nightly when I was quite young; and both, especially my father, steadily encouraged me to read. For a white male Southerner of his generation, my father held remarkably advanced views on virtually every subject, including religion, race relations, sex, and the rearing of children. Like Samuel Johnson, he believed (with no opposition from my mother) that boys and girls should be free, indeed be heartened, to read whatever their inclinations suggested. I therefore read widely and most indiscriminately, my choices limited only by the materials available. Their number and scope, I now realize, deserved a more perceptive selection than I was usually able to accord them.

To be sure, my parents possessed very few books, only two that I remember, Bunyan's *Pilgrim's Progress* and a thick red volume entitled *The History of the Great War* (that is, World War I). With the arrival of the Great Depression they could afford to buy virtually none; indeed, I recall only one, the single-volume *Lincoln Library of Essential Information,* "named in appreciative remembrance of Abraham Lincoln, the foremost American exemplar of Self-Education," which my mother paid for in three installments (the money came from her sale of milk and butter) and which bears beneath my signature the date "Oct. 3, 1934."

However, during the twenties and thirties, our slender stock was supplemented by borrowings from neighbors and from the public school and town libraries of Aberdeen and Durant, Mississippi. Known as a bookish lad, I happily scanned the partially comprehended pages of *A Military History of the United States* (belonging to our family dentist); the works of Zane Grey (a favorite of my father), Gene Stratton Porter, Thomas Dixon, Robert Louis Stevenson, Sir Walter Scott, G. A. Henty, and so on; and a mass of popular biographies, but not Boswell's *Life of Johnson*. My introduction to Johnson occurred with the reading, when I was in high school, of Macaulay's *Encyclopaedia Britannica* article, which was contained in an anthology of English literature.

The reasons for my early attraction to biography, history, and fiction, not so much to poetry and plays, I do not wholly understand. Perhaps I was merely another instance of biography's power, in Johnson's phrase, to "enchain the heart by irresistible interest" or "diffuse instruction to every diversity of condition."[2] I certainly felt marked empathy for many of the figures, both large and small, whose actions and characters were described in the lives and novels I read.

My bias toward these genres and the more inclusive class of historical writings sprang also, I suspect, from my pervasive awareness of the size of the past and its encroachments on the present. The public event I was most aware of as a child was the American Civil War—the War Between the States, we were taught to call it. Annually, until about the beginning of the Second World War, on April 9, the date of Lee's surrender to Grant at Appomattox in 1865, the Confederate monuments in the two towns where I lived were draped in black cloth, and fresh flowers were placed on family graves. Two of my sharpest memories resulted from visits to two great-grandfathers who had served in the Southern army—one was at the battle of Shiloh, the other at the siege of Vicksburg. I picked up early and quoted often, without any conscious incongruity, Lincoln's dictum "We cannot escape history."

By the time I entered Millsaps College in Jackson, Mississippi, in September 1937, I knew I was destined to be a schoolteacher (my trusting parents concurred heartily), but I was torn between the rival claims of history and literature. The opposing arguments of high school counselors—history and English teachers, respectively—did not ease my task. At Millsaps, my uncertainty continued until I had accumulated enough course credits to major both in history and in English. A decision had to be made. The chairman of the English department, who had a master's from Harvard and a doctorate from Wisconsin, helped me to arrive at a seemingly rational choice. "You're drawn both by the study of history and the study of literature," he said. "If you take your final exams in history, you cannot really satisfy your taste for literature. But if you officially major in English, you will surely be able to investigate the historical aspects of the works you read." So that is why I became a B. A. in English and the proud possessor of a certificate to teach English indefinitely in the public secondary schools of Mississippi.

The Second World War had broken out, of course, long before I graduated from Millsaps. The United States had not entered the conflict, however, and my teachers encouraged me to go to graduate school at least long enough to get a master's degree. My English advisor, largely responsible for my being an English major, strongly recommended an application to the University of Wisconsin, where he had written a dissertation on Dr. Johnson's friend Arthur Murphy and where he thought I might specialize in eighteenth-century literature, since I struck him as being "an eighteenth-century type." My history professor, who remained kindly disposed toward a deserter, urged me to consider the University of Chicago, where he had taken a master's in the late twenties and where, he said, exciting things were happening in the humanities. Eager to please everyone, I requested catalogs and forms from both institutions, and I actually applied to both departments, of which Merritt Y. Hughes and R. S. Crane were the respective chairs.

The description of the English program at Wisconsin was exceedingly impressive to a callow twenty-one-year-old youngster from Mississippi; that of the program at Chicago differed sharply from any description I had ever seen before. "For the student of English," I read, "the essential disciplines, as determined by the kinds of books and problems with which he may be concerned, are four: (1) literary criticism, or the principles of analysis useful for the understanding and appreciation of imaginative works; (2) the analysis of ideas, or the principles applicable to the reading and judgment of writings of an intellectual or rhetorical type; (3) history, or the principles involved in the construction of good historical arguments and narratives; and (4) linguistics, or the principles involved in any systematic approach to the problems of language." Naive though I was, I concluded immediately that the department at Chicago had quite precise—and inclusive—notions about the ends and means of graduate study, and I vaguely sensed the existence of a broader theoretical, even philosophical, foundation underneath the specification of the four "essential disciplines." I was startled by the numerical position granted "literary criticism;" puzzled by the phrase "analysis of ideas," which I had not heard before; intrigued by the clear distinction between imaginative and intellectual works; reassured by the presence of "history" on the list; and resigned to the fact that "language" surely meant courses in Anglo-Saxon.

Altogether, curiosity outweighed uneasiness. Consequently, I entered the master's program at Chicago in the autumn of 1941. My courses that first quarter were Chaucer (with James R. Hulbert), Donne and the Metaphysical Poets (with George Williamson)—both wholly traditional in their approaches—and something entitled "Introduction to the Methods of Literary Study" (taught by the distinguished Americanist Walter Blair), which was required of all M. A. candidates and which comprised detailed discussions of the organizing principles or structures of selected poems, fiction, and plays, on the one hand and philosophical (namely Bishop Berkeley's *Three Dialogues between Hylas and Philonous*), historical, rhetorical, and scientific pieces, on the other. I certainly did not flourish in this course, but I survived, having learned gradually and painfully that literary studies encompassed far more than simple notions regarding dates, authors, content, style, and the like. Then came the bombing of Pearl Harbor and my departure from graduate school for the United States Navy.

When I returned to Chicago in 1945, my early courses included History of the English Language (with Hulbert), Bibliography and Literary Historiography (with Donald Bond), and The Theory and Analysis of Literary Forms, extending through two quarters, with Crane. All three exerted significant influences on the development of my professional choices and activities. By the end of the winter quarter, I had strongly reaffirmed my original hope (the financial aid provided through the G. I. Educational Bill gave the hope reality) to earn a Ph.D. and become an English teacher. Exposure to the history of the language persuaded me that I, tone-deaf then and not much better now, should not try to become a linguist, even of the historical sort.

Bibliography and Literary Historiography afforded a revealing initiation into the marvelous new (to me) world of rare books; such works as the *OED, DAE, DNB, DAB,* and *CBEL;* such journals as *PMLA, JEGP, ELH, MP,* and *PQ* (featuring annually its "English Literature, 1660–1800: A Current Bibliography," founded by Crane and continued by the likes of Louis Bredvold, Richmond Bond, Arthur Friedman, and Louis Landa); and the absorbing pages of Henry Hallam's *Introduction to the Literature of Europe in the Fifteenth, Sixteenth, and Seventeenth Centuries,* Hippolyte Taine's *History of English Literature,* Vernon Parrington's *Main Currents in American Thought,* Arthur Lovejoy's *Great Chain of Being,* David C. Douglas' *English Scholars,* and René Wellek's *Rise of English Literary History* (where I first read a description of Thomas Warton's *History of English Poetry*). By its classification of scholarly investigations into one or more of four main kinds—concerned with the author of a work, the materials of a work, a completed work, and a work's readers—the course also enabled me to discern a rationale

and logical relationship for the mass of secondary studies I was scruti-
nizing or hearing about in other classes. Unlike a number of my peers,
I emerged from Bibliography and Historiography with a heightened
wish to own a few books, including those dubbed rare, that I had been
examining and, more important, to produce a modest addition to the
rich accretion of scholarship illuminating English literature, specifically, I had tentatively decided, eighteenth-century literature.

Crane's brilliant course entitled "The Theory and Analysis of
Literary Forms" marked my baptism—suffused with headaches and
indigestion—into the realms of theory, not for me Keats' "realms of
gold." Crane's critical god was Aristotle, his theoretical basis mimetic,
his sacred text the *Poetics*. We moved through that truly seminal work
line by line, often word by word. I remembered ruefully a remark of
my undergraduate philosophy professor, who ardently admired the
Nicomachean Ethics, that it took a thousand years to learn Aristotle, a
thousand years to unlearn him, and was taking a thousand years to
learn him over again. I wondered whether the last thousand were not
being compressed into a few quarters at the University of Chicago.
Besides expounding his interpretation of Aristotle's notions about
Greek tragedy and Homer's epics, Crane sought to extend the principles and procedures—a posteriori, he never tired of emphasizing—to
the delineation of literary forms, including comedy and lyric modes,
not treated by Aristotle. During that period and afterward for a longer
stretch of time, Crane was intent on establishing the theoretical foundations of what was to be his volume, covering the years from about
1740 to about 1785, in the *Oxford History of English Literature.* So he
usually analyzed eighteenth-century works in terms of their formal
structures, frequently lamenting the virtual dearth of satisfactory analyses and encouraging the members of his seminars to repair the lack.
It was an arduous undertaking, which engrossed much of Crane's
imposing intellectual ability.

I was frequently bewildered and acutely aware of my obtuseness
throughout the experiences. Nevertheless, I was strongly responsive
to Crane's pervasive recognition of the inevitable presence of theory
of some sort in all critical statements about literary works; his insistence
on the desirability of concrete evidence for the solution of literary
problems; his emphasis on the inductive, the empirical approach to
literary issues; his abiding distrust of the a priori lines of argument
and the adduction of single causes for complex phenomena; his enter-
tainment of multiple hypotheses before arriving at probable, not absolute conclusions; and his acknowledgment that no one system or theory, not even Aristotle's, could embrace the total, the final truth about
a work of art.

Occasionally, it seemed to me, in his relentless search for particular forms, he failed to exhibit the circumspection that he habitually displayed and that he cogently proclaimed to his students and his readers. Two momentary lapses left a permanent impression on my developing mind. Looking for examples of protagonists in what he called "punitive comedy" (which produces laughter at the expense of a reprehensible central figure), he opined that Pinchwife rather than Horner is the dominant figure in Wycherley's *Country Wife*. This opinion he maintained at length and with marked ingenuity until the steadfast disbelief of the class led him to abandon it. Again, preoccupied with the identification of various forms of lyric poetry, he classified Johnson's *Vanity of Human Wishes* as a "lyric of character," the other forms being "lyrics of feeling" and "lyrics approximating actions." And again, he held this view tenaciously until several students persuaded him that, according to his own criteria, *The Vanity* should be labeled a piece of moral rhetoric, not a lyric poem of any kind.

Although Crane suggested that I write a critical dissertation under his supervision (I became his assistant on *Modern Philology* in 1946), my tastes continued to draw me toward the area of traditional historical scholarship. These inclinations were strengthened by my conscious inadequacies as a theorist and a critic; doubts about the longevity of most critical, heavily theoretical theses; courses with Arthur Friedman and Donald Bond; and my experiences as the editorial assistant on *MP*.

Admiring enormously the philosophical speculations and practical discourses of both ancient and modern critics (including Crane and the other Chicago neo-Aristotelians), I realized quite early that I possessed scant gifts for that sort of professional activity. In addition, I simply preferred ascertaining the exact publication date of an eighteenth-century book to ruminating on the distinctive elements of a punitive comedy or a punitive tragedy. Further, I noted a complete absence of ordinary academics among the classical English critics—for example, Sidney, Dryden, Johnson, Coleridge, Arnold, and T. S. Eliot, all of whom demonstrated their creative prowess in noncritical compositions. Moreover, among my peers who wrote critical dissertations, few indeed, I observed, went much beyond the models and boundaries established by their mentors. In conception and execution, most of their works followed well-traveled roads.

I hasten to confess that I could not claim marked originality in the kind of dissertation I elected to write. My choice was determined in large measure by the sort of investigations Arthur Friedman and Donald Bond had under way when I enrolled in their courses. Friedman was preparing his edition of Goldsmith, which Crane had begun back in the 1920s but had relinquished to Friedman when Crane's concerns shifted to criticism. Bond was getting started on his edition of the *Spectator* papers. Both men (and Crane too, I should make clear), knowing of my rising interest in Johnson, encouraged me to put together a commentary on *Rasselas* that was mostly historical in character. They thought it might provide the nucleus of a new edition of the moral tale. Friedman and Bond, though devoting little attention to criticism and theoretical matters, always spoke of Crane and his labors with the highest respect. Simultaneously, they lamented his departure from the ranks of conventional scholars (a departure which entailed his forsaking several major enterprises besides the edition of Goldsmith), and they wondered whether his critical projects would bear results as lasting as they believed his more traditional work might have been.

Their dubiety gradually turned to certainty more than a decade later when it became apparent that Crane, despite immense reflection on the *Critical and Historical Principles of Literary History* (to use the title of the incisive and instructive monograph he published in 1967), would never finish his projected volume of the *Oxford History*, which, of course, John Butt took over but did not live to complete. Subsequently, Friedman and Bond contrasted Crane's and George Sherburn's achievements in writing literary history (during the early part of their careers, I should note, Crane and Sherburn had been colleagues at Chicago). "Crane produced the theory—and a magnificent theory it is," they liked to say, "but Sherburn, who scoffed at elaborate theorizing, produced the history—and a very good history it is." Such comments were not lost on me, then an instructor at Chicago.

The pull toward historicity exerted by my native temperament, upbringing, and teachers, the last being probably the most powerful influence of all, received its final impetus from my stint as editorial assistant on *Modern Philology,* first under Crane and subsequently under George Williamson. Through my duties, I was able to read a representative sampling of essays being submitted to journals throughout the country; to keep up, in an unsystematic way, with the books on medieval and modern literature being written by members of the post-World War II generation of specialists; to become slightly acquainted, either by letter or in person, with several senior British scholars, including David Nicoll Smith, R. W. Chapman, L. F. Powell, and F. W. Bateson; and to benefit from my association with Crane and Williamson.

In those days, as is still the case today, the dominant cast of studies appearing in *MP* was historical, certainly not New Critical. Most of the books reviewed in its pages were rooted in temporal circumstantiality.

The persons I just named, like Williamson, Friedman, and Bond, notwithstanding the talent some of them possessed for criticism, were committed to comprehending and recording the literary past, albeit partially and credibly, never fully or exactly. "We concentrate on the past," I remember Nicoll Smith once remarked, "realizing its multiplicity of insoluble mysteries, because future writings don't exist and present works have already receded into the past." Crane himself, as I have already intimated, consistently stressed a fundamental relationship between history and criticism.

At the end of ten years, I left the *MP* staff and succeeded Arthur Friedman as an editor of the *PQ* bibliography. When I put together my eight years in that post, my *MP* assistantship, and the sixteen years I shall soon have accumulated as coeditor of *MP*, I conclude that my perspective, while limited, shorter, and much less significant, bears a slight resemblance to that spacious expanse of memory regarding America that Burke, in his *Speech on Conciliation with the Colonies*, ascribes to Lord Bathurst whose guardian angel (Burke apostrophizes) forecast to him, when a youth, the astonishing economic growth of America within his lifetime.

Had I been visited in 1925 by a similar genius, he might have pointed out the relatively small quantity of published research and research tools and then have declared in Burkeian tones: "Young man, that little speck of work will swell into a mighty pile in the next sixty years. Next year R. S. Crane will launch his 'English Literature, 1660–1800: A Bibliography of Modern Studies,' which will appear annually for an indefinite period. Later F. W. Bateson will edit the four-volume *Cambridge Bibliography of English Literature*, which will subsequently be updated and enlarged in five volumes; the British Museum will distribute its 263-volume *Catalogue of Printed Books;* and the Americans will bring out the 610-volume *National Union Catalog, Pre-1956 Imprints*. And that's only the beginning. As far ahead as eye can see, as far as April of 1987, the participants in a conference at Georgetown University will be adding more materials to the enormous pile."

Had the supposed genius been a literary historian of the old-fashioned persuasion, he would have then proceeded to divide up the century and a half between 1660 and 1800 into the Age of Dryden, the Age of Pope and Swift, and the Age of Johnson and would have gone on to list ad infinitum the books and articles that have been published between 1925 and the present. Fortunately, the genius was not a historian. However, I am—and an enumerative bibliographer to boot. But I intend to practice my trade only to the extent necessary for suggesting briefly, to a benevolently disposed audience and in accordance with ancient notions, the nature of the contributions that twentieth-century specialists, past and current (including, emphatically, the other speakers at this conference), have made to the understanding of Restoration and eighteenth-century literature, both belletristic and nonbelletristic. Admittedly, disappointments can be stated, strictures leveled, and reservations voiced. Nevertheless, the combined amount, quality, and range of the scholarship have been remarkable.

I must obviously restrict my evidence to some of the major figures, selected somewhat arbitrarily, in the three ages I distinguished a moment ago, and I begin with the works of these figures because their existence is the raison d'être of the whole scholarly enterprise. We are all aware, of course, that some contemporary theorists have doubted the independent existence of literary works, yet I notice that these theorists always manage to find their way back to the works—often to critical editions that other persons have prepared, containing, typically, a reasonably accurate text and textual notes; information about composition, publication, historical context, and reception; detailed annotation; and a full index.

In considering the first age, one thinks immediately of the University of California Dryden and shortly afterward of Kinsley's edition of the *Poems* and Watson's edition of the *Essays.* Aside from collections of the period's most versatile, most influential author, I (as an extremely selective enumerator) must mention the Clarendon Press edition of Locke, the Latham-Matthews edition of Pepys' *Diary* and de Beer's edition of Evelyn's, the Wharey-Sharrock edition of *The Pilgrim's Progress,* Vieth's and Walker's editions of Rochester's poems, Friedman's edition of Wycherley's plays, Davis' edition of Congreve's, and Kenny's edition of Farquhar's.

Moving from works (it would be presumptuous to discriminate among many splendid historical-critical studies) to biographies, I pause to note that several contemporary theorists seem bent on obliterating both work and author as elements in literary transactions. Then I reiterate a commonplace: notwithstanding the putative theoretical demise of its subjects, the art of biography has flourished during my lifetime as seldom—if ever—before. Among the notable volumes treating personages in the Age of Dryden are Ward's *Life of John Dryden* (which will probably be superseded by James Winn's forthcoming life); Westfall's account of Sir Isaac Newton, *Never at Rest;* Bryant's *Samuel Pepys;* and Hodge's *William Congreve.*

The initial editions that occur to me as I turn to the Age of Pope and Swift are the Twickenham edition of Pope's poems; Sherburn's edition of Pope's *Correspondence;* Williams' editions of Swift's poems, *Journal to Stella,* and Swift's *Correspondence;* and Davis' edition of Swift's prose works. Other major writers of the same age who have been ably

handled by their editors include Addison and Steele (Bond's edition
of the *Spectator* and his forthcoming edition of the *Tatler*, Stephens'
edition of the *Guardian*, Blanchard's editions of Steele's *Correspondence*
and other assorted writings, and Kenny's edition of Steele's plays),
Bishop Berkeley (the Luce-Jessop edition of the works), John Gay (the
Dearing-Beckwith edition of the *Poetry and Prose* and Fuller's edition
of the *Dramatic Works*), Matthew Prior (the Wright-Spears edition of
the *Literary Works*), and James Thomson (McKillop's edition of *The
Castle of Indolence and Other Poems* and Sambrook's editions of *The
Seasons* and *The Castle of Indolence*).

In the field of biography, Mack and Ehrenpreis have recently
completed authoritative, if not definitive, lives of the two individuals
whose names identify the Age of Pope and Swift. In addition, Smith-
ers, Winton, Wild, Irving, Eves, and Grant have produced comparable
accounts of Addison, Steele, Berkeley, Gay, Prior, and Thomson.
Sutherland's biography of Defoe (revised edition, 1950) may well be
superseded by work in progress.

When one surveys only the editorial and biographical labors of
students of the Age of Johnson (omitting entirely the steady flow of
fine historical-critical examinations), the list of major or near-major
authors treated during the past sixty years becomes very extended
indeed. Twelve volumes of the Yale Johnson have appeared, another
should be published in the next year or two, and still others are nearing
completion. Chapman's edition of Johnson's letters will soon give way
to the Hyde-Princeton edition, prepared by Redford. A substantial
monograph could be written on the editing of Boswell's works and
private papers since World War I; here I can just allude to Powell's
updating of Hill's great nineteenth-century edition of the *Life of Johnson* and the Yale trade (thirteen volumes so far) and research (three
volumes so far) editions of the correspondence and private papers.

Additional members of Johnson's circle have received or are re-
ceiving editorial attention befitting the importance of their compositions. Burke (Copeland's edition of the correspondence and Boulton's
edition of the *Sublime and Beautiful* must be mentioned), Garrick (letters
by Little and Kahrl and plays by Pedicord and Bergmann), Goldsmith
(whose *Collected Works* have been edited by Friedman, as I have already
noted), Sheridan (both his *Dramatic Works* and *Letters* by Price), and
Mrs. Thrale-Piozzi (Balderston brought out *Thraliana*, of course, in
1942, and the Blooms are pushing ahead with their edition of the
letters) fall in this group. Of the creations of the principal novelists,
the Wesleyan edition of Fielding and the Florida edition of Sterne
deserve more than the passing reference I can accord them. Among
the poets, Burns (*Poems and Songs* edited by Kinsley), Collins (edited

both by Wendorf-Ryskamp and Lonsdale), Cowper (whose poetry is being edited by Baird and Ryskamp and whose *Letters and Prose Writings* have been edited by King and Ryskamp), Gray (the poetry edited by Lonsdale and the *Correspondence* by Toynbee and Whibley), and Smart (being edited by a number of persons) have all fared well at the hands of their editors. Finally, as an extoller of feats of editorial scholarship during the last six decades, I must pay tribute, out of a rich store of possibilities, to *The London Stage 1660–1800* (eleven volumes) and to W. S. Lewis' edition of *Horace Walpole's Correspondence* (forty-eight volumes).

For many, probably most, readers, Boswell's *Life of Johnson* remains the greatest biography in the language. But Boswell should be supplemented by several modern accounts, beginning with Krutch's *Samuel Johnson* and extending through Clifford's two volumes (*Young Sam Johnson* and *Dictionary Johnson*) and Wain's and Bate's lives. Moreover, rumors persist that one of the speakers at this conference is writing still another full-length study of Johnson. Boswell himself has found his Boswell in Pottle and Brady, whose combined volumes will indefinitely merit the label of the standard life.

Aside from Johnson and Boswell, latter-century authors who have been fortunate in their biographers include Collins (life by Carver), Cowper (King), Garrick (Stein), Gibbon (Craddock), Goldsmith (Wardle), Gray (Ketton-Cremer), Hogarth (Paulson), Hume (Mossner), Lady Mary Wortley Montagu (Halsband), Richardson (Eaves-Kimpel), Smart (Sherbo), Smollett (Knapp), Sterne (Cash), and Mrs. Thrale-Piozzi (Clifford).

After this recital—exceedingly fragmentary, I emphasize, being restricted to editions and biography—it is hardly necessary to ask what historical scholarship since (for example) World War I has contributed to our understanding of eighteenth-century literature. Put quite simply, the texts of very few major works have escaped rigorous, fruitful examinations by skilled explorers, and a large majority have been made far more accessible and intelligible by virtue of the full apparatus of critical editing. Concurrently, the lives—particularly the literary aspects of the lives—of the authors have been probed and narrated with a degree of deftness, sympathy, insight, and knowledge rare indeed before the twentieth century. These glib generalizations, buttressed by the evidence I have just cited, may satisfy the converted among us, but for the young person uncertain of a choice of professional life, a skeptical taxpayer, or a prospective donor, a fundamental question may nag persistently: How do you justify the sort of professional activity that you told us at the beginning of your talk your parents found so puzzling?

In reply to this basic question, I say first that for me the importance of literary scholarship, including literary criticism and literary theorizing, derives predominantly from the prior, higher functioning of literature itself, to which the scholarly-critical disciplines as disciplines (excluding a relatively few specimens that have attained the status of literature) are subordinate and inferior arts. The main job of scholarship is to illuminate the extraordinary, the enormous universe of literature, containing, among countless other wonders, the masterpieces created by individual British men and women during the Restoration and eighteenth century. Secondly, I believe that reading good books has functioned, and continues to function, to make the human race a little bit better, a little bit wiser, and a little bit more receptive to knowledge and beauty—in short, a bit more human and hence a bit happier. If I did not believe that literature promotes (however feebly and erratically) moral, intellectual, and aesthetic values, I would not have entered the academic profession. But, believing what I do, I am determined to practice historical scholarship until prudence tells me it is time to stop.

Notes

1. *Rambler* No. 60 (1750), par. 5.
2. *Rambler*, par. 3.

Index